SPORTS LITERATURE

Edited by

John Brady and James Hall

McGRAW-HILL BOOK COMPANY

New York St. Louis Dallas San Francisco Atlanta

ACKNOWLEDGMENTS

Cyrilly Abels and *The Saturday Evening Post* for permission to reprint "John Sobieski Runs" by James Buechler. Copyright © 1964 by James Buechler. Reprinted by permission of Cyrilly Abels, Literary Agent, and *The Saturday Evening Post.*

Barnard Law Collier for permission to reprint "On Chuck Hughes, Dying Young" by Barnard Collier. First published in *Esquire* magazine, © 1972 by Esquire, Inc. Reprinted by permission of the author.

Olga F. Connolly for permission to reprint "Destroying a Myth" by Olga Connolly. Reprinted by permission of the author.

Doubleday & Company, Inc. for permission to reprint "In the Pocket," copyright © 1970 by James Dickey from *The Eye Beaters, Blood, Victory, Madness, Buckhead and Mercy* by James Dickey. Reprinted by permission of Doubleday & Company, Inc.

Harper & Row, Publishers, Inc. for permission to reprint an excerpt from "I Always Wanted to Be Somebody" by Althea Gibson, edited by Edward Fitzgerald. Copyright © 1958 by Althea Gibson and Edward E. Fitzgerald. Copyright © 1958 by The Curtis Publishing Company; and for permission to reprint "Ex-Basketball Player" from *The Carpentered Hen and Other Tame Creatures* by John Updike. Copyright © 1957 by John Updike. Originally appeared in *The New Yorker.* Both reprinted by permission of Harper & Row, Publishers, Inc.

Holt, Rinehart and Winston, Inc. for permission to reprint "400-Meter Freestyle" from *Halfway* by Maxine Kumin. Copyright © 1957, 1958, 1959, 1960, 1961 by Maxine W. Kumin. Reprinted by permission of Holt, Rinehart and Winston, Inc.

Indiana University Press for permission to reprint "Polo Grounds" from *Poems of Rolfe Humphries* by Rolfe Humphries. Copyright © 1965 by Indiana University. Reprinted by permission of Indiana University.

Alfred A. Knopf, Inc. for permission to reprint pages 3–6 from *Rabbit, Run* by John Updike. Copyright © 1960 by John Updike. Reprinted by permission of Alfred A. Knopf, Inc.

Robert Lescher Literary Agency for permission to reprint "George Chuvalo: Pain and Violence as a Way of Life" by Leonard Gardner. Copyright © 1972 by Leonard Gardner. Reprinted by permission of Robert Lescher Literary Agency.

The Sterling Lord Agency, Inc. for permission to reprint "The Last Days of Ernie Banks" by Paul Hemphill. Copyright © 1971 by Paul Hemphill. Reprinted by permission of

Library of Congress Cataloging in Publication Data

Brady, John Joseph, date   comp.
   Sports literature.

   (Patterns in literary art, 15)
   SUMMARY: An anthology exploring the athletic experience through poetry, essays, and stories written by sports columnists, literary figures, and athletes themselves.
   1. Sports stories. [1. Sports. 2. Sports stories]
I. Hall, James Phillip, date   joint comp.
II. Title.
GV707.B68   796   74-9910
ISBN 0-07-007085-7

Editorial Development, Susan Gelles and Hester Eggert; Editing and Styling, Linda Richmond; Design, Cathy Gallagher; Production, Renee Laniado; Permissions, Laura Mongello.

The Sterling Lord Agency, Inc.

Macmillan Publishing Co., Inc. for permission to reprint "Willie Kamm" from *The Glory of Their Times* by Lawrence S. Ritter. Copyright © 1966 by Lawrence S. Ritter. Copyright © 1966 by Macmillan Publishing Co., Inc. Reprinted by permission of Macmillan Publishing Co., Inc.

Harold Matson Company, Inc. for permission to reprint "The Only Way to Win" by Charles Mercer. Copyright by Charles Mercer. Reprinted by permission of Harold Matson Company, Inc.

McIntosh and Otis, Inc. for permission to reprint "I'm a Dedicated Man, Son" by Stewart Pierce Brown. Copyright 1954 by The Crowell-Collier Publishing Company. Appeared originally in *Collier's*. Reprinted by permission of McIntosh and Otis, Inc.

Peter Meinke for permission to reprint "To an Athlete Turned Poet" by Peter Meinke. Reprinted by permission of the author.

William Morris Agency, Inc. for permission to reprint "The Crucial Part Fear Plays in Sports" by Roger Kahn. Copyright © 1959 by Roger Kahn. Reprinted by permission of William Morris Agency, Inc.

MS. magazine for permission to reprint "Giving Women a Sporting Chance" by Brenda Feigen Fasteau and "Billie Jean King Evens the Score" by Bud Collins. Reprinted with permission from *MS.* magazine, Volume II, Number 1.

National Council of Teachers of English for permission to reprint "He Tries Hard" from "Dear Coach Musselman" by William E. Stafford. Copyright © 1955 by National Council of Teachers of English. Reprinted by permission of the publisher and the author.

The New York Times for permission to reprint "Athletic Recruiting: A Campus Crisis" by Joseph Durso of March 10, 1974; and "Meanwhile, for the Brainy Nonathlete, a 'Financial Struggle'" by Steve Cady of March 12, 1974; and "Opinion: A College Coach Tells Why Recruiting Abuses Happen" by Joe Paterno of March 17, 1974. Copyright © 1974 by The New York Times Company. Reprinted by permission.

Richard Peck for permission to reprint "TKO" by Richard Peck. Reprinted by permission of the author.

Max Rafferty for permission to reprint "Interscholastic Sports: The Gathering Storm" by Max Rafferty. Reprinted by permission of the author.

Ramparts Press for permission to reprint an excerpt from *Out of Their League* by Dave Meggyesy. Copyright © 1970 by Dave Meggyesy. Reprinted with permission from *Out of Their League*, Ramparts Press.

Random House, Inc. for permission to reprint "Don Larsen's Perfect Game" by Paul Goodman. Copyright © 1967 by Paul Goodman. Reprinted from *Hawkweed*, by Paul Goodman, by permission of Random House, Inc.

Charles Scribner's Sons for permission to reprint "Sky Diving" by Richmond Lattimore. Copyright © 1966 by Richmond Lattimore. Reprinted by permission of Charles Scribner's Sons from *Poems from Three Decades*.

Harry Sylvester for permission to reprint "Eight-Oared Crew" by Harry Sylvester. Reprinted by permission of the author.

Time-Life Books for permission to reprint "'I Didn't Know What a Birthday Cake Was': A Look at Life on the Black Side" from *The Black Athlete: A Shameful Story* by Jack Olsen. Copyright © 1968 Time-Life Books. Reprinted by permission.

Vanderbilt University Press for permission to reprint "The Old Pro's Lament" by Paul Petrie, copyright © 1969 by Paul Petrie. From *From Under the Hill of Night*. First appeared in *The New Yorker*, June 28, 1969. Reprinted by permission of Vanderbilt University Press.

The Viking Press, Inc. for permission to reprint "Reflections Outside a Gymnasium" from *Times Three* by Phyllis McGinley. All rights reserved. Originally appeared in *The New Yorker*; and for permission to reprint "Pick" from *I Am Third* by Gale Sayers, with Al Silverstein. Copyright © 1970 by Gale Sayers and Al Silverstein. Both reprinted by permission of The Viking Press, Inc.

Robert Wallace for permission to reprint "The Double Play" and "A Snapshot for Miss Bricka Who Lost in the Semi-Final Round of the Pennsylvania Lawn Tennis Tournament at Haverford, July, 1960" by Robert Wallace. Both copyright © 1965 by Robert Wallace and reprinted with his permission.

Acknowledgements   iii

CONTENTS

INTRODUCTION

Americans are *addicted* to sports. We watch football, baseball, basketball, and hockey. We bowl, golf, jog, and swim. We play handball, badminton, croquet, and chess. Ours is the age of the tennis elbow, the golf widow, and the football freak. There is even a time each autumn when four major professional sports overlap. Five, if you include golf; six, if you count bowling; seven, if you . . . . And the beat goes on.

At breakfast, the sports page is often the largest section of the newspaper. At lunch, the conversation is about the girls' volleyball team, Dick Butkus's knees, and Friday night's game against the Liberty Indians. After dinner, we catch the sports news on TV, then settle down to read books and magazines with box scores by the score.

For many Americans, of course, sports represent but a casual interest —life's "toy department," as sportscaster Howard Cosell once put it. For others, though, sports occupy a central position: much of the meaning in their lives is derived from these games. Sports offer such people an avenue of expression unique in our society. This is often as true of the fan on the sidelines as it is of the athlete on the field. Both must struggle through an early period of trial and error, enjoy some seasons in the sun, and finally confront that most unyielding opponent of all—time.

Why does the world of sport have such a claim on our lives? Few people, at least in the classroom, have bothered to ask. That is what this book is about. We want to know why the sports experience is as meaningful as it seems to be for the millions of us who fill the stands year after year, measuring out our lives in season tickets. Is sports a microcosm that gives us a glimpse of life and of our inner selves? Or is it an escape hatch from reality, offering us experiences that life itself lacks? We want to know how people have expressed the meaning of sports in writing: through poetry, autobiography, fiction, and nonfiction. *Sports Literature* is a book that we hope not only will help you to discover the meanings that others have derived from the sports experience, but also will lead you to understand your own involvement with sports more clearly.

In scouting the literature of the field, we have found an abundance of fine material, but, like a team coach on the day of final cuts, we have had to make some painful decisions. William Hazlitt's brilliant essay "The Fight," written in 1822, may be the first great account of a sports event, but we felt that a more contemporary portrait of heavyweight fighter George Chuvalo, by Leonard Gardner, would bring the realities of the ring closer to today's student. Likewise, John Updike's popular profile of Ted Williams playing his last game in Boston's Fenway Park (and hitting a home run in his final appearance at the plate) was cut to make room for Paul Hemphill's study of Ernie Banks in his final hours as a ballplayer. No home runs here, but again, perhaps this account is closer to the realities of sport and of life at large.

"People are no longer terribly interested in the swashbuckling, hairbreadth Harry, 'garrison finish' approach to sport," observes editor-writer Al Silverman. "Today they appreciate sentiment and color handled with restraint, but they also demand depth and realism and, above all, truth. They want to know how the gladiator stands as a human being, so that they can appreciate him more as an athlete." *Sports Literature* has a few gladiators along its way, but their portrayal is always combined with a glimpse of the truth—even if this truth is more than the hurt in Butkus's knees.

We hope that, in addition to providing some fruitful hours of reading for the student, *Sports Literature* will also promote lively classroom discussions and interesting writing assignments. Many writers of national and international prominence began their careers as sportswriters, namely, Ernest Hemingway, Ring Lardner, Jimmy Breslin, James Reston, Gay Talese, Tom Wicker, and Heywood Broun. "Sportswriting is the best training for a writer there is, outside of being a war correspondent," says Roger Kahn, author of *The Boys of Summer*. "It's fast and there are immediate deadlines and it's violent. Everybody is against violence, but everyone wants to read about it."

Here, then, is *Sports Literature*. We hope that after reading the selections, thinking about them, and exploring some of our suggestions for talking and writing, you will not only discover the meanings that others have derived from the sports experience, but also define your own emerging attitudes toward the games that people play.

Looking
Back

CHAPTER ONE

In the movie *Requiem for a Heavyweight*, the first shot is a close-up of the battered faces of ex-boxers, their eyes surrounded with scar tissue and riveted to a television set. On the screen a young fighter, then called Cassius Clay, is whipping an aging heavyweight named Mountain Rivera. Some of the ex-boxers wince and dodge, as if they are absorbing the vicious blows landing on Rivera. Their eyes reflect the intensity of their involvement: it is total. They are in the ring with Clay, too. Perhaps, in a sense, they really are. Long after our bodies have surrendered to the sadness of time, sports continue to affect us. Vicariously, we are *there*; perhaps we never left.

There can be a strong sense of the past in sports. Athletes tend to look back at "the good old days," at a crucial moment in a play-off or at a traumatic childhood that was the first hurdle to a sports career. Call it hindsight, or second-guessing if you will, but looking back is often an important way of discovering meaning in sports.

The story of Mountain Rivera is fiction, but countless fights like the bout with Clay have happened—and the loser often suffers the same fate as Mountain Rivera. For the defeated fighter, looking back becomes everything; it is the only way he can get through a future that is beginning to close in on him. In a later scene, Mountain says to a young woman who is arranging a job interview for him, "Don't try to build me up too much. Just tell 'm I had a hundred and eleven fights, and I never took a dive. I'm kinda proud 'a that."

One needn't have 111 fights to perceive some meaning in the remembrance of things past. For some the past is but a moment—Ralph Branca remembers a pitch he threw to Bobby Thompson in the 1951 National League play-off. For Roger Kahn, author of the bestselling book, *The Boys of Summer*, ultimate values nearly always appear in the past tense, and happiness, more often than not, is a memory, not an experience.

In this chapter of *Sports Literature* we will be looking back, examining some long-ago moments to discover their meaning for today. Althea Gibson looks back at ghetto life in New York; Harry "Rabbit" Angstrom attempts to revisit the past in a pick-up, back-alley basketball game; we review the career of Ernie Banks as he plays his final games; and we share momentary visions of the past with poets like Phyllis McGinley and Paul Goodman. Looking back can often shed light on the present, and the experiences of Willie Kamm, a star player for the White Sox in the 1920s, parallel those of many players in the game today.

Somebody once said that the only thing we learn from the past is that we learn nothing. In view of the readings that follow, you may wish to disagree.

INTRODUCTION

Althea Gibson rose to worldwide prominence in women's tennis. At her peak, no one could touch her. Tall, strong, and rangy, she was the first woman to play the game the way men did—with strong serves and volleys. She was devastating. She was also black—the first black woman to play in competitive national tennis. The strength of character that made her achievements possible is all the more remarkable when one considers the circumstances of her childhood. Here is Althea Gibson, looking back at street life in Harlem.

We Weren't Bad, Just Mischievous

Althea Gibson

I didn't start getting into real trouble until the Gibson family settled into a place of its own, the apartment on West 143rd Street in which my mother and father, my sisters, Millie and Annie and Lillian, and my brother Daniel still live. I was a traveling girl, and I hated to go to school. What's more, I didn't like people telling me what to do. Take it from me, you can get in a lot of hot water thinking like that.

I played hooky from school all the time. It was a habit I never lost. Later on, when I got bigger, my friends and I used to regard school as just a good place to meet and make our plans for what we would do all day. When I was littler, the teachers used to try to change me; sometimes they would even spank me right in the classroom. But it didn't make any difference, I'd play hooky again the next day. Daddy would whip me, too, and I'm not talking about spankings. He would whip me good, with a strap on my bare skin, and there was nothing funny about it. Sometimes I would be scared to go home and I would go to the police station on 135th Street and tell them that I was afraid to go home because my father was going to beat me up. The first time I did it, the cops let me stay there for about an hour and then they called Mom and told her to come and get me. But she was afraid to go. She didn't want any part of police stations. So, finally, the desk sergeant sent a young cop over to the house to ask her, "Don't you want your daughter?" I got it good that night.

The only thing I really liked to do was play ball. Basketball was my favorite but any kind of ball would do. I guess the main reason why I hated to go to school was because I couldn't see any point in wasting all that time that I could be spending shooting baskets in the playground. "She was always the outdoor type," Daddy told a reporter once. "That's why she can beat that tennis ball like nobody's business." If I had gone to school once in a while like I was supposed to, Daddy wouldn't have minded my being a tomboy at all. In fact, I'm convinced that he was disappointed when I was born that I wasn't a boy. He wanted a son. So he always treated me like one, right from when I was a little tot in Carolina and we used to shoot marbles in the dirt road with acorns for marbles. He claims I used to beat him all the time, but seeing that I was only three years old then, I think he's exaggerating a little bit. One thing he isn't exaggerating about, though, is when he says he wanted me to be a prizefighter. He really did. It was when I was in junior high school, like maybe twelve or thirteen years old, and he'd been reading a lot about professional bouts between women boxers, sort of like the women's wrestling they have in some parts of the country today. (Women's boxing is illegal now but in those days it used to draw some pretty good small-club gates.) Daddy wanted to put me in for it. "It would have been big," he says. "You would have been the champion of the world. You were big and strong, and you could hit."

I know it sounds indelicate, coming from a girl, but I could fight, too. Daddy taught me the moves, and I had the right temperament for it. I was tough, I wasn't afraid of anybody, not even him. He says himself that when he would whip me, I would never cry, not if it killed me. I would just sit there and look at him. I wouldn't sass him back or anything but neither would I give him the satisfaction of crying. He would be doing all the hitting and all the talking, and I guess after a while it must have seemed like a terrible waste of time. He liked our boxing lessons better. He would say, "Put up your dukes," and I had to get ready to defend myself or I would take an even worse beating. He would box with me for an hour at a time, showing me how to punch, how to jab, how to block punches, and how to use footwork. He did a good job on me, maybe too good. I remember one day he got mad at me for not coming home for a couple of nights, and he didn't waste any time going for the strap. When I finally sashayed in, he just walked up to me and punched me right in the face and knocked me sprawling down the hall. I got right back up and punched him as hard as I could, right in the jaw, and we had a pretty good little fight going and we weren't fooling around, either. Daddy weighs about 190 pounds. He's fond of saying, "I can take any one man. Maybe a gang could take care of me, but one man, that's out of the question. If I give him one punch, he ain't going to bother me any more." But I took a shot at him just the same.

Of course, once he got the idea of me boxing professionally out of his head, all Daddy was trying to do, aside from teach me right from wrong, was to make sure I would be able to protect myself. Harlem is a mean place to grow up in; there's always somebody to gall you no matter how much you want to mind your own business. If Daddy hadn't shown me how to look out for myself, I would have got into a lot of fights that I would have lost, and I would have been pretty badly beaten up a lot of times. I remember once I was walking down the street with a bunch of pebbles in my hand, throwing them at targets like street signs and mailboxes and garbage cans, and this big girl came up to me and said, "What, are you supposed to be tough or something? You're supposed to be bad?" I tried to pay no mind to her. I wanted to avoid her. But she wouldn't let me. She hauled off and hit me right in the breadbasket and I went down to my knees, in agony. I prayed that she wouldn't hit me again while I was trying to get my breath back. But she didn't; she just walked away, and I ran home crying.

Daddy didn't give me any sympathy at all. When I told him what had happened, he said, "If you don't go back out there and find her and whip her, I'll whip the behind off you when you come home." So I went back and I found her and I beat the hell out of her. I really tore into her. I kept hitting and hitting, and I wasn't hitting like a girl, either, I was punching. Every time I hit her in the belly and she doubled up with the pain, I straightened her up again with a punch in the face. I didn't show her any mercy, but I guarantee you one thing, she never bothered me again.

Sometimes, in a tough neighborhood, where there is no way for a kid to prove himself except by playing games and fighting, you've got to establish a record for being able to look out for yourself before they will leave you alone. If they think you're an easy mark, they will all look to build up their own reputations by beating up on you. I learned always to get in the first punch. There was one fight I had with a big girl who sat in back of me in school. Maybe because I wasn't there very often, she made life miserable for me when I did show up. I used to wear my hair long, in pigtails, then, and she would yank on those pigtails until I thought she was going to tear my hair out by the roots. If I turned around and asked her to leave me alone, she would just pull harder the next time. So one day I told her I'd had all of that stuff I was going to take, and I'd meet her outside after school and we would see just how bad she was. The word that there was going to be a fight spread all around the school, and by the time I walked outside that afternoon, she was standing in the playground waiting for me, and half the school was standing behind her ready to see the fun. I was scared. I wished I hadn't started the whole thing. She was a lot bigger than me, and she had the reputation of being a tough fighter. But I didn't have any choice. I had to save my face the best way I could. Anyway, my whole gang was behind me, pushing me right up to her.

We stood there for a minute or so, our faces shoved up against each other, the way kids will do, and we cursed each other and said what we were going to do to each other. Meanwhile I tried to get myself into position, so I'd have enough leverage to get off a good punch. She had just got through calling me a pigtailed brat when I let her have it. I brought my right hand all the way up from the floor and smashed her right in the face with all my might. I hit her so hard she just fell like a lump. Honest to God, she was out cold. Everybody backed away from me and just stared at me, and I turned around like I was Joe Louis and walked on home.

6

It wasn't only girls that I fought, either. I had one terrible fight with a boy, on account of my uncle Junie, who was Aunt Sally Washington's brother, Charlie. They were living on 144th Street, just off Edgecombe, and there was a tough gang on the block called the Sabres. The leader of the gang and I used to pal around together a lot; we played stickball and basketball and everything. No loving up, though. I wasn't his girl. We were what we called boon-coons, which in Harlem means block buddies, good friends. Well, this one day I'd been up visiting Aunt Sally, and on my way out, just as I turned around the last landing, I saw Uncle Junie lolling on the stairs, slightly intoxicated, and this Sabre leader was standing over him going through his pockets. "What you doin'?" I hollered down at him. "That's my uncle! Go bother somebody else if you got to steal, but don't bother him!" I ran down and lifted Uncle Junie up, got him turned around, and started to help him up the stairs. Then I looked back over my shoulder to see if the kid was leaving, and I was just in time to see him take a sharpened screw driver out of his pocket and throw it at me. I stuck my hand out to protect myself and got a gash just above my thumb that still shows a scar as plain as day. Well, I got Uncle Junie upstairs as quick as I could and went back down after that boy and we had a fight that they still talk about on 144th Street. We fought all over the block, and first he was down and then I was down, but neither of us would stay down if we died for it. He didn't even think of me as a girl, I can assure you. He fought me with his fists and his elbows and his knees and even his teeth. We were both pretty bloody and bruised when some big people finally stopped it, and I guess you would have to say it was a draw. But at least those Sabres respected me from then on. None of them ever tried to use me for a dartboard again.

Once I took a punch at Uncle Junie himself. I walked into his apartment one night when he was having a big fight with his wife, Mabel. Just as I came in, Uncle Junie hauled off and slapped Mabel as hard as he could, right across her face. Well, that was all I had to see. I was little lady Robin Hood in the flesh. I sashayed right up to him and punched him in the jaw as hard as I could, and knocked him down on his back. "What the hell are you hittin' Mabel like that for?" I hollered at him. I was lucky he didn't get up and knock all my teeth out.

Except for the fights I got into, and playing hooky all the time, I didn't get into much serious trouble when I was a kid or anything very bad. I guess about the worst thing we did was snitch little packages of ice cream while we were walking through the big stores like the five-and-ten, or pieces of fruit while we were walking past a stand on the street. I remember once a gang of us decided we would snitch some yams for roasting, and I strolled nonchalantly past the stand and casually lifted one. Once I had it, though, I couldn't resist the impulse to run, and a cop who was standing on the corner got curious and grabbed me, for good luck. He had me cold; I had that damn yam right in my hand. I'd have run if I could, but he had a death grip on my arm and he dragged me over to the police call box and made like he was going to call up for the wagon to come and get me. I was scared. I begged him to let me go. I swore I'd be a good girl for the whole rest of my life. Finally he said he would give me a break, and he took me over to the stand and made me put back the yam, and then he let me go. But when I walked around the corner and found the rest of the girls I'd been with, they dared me to go back and get it again, and I was just bold enough to take the dare. I got it, too, and got away clean, and we went and built a fire on an empty lot in the next block and roasted it.

Sometimes we used to go across the 145th Street Bridge to the Bronx Terminal Market, where all the freight cars full of fruits and vegetables are broken down for the wholesalers. That was a snitcher's heaven. They used to stack rejects off to one side, stuff that the wholesalers wouldn't accept, and we'd sneak in with empty baskets and try to fill them up before they spotted us and came after us. Sometimes I'd get a whole basketful of overripe bananas and peaches, wilted lettuce and soft tomatoes, and we'd really gorge ourselves on the stuff. Once I carried a whole watermelon in my hands over that bridge.

Like I said, we never got in any real trouble. We were just mischievous. I think one good thing was that I never joined any of those so-called social clubs that they've always had in Harlem. None of my girl friends did, either. We didn't care for that stuff, all the drinking and narcotics and sex that they went in for in those clubs—and we didn't care for the stickups that they turned to sooner or later in order to get money for the things they were doing. I didn't like to go to school but I had no interest in going to jail, either. Mostly my best girl friend, Alma Irving, and I liked to play hooky and spend the day in the movies, especially on Friday, when they had a big stage show at the Apollo Theatre on 125th Street. Alma liked to play basketball, too, almost as much as I did. She was a good basket shooter, and we'd spend hours in the park shooting for Cokes or hot dogs. At night we used to go to the school gymnasium and challenge anybody, boy or girl, man or woman, to play us in what we used to call two-on-two. We'd use just one basket and see which team could score the most baskets on the other. We played hard, and when we got finished we'd go to a cheap restaurant and get a plate of collard greens and rice, or maybe, if we were a little flush, a hamburger steak or fried chicken and French fried potatoes. In those days, of course, you could get a big plate of food like that for only thirty-five cents. Fish and chips were only fifteen cents, and soda was a nickel a quart if you brought your own can. You could buy big sweet potatoes—we called them mickeys—for a couple of cents apiece, and they tasted awful good roasted over an open fire made out of broken-up fruit crates that we picked up in the alleyway behind the A&P. Now I realize how poor we were in those days, and how little we had. But it didn't seem so bad then. How could you feel sorry for yourself when soda was a nickel a quart?

We had some great adventures. I had a friend, Charles, who was twelve years old and, like me, was always ready to go. One time we made up our minds to go to the World's Fair out on Long Island. We got together some change by scrounging all the empty soda bottles we could find and turning them in at the store; we got two cents for Coke bottles and ginger ale and soda splits, and a nickel apiece for the big quart bottles. Then we went to the bicycle store and rented a bike for the day for thirty-five cents, and we rode all the way out to the World's Fair in Flushing Meadows, taking turns with one of us driving and the other one sitting on the bar. When we got there we walked around until we spotted a place where we could sneak in, and we had a big time all afternoon and then pedaled all the way back home to Harlem.

Another time, Charles and I rented a bike up around 145th Street, rode it down to another bicycle store a couple of blocks below 125th Street, and sold it for three dollars so we could go to Coney Island. We didn't get back home until midnight, and in the meantime the man we had rented the bike from had come to the house looking for it. We'd had to give him our names and addresses when we took it out. Looking back on it, I have no idea how we thought we were going to get away with it. I guess we had some notion that maybe the man who owned the bike wouldn't look for it for a couple of days, and in the meantime we could make a few bucks somewhere and buy it back from the man we'd sold it to. What happened was that the next morning Daddy took me downtown and gave the man his three dollars and got the bike back. The man didn't want to let us have it at first, but when Daddy explained that we'd stolen it, he gave it up in a hurry. He didn't want to have any trouble with the police. I had a sore bottom for a week after that little business deal, and it wasn't from riding the handlebars, either.

Poor Daddy must have wished there was some way he could whip me hard enough to make me behave like the other kids in the family. My brother Dan and my three sisters, Millie and Annie and Lillian, never got into any trouble at all. They were good in school, too. I was the only one who was always stepping out of line.

I think my worst troubles started when I graduated from junior high school in 1941. How I ever managed to graduate, I don't know, but I guess I was there just often enough to find out a little bit about what was going on. Either that or they simply made up their minds to pass me on to the next school and let them worry about me. It might have worked except that I didn't like the idea of going to the Yorkville Trade School, which was where I'd been transferred to. It wasn't that I really cared which school I went to, or played hooky from; it was just that a lot of my girl friends were going to one of the downtown high schools, and I wanted to stay with them. I tried to get changed over, but they wouldn't let me, and that didn't set well with me at all.

I guess I went pretty regularly for the first year, mostly because I was interested in the sewing classes. I got to be pretty good on the sewing machine. I remember once something went wrong with the machine I was using, and I volunteered to fix it, and I did. The teacher was amazed. But after a while I got tired of the whole thing, and from then on school and I had nothing in common at all. I began to stay out for weeks at a time, and because the truant officer would come looking for me, and then Daddy would whip me, I took to staying away from home, too. Mom says she used to walk the streets of Harlem until two or three o'clock in the morning looking for me. But she never had much chance of finding me. When I was really trying to hide out I never went near any of the playgrounds or gymnasiums or restaurants that I usually hung out at. I sneaked around to different friends' houses in the daytime, or sat all by myself in the movies, and then, if I didn't have any place lined up to sleep, I would just ride the subway all night. I would ride from one end of the line to the other, from Van Cortlandt Park to New Lots Avenue, back and forth like a zombie. At least it was a place to sit down.

Naturally, the longer I would stay away the worse beating I would get when I finally did go home. So I would just stay away longer the next time. It got so that my mother was afraid to let me out of the house for fear I wouldn't come back. Sooner or later, though, she would take a chance and give me fifteen or twenty cents and send me down to the store for a loaf of bread or a bottle of milk. I would go downstairs and see the boys playing stickball in the street, and that would be the last I thought of the loaf of bread or the bottle of milk. I would play until it got dark, spend the money on something to eat, and take off on another lonesome expedition.

Once a girl friend of mine whose parents had been really cruel to her, so bad that she'd had to go to the police about it, told me there was a place on Fifth Avenue at 105th Street called the Society for the Prevention of Cruelty to Children, that would take in kids who were in trouble and had no place to go. The next time I stayed out so late that I didn't dare go home I remembered about this place and went there and asked them to take me in. "I'm scared to go home," I told the lady in charge. "My father will whip me something awful." They took me in and gave me a bed to sleep in, in a big girls' dormitory, and it was a whole lot better than riding the subway. The beds had white sheets and everything. The trouble was, they notified my mother and father that they had me there, and Daddy came for me in the morning and took me home. I promised him I wasn't ever going to run away again, but he licked me anyway, and a week later I took off again. I went straight to the S.P.C.C. I told them that my father had whipped me bad, after he'd promised that he wouldn't, and I even skinned off my shirt and showed them the big red welts the strap had put on my back. They took me in again, and this time when Daddy came after me they asked me if I wanted to go back with him. When I said no, that I was afraid to, they said I could stay if I wanted to. I wanted to, all right. As far as I was concerned, that place was a regular country club. I had to do a little work, like making my bed and helping clean up the dormitory, and taking my turn scrubbing the toilets, but mostly it was a snap. At home I'd had to work a lot harder, the food was nowhere near as good, and somebody was always yelling at me or worse, hitting me. This was my idea of living.

The only time it was bad was when I got into a fight with one of the other girls and they punished me by putting me down in the solitary cell, which wasn't really a cell at all but just a little room in the basement where all you had was a mattress on the bare floor and nothing very much to eat. I behaved myself after that experience; I didn't want to go back there again. It was too nice up in the dorm.

After a while, though, I got tired of the life there. I guess it was a little too restricted for me. So I told the head lady I wanted to go back home, and she said, all right, I could, but that if I had any more trouble they would have to send me away to the girls' correction school, which is polite language for reformatory, at Hudson, in upstate New York. They sent for Daddy and released me in his custody. I was a little nervous about what he might do, but I was glad to be going home anyway.

I want to say right here that none of this is meant to say that my father was harder on me than he ought to have been. Even though when he got mad he got very mad, he was actually a patient man. If he had whipped me every day of my life from the time I was seven years old, I would have deserved it. I gave him a whole lot of trouble. I don't hate him for anything today. In fact, I love him. I feel a lot of those whippings he gave me helped make me what I am today. Somebody had to knock a little sense into me, and it wasn't easy.

I had no intention of going back to that Yorkville Trade School, but I was too young to get my working papers, so I had to make a deal with the school people. They let me have working papers on condition that I would go to night school a certain number of hours a week. I went for a couple of weeks, but then I stopped, and nobody ever came after me. So that was that. I was officially a working girl. I liked it, too. I felt better, working. I had the feeling of being independent, like I was somebody, making my own money and buying what I wanted to buy, paying in a little at home and doing what I wanted to do instead of being what you might call dictated to. It was very important to me to be on my own.

I must have worked at a dozen jobs in the next few years, maybe more. I was restless and I never stayed in any one place very long. If it wasn't to my liking, I quit. I was a counter girl at the Chambers Street branch of the Chock Full O' Nuts restaurant chain. I was a messenger for a blueprinting company. I worked in a button factory and a dress factory and a department store. I ran an elevator in the Dixie Hotel, and I even had a job cleaning chickens in a butcher shop. I used to have to take out the guts and everything, but I still like to eat chicken. Out of all of them, I only had one job that I really liked, and I lost that one for being honest. It was at the New York School of Social Work. I was the mail clerk, and I even had a little office of my own. It was my job to sort all the mail for the whole school, break it down and deliver it to the different offices and people, and also take care of sending out the outgoing mail. I liked the job because it was the first one I'd had that gave me some stature, that made me feel like I was somebody. I was there for six months, the longest I ever worked at any job. I lost it because one Friday some of my girl friends were taking the day off to go to the Paramount Theater in Times Square to see Sarah Vaughan in the stage show, and I decided I would go, too.

When I went in to work on Monday morning, the lady supervisor sent for me to come into her office, and I knew right away I was in trouble. "What happened to you on Friday?" she wanted to know. I could have lied to her and told her I'd been sick, but I didn't feel like it. I told her the truth. "All my girl friends were going to Paramount to see the show," I told her.

"Sarah Vaughan was there. I thought maybe it wouldn't be so bad if I took just one day off. I'm sorry about it. I won't do it again, I promise." For a minute, I thought she was going to let me off. "I must say I admire your honesty," she said. "I would much rather you told me the truth than have you lie to me. But that doesn't change the fact that your job here is particularly important to the whole organization. We've got to have an especially trustworthy person in it. I had to do all the mail by myself on Friday, and it was late getting around. I simply can't have somebody in that job who would leave it untended for such a foolish reason. I'll have to let you go and get somebody else."

The kind of girl I was at the time, it wasn't easy for me to beg anybody for anything. But I really begged that lady to let me stay. "I'll never do it again," I told her, "honest I won't. I'll come to work even if I'm sick." But she wouldn't change her mind. "The only thing I can do for you," she said, "is give you a week's pay to give you a chance to find another job. But you're through here. You'll have to leave today."

It wasn't exactly the best way for me to learn that it pays to be honest, but it was a good way for me to learn that it pays to stick to your responsibilities. I sure liked that job. I hated to lose it.

For a while I didn't exactly knock myself out looking for another job. I suppose you could say I was sulking. Anyway, I just stayed away from home and bummed around the streets. It wasn't long before a couple of women from the Welfare Department picked me up and laid down the law. If I wouldn't live home, and I wouldn't go to school, I would have to let them find me a place to stay with a good, respectable family and report to them every week so they could keep a check on me. Either that or I would have to go away to the reformatory; one or the other. Naturally, when they put it like that, I said I would go along with what they wanted. So they got me a furnished room in a private home, and even gave me an allowance to live off while I was looking for a job. I could hardly believe this allowance jazz. It was too good to be true. But I figured I might as well enjoy it while I could, so I forgot all about looking for a job and just spent all my time playing in the streets and the parks and going to the movies. I went back to see my mother and father fairly often, and they made no objection to what I was doing because they figured I was in good hands with the Welfare ladies. I sure was; never better. All I had to do was report in once a week and pick up my allowance. It was during this time, when I was living in a never-never land through the courtesy of the City of New York, that I was introduced to tennis. My whole life was changed, just like that, and I never even knew it was happening.

FOR DISCUSSION

1. Which of the strikes against Althea Gibson—that she is black, a woman, or raised in the ghetto—seems most critical? How would you rank these three strikes?
2. How are your ideas about the "conventional" role of women challenged by Althea Gibson's story?
3. Can you tell from evidence in this selection that Althea Gibson would go on to greatness in at least one sport? What is that evidence?
4. Using specific examples from what you have read—and from what you have observed in life—how would you distinguish between "bad" and "mischievous"?

INTRODUCTION

The hero of John Updike's *Rabbit, Run* is Harry "Rabbit" Angstrom, a 26-year-old onetime high school basketball star who, on an impulse, deserts his wife and family. In this opening scene from the novel we are given a glimpse of what becomes a major conflict: Rabbit is caught between the dull conformity he finds in marriage and the dreams which spring from a nostalgic longing for his days of athletic triumph. In view of the novel's theme, what special significance can you see in the game of basketball played here? Can it stand for something else in life?

from Rabbit, Run

John Updike

Boys are playing basketball around a telephone pole with a backboard bolted to it. Legs, shouts. The scrape and snap of Keds on loose alley pebbles seems to catapult their voices high into the moist March air blue above the wires. Rabbit Angstrom, coming up the alley in a business suit, stops and watches, though he's twenty-six and six three. So tall, he seems an unlikely rabbit, but the breadth of white face, the pallor of his blue irises, and a nervous flutter under his brief nose as he stabs a cigarette into his mouth partially explain the nickname, which was given to him when he too was a boy. He stands there thinking, the kids keep coming, they keep crowding you up.

His standing there makes the real boys feel strange. Eyeballs slide. They're doing this for their own pleasure, not as a demonstration for some adult walking around town in a double-breasted cocoa suit. It seems funny to them, an adult walking up the alley at all. Where's his car? The cigarette makes it more sinister still. Is this one of those going to offer them cigarettes or money to go out in back of the ice plant with him? They've heard of such things but are not too frightened; there are six of them and one of him.

The ball, rocketing off the crotch of the rim, leaps over the heads of the six and lands at the feet of the one. He catches it on the short bounce with a quickness that startles them. As they stare hushed he sights squinting through blue clouds of weed smoke, a suddenly dark silhouette like a smokestack in the afternoon spring sky, setting his feet with care, wiggling the ball with nervousness in front of his chest, one widespread pale hand on top of the ball and the other underneath, jiggling it patiently to get some adjustment in air itself. The moons on his fingernails are big. Then the ball seems to ride up the right lapel of his coat and comes off his shoulder as his knees dip down, and it appears the ball will miss because though he shot from an angle the ball is not going toward the backboard. It was not aimed there. It drops into the circle of the rim, whipping the net with a ladylike whisper. "Hey!" he shouts in pride.

"Luck," one of the kids says.

"Skill," he answers, and asks, "Hey. O.K. if I play?"

There is no response, just puzzled silly looks swapped. Rabbit takes off his coat, folds it nicely, and rests it on a clean ash can lid. Behind him the dungarees begin to scuffle again. He goes into the scrimmaging thick of them for the ball, flips it from two weak white hands, has it in his own. That old stretched-leather feeling makes his whole body go taut, gives his arms wings. It feels like he's reaching down through years to touch this tautness. His arms lift of their own and the rubber ball floats toward the basket from the top of his head. It feels so right he blinks when the ball drops short, and for a second wonders if it went through the hoop without riffling the net. He asks, "Hey whose side am I on?"

In a wordless shuffle two boys are delegated to be his. They stand the other four. Though from the start Rabbit handicaps himself by staying ten feet out from the basket, it is still unfair. Nobody bothers to keep score. The surly silence bothers him. The kids call monosyllables to each other but to him they don't dare a word. As the game goes on he can feel them at his legs, getting hot and mad, trying to trip him, but their tongues are still held. He doesn't want this respect, he wants to tell them there's nothing to getting old, it takes nothing. In ten minutes another boy goes to the other side, so it's just Rabbit Angstrom and one kid standing five. This boy, still midget but already diffident with a kind of rangy ease, is the best of the six; he wears a knitted cap with a green pompom well down over his ears and level with his eyebrows, giving his head a cretinous look. He's a natural. The way he moves sideways without taking any steps, gliding on a blessing: you can tell. The way he waits before he moves. With luck he'll become in time a crack athlete in the high school; Rabbit knows the way. You climb up through the little grades and then get to the top and everybody cheers; with the sweat in your eyebrows you can't see very well and the noise swirls around you and lifts you up, and then you're out, not forgotten at first, just out, and it feels good and cool and free. You're out, and sort of melt, and keep lifting, until you become like to these kids just one more piece of the sky of adults that hangs over them in the town, a piece that for some queer reason has clouded and visited them. They've not forgotten him; worse, they never heard of him. Yet in his time Rabbit was famous through the county; in basketball in his junior year he set a B-league scoring record that in his senior year he broke with a record that was not broken until four years later, that is, four years ago.

He sinks shots one-handed, two-handed, underhanded, flat-footed, and out of the pivot, jump, and set. Flat and soft the ball lifts. That his touch still lives in his hands elates him. He feels liberated from long gloom. But his body is weighty and his breath grows short. It annoys him, that he gets winded. When the five kids not on his side begin to groan and act lazy, and a kid he accidentally knocks down gets up with a blurred face and walks away, Rabbit quits readily. "O.K.," he says. "The old man's going."

To the boy on his side, the pompom, he adds, "So long, ace." He feels grateful to the boy, who continued to watch him with disinterested admiration after the others grew sullen, and who cheered him on with exclamations: "God. Great. Gee."

Rabbit picks up his folded coat and carries it in one hand like a letter as he runs. Up the alley. Past the deserted ice plant with its rotting wooden skids on the fallen loading porch. Ash cans, garage doors, fences of chicken wire caging crisscrossing stalks of dead flowers. The month is March. Love makes the air light. Things start anew; Rabbit tastes through sour after-smoke the fresh chance in the air, plucks the pack of cigarettes from his bobbling shirt pocket, and without breaking stride cans it in somebody's open barrel. His upper lip nibbles back from his teeth in self-pleasure. His big suede shoes skim in thumps above the skittering litter of alley gravel.

FOR DISCUSSION

1. Rabbit is looking back at his old self here, yet everything occurs in the present tense. Why is this effective as a literary device?
2. Another device that the author uses here is the sentence fragment. Locate several and explain why you find them effective or ineffective.
3. If Rabbit were in a *real* game, instead of an alley match-up such as this, how do you think he would fare? Explain.
4. How would you characterize Rabbit? Is he selfish? insecure? mature? immature? Or what? What details form the basis for your conclusion?

INTRODUCTION

Sports poetry, like box scores, uses real names. Don Larsen pitched his no-hit, no-run game against the Brooklyn Dodgers in the 1956 World Series. It was the greatest moment of his career; but, as you will read, the moment was not without pain. Nor is the looking back.

The players named in Rolfe Humphries's poem "Polo Grounds" are but memories for old baseball fans and legends for young rooters. Yet the game itself, with all of its chatter and line drives and moving shadows, has not basically changed. Nor has the fan. Only time has moved on,—and it is of the essence.

No matter how long a man trains for a fight, and no matter what hopes and dreams he carries into the ring, a fighter can still end up on the ropes with his corner throwing in the towel. What ever happened to those tough old boxers who used to go a hundred rounds? Were they for real, or was it all an old Irene Dunne movie on the late show?

Don Larsen's Perfect Game

Paul Goodman

Everybody went to bat three times
except their pitcher (twice) and his pinch hitter,
but nobody got anything at all.
Don Larsen in the eighth and ninth looked pale
and afterwards he did not want to talk.   5
This is a fellow who will have bad dreams.
His catcher Berra jumped for joy and hugged him
like a bear, legs and arms, and all the Yankees

crowded around him thick to make him be
not lonely, and in fact in fact in fact
nothing went wrong. But that was yesterday.

Polo Grounds

Rolfe Humphries

Time is of the essence. This is a highly skilled
And beautiful mystery. Three or four seconds only
From the time that Riggs connects till he reaches first,
And in those seconds Jurges goes to his right,
Comes up with the ball, tosses to Witek at second
For the force on Reese, Witek to Mize at first,
In time for the out—a double play.

(Red Barber crescendo. Crowd noises, obbligato;
Scattered staccatos from the peanut boys,
Loud in the lull, as the teams are changing sides)...

Hubbell takes the sign, nods, pumps, delivers—
A foul into the stands. Dunn takes a new ball out,
Hands it to Danning, who throws it down to Werber;
Werber takes off his glove, rubs the ball briefly,
Tosses it over to Hub, who goes to the rosin bag,
Takes the sign from Danning, pumps, delivers—
Low, outside, ball three. Danning goes to the mound,
Says something to Hub. Dunn brushes off the plate,
Adams starts throwing in the Giant bullpen,
Hub takes the sign from Danning, pumps, delivers,
Camilli gets hold of it, a *long* fly to the outfield,
Ott goes back, back, back, against the wall, gets under it,
Pounds his glove, and takes it for the out.
That's all for the Dodgers. . . .

Time is of the essence. The rhythms break,
More varied and subtle than any kind of dance;

5

10

15

20

25

Movement speeds up or lags. The ball goes out
In sharp and angular drives, or long, slow arcs,
Comes in again controlled and under aim;
The players wheel or spurt, race, stoop, slide, halt,   30
Shift imperceptibly to new positions,
Watching the signs, according to the batter,
The score, the inning. Time is of the essence.

Time is of the essence. Remember Terry?
Remember Stonewall Jackson, Lindstrom, Frisch,   35
When they were good? Remember Long George Kelly?
Remember John McGraw and Benny Kauff?
Remember Bridwell, Tenney, Merkle, Youngs,
Chief Myers, Big Jeff Tesreau, Shufflin' Phil?
Remember Matthewson, and Ames, and Donlin,   40
Buck Ewing, Rusie, Smiling Mickey Welch?
Remember a left-handed catcher named Jack Humphries,
Who sometimes played the outfield, in '83?

Time is of the essence. The shadow moves
From the plate to the box, from the box to second base,   45
From second to the outfield, to the bleachers.

Time is of the essence. The crowd and players
Are the same age always, but the man in the crowd
Is older every season. Come on, play ball!

TKO

Richard Peck

It's all mostly on the ropes now:
The old sweaty-strapped grandeur of Stillman's gym—
The berserk punching bag
Tapping out its staccato code.

The flattened-out faces, unexpected ears;   5
The little touts behind the big pinstripes;
The Kid's either on medicare
Or dead.

Nobody goes twenty-eight rounds anymore,
Or comes back with a punishing left on the nine-count;   10
With Irene Dunne at ringside discovering
Blood spatters on her verywhite collar.

Nobody's running for a telephone or liniment
Or soaking a sponge in witch hazel
Or stretched out on the table   15
Wondering if it's the doctor or the priest.

It's all mostly on the ropes now;
They pretty much threw in the towel.

FOR DISCUSSION

1. Goodman does not seem particularly pleased over Larsen's
   achievement. Why would he write so somber a poem? How
   is his mood revealed?
2. Larsen had what could be considered a moment of glory in
   an otherwise undistinguished career. Name other athletes
   (in any sport) who have suffered the same fate. What con-
   clusions can you draw about the nature of sports?
3. Is there such a thing as "luck" in sports? Or is one man's
   mistake always another man's reward for good play? Give
   examples to support your answer.

4. Can you see any ambiguity in the line "Time is of the
   essence" in "Polo Grounds"? How does the line's meaning
   change as the poem develops?
5. What significance do you see in the moving shadow toward
   the end of the poem? What bearing does it have on the final
   stanza?

6. Why do you suppose the poet uses the pronoun "It" in the first and last stanzas of "TKO"?
7. "TKO" strips away the sentiment and romanticism that some fans might feel about boxing as a sport. How is this achieved? What images are most forceful?

INTRODUCTION

Ernie Banks broke in with the Chicago Cubs in 1953 as a slender, graceful shortstop. He set fielding records and teamed with Gene Baker in the early years to form one of the league's finest double-play combinations. Twice he was voted the Most Valuable Player in the league. He hit more home runs than any other shortstop in the game. Yet during his nineteen years with the Cubs, the team never won a pennant. What would Ernie Banks have to look back on? To find out, Paul Hemphill went out to the park to see "Mr. Cub" in the closing days of his long career.

The Last Days of Ernie Banks

Paul Hemphill

There is something infinitely sad about the closing days of a baseball season, a melancholia not unlike that accompanying the last dance or the end of an affair, and it was no different on this the final weekend of September in Chicago. The Cubs and the Phillies were headed nowhere except home for the winter. The upper deck of Wrigley Field had been closed due to lack of interest on Friday, when the smallest crowd of the season stopped by to see if the Phils' Barry Lersch could avoid losing his twelfth straight decision. The next day it had rained right up to game time, and the players had managed to finish the game in less than two hours; their anxiety to get in out of the cold was so acute that they seldom bothered to throw the ball around the infield after a putout. And now, on a slightly overcast fall Sunday morning, the end was at hand. Somebody had a portable television in the press box so they could watch the Bears' football game from Minneapolis. The names of recently recalled rookies dotted both lineups. The few veterans ticketed to start were playing for themselves, working on next year's salaries. Vendors were desperately touting their remaining souvenir caps and bats and Cubs pennants. A brisk wind snapped in from Lake Michigan. But perhaps the surest sign that it was about to end for another summer was found on Phil Wrigley's brick outfield walls where the ivy, that ivy which has been there for more than three decades, was turning a distinct brown.

It was fitting that the place didn't come to life until the door to the clubhouse in the left field corner eased open and Ernie Banks stepped into the hazy sunlight to begin the long walk to the batting cage. It would probably be the last time he would make that walk as a player, a fact broadly trumpeted in the Chicago papers in advance of this season-ending home series, and that is why about a thousand of the faithful were on hand more than two hours early. Blinking at the harsh light, carrying two bats and a glove in his right hand, he paused there for a few seconds and took it all in one more time and then began striding through the blue green grass along the foul line. That was the signal for them to begin.

"Ernie, Ernie, come over here," one of them yelled. "I'm your best fan, Ernie. Honest, Ernie. Hey, *Ernie.*" Ernie was smiling like a little boy, waving to them and even calling some of the kids by their first names, now and then doing a little jive step and winking and circling his index finger and thumb into the "O.K." sign. By the time he reached the cage they were near hysteria. "Ernie, you still got my lipstick on your cheek?... Ernie, Ernie, *please*, Ernie...."

Loosening up near the cage, he spied one of the Phillies. "Hey," he said, "are you inspired?"

"Now I *know* you're crazy, Banks," the player said.

"*Inspired.* You *must* be *inspired.*"

"It's too damned cold to be inspired."

"Ah, but you must remember those who have to work for a living. You must put it in the proper perspective."

The Phillie shrugged and went back to warming up. "Isn't it a beautiful day?" Banks yelled to nobody in particular, breaking into song.

"*On a clear day, you can see forever....* The Cubs of Chicago versus the Phillies of Philadelphia, in beautiful, historic

Wrigley Field," he said, grabbing a bat and jumping into the batting cage. "Let's go, let's go. It's Sunday in America."

Sunday in America, indeed. Witnessing a weekend of baseball at Wrigley Field may be one of the last recurring opportunities we have for seeing an America that used to be, an America pregnant with memories of handlebar mustaches and sudsy beer mugs and promenades in the park. The Cubs have been playing their games at Wrigley Field since 1916, and what is so amazing in this age of artificial grass and domed stadiums and scoreboard fireworks is how little has changed there since the glorious days of Roger Hornsby and Grover Alexander and Hack Wilson.

Primarily responsible for this hold on tradition in Chicago is, of course, Philip K. Wrigley, perhaps the last of the truly benevolent club owners. The Cubs still wear the same basic uniform and play in a park that has remained startlingly constant for half a century: ivy-draped walls, no billboards, wonderful close-in seating, organ music and no lighting system. (Wrigley may soon install lights, but only for the purpose of completing long doubleheaders.) Pat Pieper, at eighty-five, is still handling the public address system as he did fifty-five years ago. In Chicago the fans still actually *sing* the National Anthem, and stand to applaud the Cubs before and after a game as though it were a concert, and scornfully throw back opposition home run balls hit into the left field seats. A good Cubbie fan cares not so much whether his lads are winning or losing, but what time they play the game, and this season over 1.6 million showed up to see a club that finished in a distant tie for third place.

Of all the heroes in the ninety-six-year history of the Cubs, none has been bigger than Ernie Banks. Not only because of his excellence afield during nineteen seasons—he holds nine of the fifteen Cub career records available to a nonpitcher—but because of his general demeanor, he has become known in recent years as "Mr. Cub." That is no mystery, because Ernie Banks is the epitome of what the Wrigley family always intended Cub baseball to be: pure of heart, exuberant in spirit, a living symbol of the way things used to be.

"I put my glasses on him one day during the National Anthem," says Chicago sportswriter Jim Enright, Banks's collaborator on a fast-selling book called *Mr. Cub*, "and he was singing and crying at the same time." The only time Banks ever showed a temper on the field was a few years ago when the Giants' Jack Sanford nailed him in the back with a fastball. "We could use the same mug shot of him in the press book that we used in 1954, and nobody would know the difference because he simply hasn't changed," says Cub publicist Chuck Shriver. "If he's got any problems, he's hiding them behind the thickest veneer known to man," marvels another Chicago journalist. Uncomplaining, forever happy, totally predictable, Banks enjoys a rapport with Cub fans that borders on the ridiculous. "He don't cuss, he don't bitch and he don't smoke," said an elephantine lady fan bundled up in the box seats. "I guess you could call him a saint."

Whether we shall have to bid farewell to Ernie Banks as an active player may have to wait until the Cubs report to spring training next March in Scottsdale, Arizona. He turns forty-one on the last day of January, and arthritic knees have kept him on the bench for most of the past two seasons. He is only a shadow of the twenty-eight-year-old who, in 1959, batted .304, hit 45 homers and drove in 143 runs while setting a major-league record for shortstops with a .985 fielding percentage. It has been rumored that he would replace Leo Durocher, thereby becoming the first black manager in big-league history, or else continue as a coach (having been designated a player-coach since 1967). "He's got a lot of options," says Enright, who probably knows Banks more intimately than any other writer. "Manager, coach, up in the broadcast booth, maybe in the front office, maybe even in politics or public service. By playing or coaching one more year, he can get his twenty-year pension. I personally think he'll be the Cubs' manager some day." Banks himself remains noncommittal. "Whatever he decides to do, he'll have to announce it himself," says a Cub official, with some exasperation and a lot of understanding of Banks's popularity in Chicago. "You don't retire an Ernie Banks in this town."

Whenever an official announcement comes of Banks's intention to retire as a player, it is certain to spark visions of a purer and more stable period in the history of American sports. Has it really been that long? Born into a large family in Dallas during the Depression ("I never invited friends home for lunch because there just wasn't enough food," he says in *Mr. Cub*), he escaped poverty by excelling in sports. "I'd seen so many people in my neighborhood get stuck on bad installment payments, I'd made up my mind I was going to be a Philadelphia lawyer." He was luckier than most black athletes at that time, of course, because just as he was graduating from high school Jackie Robinson was breaking the color line in the majors. Just the same, he was nearly twenty-three years old before he got his chance in organized baseball. Late in the 1953 season, the Cubs bought his contract from the Kansas City Monarchs of the old Negro American League for $10,000 (his salary was to be $800 a month) and called up Gene Baker to play beside him at second base. Banks and Baker thus became the first blacks to play for the Cubs.

Pennantless since 1945, the Cubs didn't have many heroes back then. Phil Cavarretta was the manager in '53, and Hank Sauer and Ralph Kiner were almost finished. So Banks quickly became the darling of Wrigley Field. In only his second full season he hit .295 with 44 homers and played superbly at shortstop. He didn't have the greatest range in the world, or the strongest arm, but he had fine quick hands and the fluid moves of a Marty Marion. At bat he was deceptive: willowy-looking at 6–1, 185, with delicate slender hands and average shoulders but a smooth swing right out of a Lew Fonseca training film. Between 1957 and 1960 he had home run productions of forty-three, forty-seven, forty-five, and forty-one, and was named the National League's Most Valuable Player in '58 and in '59. When it appeared he was slowing down a bit at shortstop he was tried late in the 1961 season at first base, where he has starred ever since. (During the Cubs' futile pennant push of two years ago he set a league fielding record of .997.) The type who never had to worry about getting back in shape for another season, Banks was a beautiful physical specimen who never spent a moment on the disabled list until 1970.

When Leo Durocher took over as manager of the Cubs for the '66 season, insiders predicted trouble; Banks, thirty-five, was past his prime, for one thing, and for another it was impossible to envision a happy marriage between him and the man who once noted that nice guys finish last. But trouble never came, or at least never came to the surface. "Leo tried to 'retire' Ernie all during spring training that year, trying out about four other guys at first base," says one Cub writer, "but when they got back to Wrigley there he was in the lineup." One reason for his survival is that Banks is the kind of man who has the capacity to put the blinders on when trouble is imminent, skirting danger by minding his own business. Durocher has very wisely taken to joking about how he "tried to retire Ernie, but he wasn't ready for it." In '69, at the age of 38, Banks hit 23 homers and drove in 106 runs and was named "Chicagoan of the Year."

Much sadder than watching a baseball season come to an end is observing the painful last attempts of a great star like Banks, and it has not been a pretty thing, over the past two seasons, to see him try to make his body work for him as it had during the good years. With rumors starting up again that he was through, he went on the disabled list in the middle of the '70 season with the arthritic knee, only to come back and hit .326 in the last month and take false hope that he could make it again in '71. This time, though, there was to be no comeback in the dry heat of Scottsdale, Arizona. Gene Baker had long since given up the ghost and taken to scouting for the Pirates. Hank Aaron was on the verge of a tremendous year and Willie Mays was still in there, but most of the others of the early '50s had departed: Richie Ashburn, Bobby Thomson, Stan Musial, Ted Williams, Minnie Minoso, et al. The Cubs had their bright moments, but they also had their bad ones, and it was obviously time to start bringing in some fresh young faces.

If, as many feel, Ernie Banks epitomized a certain definable period in the history of American sports, then Banks's decline also marked the end of that period. Baseball in the '50s was marked by a *joie de vivre*, a freewheeling independence that was a leftover from the postwar years of the old Dodgers and Cardinals and Red Sox; of the traditional two eight-team leagues; of nurtured images and huge minor-league systems and an almost boyish purity. In the '60s drastic changes came to almost all aspects of baseball.

And lost in all of it was an old-fashioned Ernie Banks. "One reason they come out for day baseball here is because of the atmosphere in the cities at night," says a Cub official. When Ernie Banks started, it wasn't that much of an issue. "I can't remember Ernie ever saying anything negative about the (Cubs) organization," says another. When he started, nobody dared question the baseball establishment or even acknowledge that there was one. "Most of the young blacks regard him as an Uncle Tom," says a writer. When he joined the Cubs it wasn't a question of "black power," but a question of whether he could find a place to eat a decent meal. So what you did last summer, in perhaps his last season, was close your eyes to the cold figures—entering the last home stand, Banks had managed only 13 hits in 72 at-bats for a .181 average—and try to conjure up images of how it used to be; not only for Ernie Banks, but also for the game of baseball.

Durocher himself ("I can tell you there's no love lost between Leo and Ernie," says one observer) had made the announcement on a postgame show Thursday that Banks would start all three games of the Cubs' home finale against Philadelphia. "We want him to play in the event he *does* announce something later," was the official explanation. He had gone all the way in only seven games that season. On Friday he went hitless in four trips, and when a ground ball shot through his legs in the seventh inning the scorer mercifully called it a hit. On Saturday, as brutally cold and wet as it was, he had a good day: two hits in four trips, one for a double, and four outstanding plays in the field. Now it was Sunday, the last day, and while the Phillies finished batting practice he sat in the Cubs' dugout along the third-base line being photographed and interviewed.

"Hey, Vukovich," he yelled to a young Phillie working at third base, "you love this game?" John Vukovich looked at Banks, incredulously for a moment, before spitting and nodding toward the dugout. "Yeah," said Banks, "everybody's going to be happy today."

"Feel anything special today, Ernie?" a reporter asked.

"Special? Special? Sure, it's the last Sunday of the season," he laughed.

"Naw, I mean, you know. . . ."

"Nostalgia? That how you say it?"

"Right." Banks's first game had been against the Phils. "I mean, like, do you remember what kind of day it was?"

"Beautiful day. Inspiring day."

"What about today? In comparison."

"Beautiful day. Inspiring day."

"Jesus, Ernie"—the crowd in the dugout had broken up laughing—"aren't you gonna say something controversial for us?"

Banks pondered it and then said, "You inspired?" Nobody expected anything else from him, and while he hunkered down to sign a dozen or so copies of *Mr. Cub* brought over from the box seats by a guard I tried to remember some of the things he had said the day before, well before the game, under the grandstand in a dank private corridor near the umpires' dressing room; tried to piece them together and make some sense of this man who has managed to show not a sliver of his inner self in nearly two decades of being in the spotlight. He knew they called him an Uncle Tom, he said, but black power was "silly." Had he ever worried about anything? "I have problems, like everybody else, but it doesn't do any good to go around spreading bad news." What about the "new athlete"? "These today have been to college and have something to fall back on if they don't make it. Baseball isn't the most important thing in their lives. I'm not so sure that's good for baseball." Did he plan to retire soon? "It depends on my knee, and whether there's a place for me on the club." What's been your attitude toward other people? "I always looked at everybody as if they had an invisible sign on their back saying, 'Please Handle With Care.' "

It would be nice to say that Ernie Banks, in what may have been his last game as a player at Wrigley Field, hit a home run to move out of an eighth-place tie with Eddie Mathews for career homers. It would be nice to be able to say that immediately after the game there was a press conference announcing him as the first black manager in major-league baseball history. Neither of those things happened, of course, because he managed a dubious infield hit in three trips and after the game raced to the parking lot for the hour drive home to his beautiful wife and three kids.

But what actually did happen during that last long day at Wrigley Field, the place he has been identified with for so long, was quite enough. It was just before the game when Pat Pieper came over the public address system with an announcement. "Your attention, ladies and gentlemen, your attention, please," he said, his heavy voice booming off the graying concrete stands and the thick brick walls. The crowd of more than 18,000 obediently turned the volume down. "Today marks the end of a distinguished career in baseball." Now there was a deathly quiet from the stands. "Today is the last day in uniform at Wrigley Field"—*No, not Ernie, he isn't going to do it, is he?*—"for umpire Al Barlick, who has spent thirty-one years as an umpire in the . . . ." The applause began behind home plate and spread all the way out to the left field bleachers, and if it was not thunderous it was most definitely not for Al Barlick, decent man though he may be. It was for what Ernie Banks had not yet chosen to do.

FOR DISCUSSION

1. Can you trace the "evolution" of Ernie Banks? How is it profitable to "look back" in a case like this, in which a man, outwardly at least, has changed so little?

2. Hemphill is a skillful writer. How does he weave the total fabric of the Wrigley Field setting into his basic ideas about Banks?

3. Do you see any parallels between the long baseball season and Banks's long career? Do you see any comparison or contrast between Ernie Banks and other players described in Hemphill's article?

4. What is the author's attitude toward Ernie Banks here? Is he objective, compassionate, condescending, or what? What words in the article lead you to your conclusion?

INTRODUCTION

Curt Flood left baseball rather than give in to the reserve clause, which says in effect that men can be bought and sold. Star players were traded in "the good old days," too, and they had their own kinds of reactions.

Willie Kamm was a star player for the Chicago White Sox from 1922 to 1931. Then he was traded for $100,000. He looks back.

Willie Kamm

Lawrence Ritter

Now Mister Willie Kamm, you don't know who I am,
But that needn't make a bit of diff to you,
For I'm just a common fan, tho' I do the best I can,
And I always root for everything you do.

I like to see you play, in that easy graceful way,
Which doesn't seem to bother you at all,
If a batter pops a fly, way up high into the sky,
It's a cinch that batter's out, and that is all.

When you swing that ashen stick, very hard and very quick,
And the ball lands in the bleachers for a tally,
Or when it's hit-and-run, right there begins the fun,
For I know it's gonna start a winning rally.

Now it's no make-believe that we hate to see you leave,
For we'll miss you, yes we'll miss you every day,
For we like you, Willie boy, and it takes away our joy,
Just to think that we'll no longer see you play.

It's hard to say good-bye, and I feel as tho' I'll cry,
Notwithstanding that the best of friends must part,
So wherever you do play, in that easy graceful way,
You will always have a warm place in my heart.
    —JUST AN ORDINARY FAN (eighty-four years old)

I played third base for the White Sox for nine years. Led the
league in fielding time after time, and hit a solid .280 or .290.
Hardly ever missed a game. And then, bang! I was traded to
Cleveland.

You know, nobody from the White Sox ever notified me that
I'd been traded. Nobody. After nine years with the club. I read it
in the newspapers! Actually, a telephone operator was really the
one who told me. She'd been listening in, I presume. About a
week before the trade the phone rang one night, and it's this
operator. I didn't know her from the man in the moon.

"You know something, you're going to be traded to Cleveland," she says.

"Oh, yeah," I said, "what's the difference?" I thought she
was just some nut.

A couple of days later she calls again. "It's getting closer
and closer," she says.

And then on Saturday night the phone rings again. "The
deal went through," she says, "you're traded to Cleveland." And
I got up the next morning and got the Sunday papers and read
where, sure enough, I'd been traded to Cleveland for Lew
Fonseca, my old buddy.

"What am I supposed to do now?" I wondered. "It has to be
official. It's in the papers."

There was still no word from the ball club. So instead of
going to the ball park at the usual time, I waited until the game
had started and then went out. Nobody was in the clubhouse
then, see. I should have said good-bye to everyone, but
somehow—I don't know—I just didn't want to see anybody.
Nine years there and contented and all, doing a good job, I
thought; I just couldn't understand why I'd been traded.

After I got all my baseball duds packed I went to the club
office to see about transportation. All they could say to me was,
"Yeah, you've been traded." That's all.

Willie Kamm   35

What the heck! It was all worth it, anyway. I was always nuts about baseball. I couldn't play enough. It was always that way, far back as I can remember. There were three cemeteries near our house when I was a kid, and I remember throwing balls, or stones, up against the walls of those cemeteries for hour after hour. All by myself, hour after hour.

When I got bigger I had a paper route, and as soon as I threw my last paper I'd hustle over to Golden Gate Park, where there were always lots of kids playing ball. Before long I got to playing semipro around San Francisco here. There was an old gentleman name of Spike Hennessy, he took a liking to me. Rough and ready man, very poor, he just barely existed, but he devoted his whole life to kids. He was a trainer, just one year, with the Sacramento club, and that year he talked them into signing me. That was 1918, and I'd just turned eighteen years old.

The Sacramento club released me after a month and then Mr. Hennessy got me a job up in Oregon in the Shipyard League. Worked in the shipyards during the week and played ball on weekends. After that I came back home and worked at the Union Iron Works, where they had a company team called the Timekeepers. And from there the San Francisco Seals signed me up. Pacific Coast League. That was in 1919.

In the beginning I was a real shy, bashful kid. In fact, when the Seals first signed me, Charlie Graham, the manager, said to me, "You're going to be our regular third baseman."

"Oh no," I told him, "I'm not that good. I just hope that when we get to spring training I'll be good enough so you'll farm me out for a couple of years."

Charlie strung along with me, though. Jeez, was I ever lousy that first year. Must have made 40 million errors. Well, I was only a kid, nineteen years old, skinny, couldn't have weighed over 140. Later on I had my tonsils out and then I started to put some weight on, but that first year I was just a gangling, awkward kid. Still, Charlie Graham stuck with me, and I'm thankful to him for it.

Of course, Mom and Pop, they didn't know what to make of all this. They were old-fashioned German people, and they didn't know baseball from shmaseball. First game they ever saw they were dumbfounded. What's going on?

36

Mom got to be quite a rabid fan, though. She never really understood the game, but that didn't stop her. Not one bit. She had lots of life and zip, and boy, she'd root like nobody's business. Everything I did was sensational as far as she was concerned. Now my father, as far as *he* was concerned I never got a hit. If I got a single, my mother would scream, "Willie's hit a triple." And Pop would say "Ach, the guy should have caught it."

That's just the way he was. All this didn't make any difference to him. Or if it did, he wouldn't let on. He was a little bitty fellow, less than five feet tall. An old-fashioned German father.

If you had a turkey for Sunday dinner, you'd ask, "How's the turkey, Pop?"

"Ach, turkey's turkey."

He was that way with everything. You know, turkey's supposed to be what it's supposed to be, that's all. My mother, she was the enthusiastic one. She got a kick out of everything. Mom picked up the game pretty well, because she used to go fairly regular. But Pop, he only went about once a week or so.

Mom went to the ball park so much she used to hear a lot of stories about me. She'd listen to the folks around her, you know. When I first started with the Seals she went out one day and two guys were sitting in back of her.

"See that skinny kid out there throwing the ball?" one of them says.

"Yeah."

"That's Willie Kamm."

Well, my mother's all ears, because she'd never seen anything like a ball park this big before, with so many people in it, and here they're talking about her son.

So the guy continues, "Yeah, that's Willie Kamm. They're going to try to make a ball player out of him."

"Is that so?" the other guy says. "How come?"

"Oh," says the first guy, "his father's a millionaire, owns half of Market Street. You know the Kamm Building there." And on and on they went. Owns this and owns that.

When I got home that night my mother looked at me and said, "Willie, I don't think you should go to that place any more. The people there, they talk very peculiar."

I played third base with the San Francisco club for four years. After the second year was when I had my tonsils out, and that winter I put on a good 20 or 25 pounds. The next season I felt real strong and my batting average went up 50 points. That would be 1921. In 1922 it went up another 50 points, to about .340, and that's when the White Sox bought me for $100,000.

I was only twenty-two years old then, more than forty years ago, but I still remember that day like it was yesterday. It was June of 1922. The San Francisco club had to make a trip to Los Angeles that week, but I had a bad charley horse so they decided to leave me home to rest up. I didn't have anything in particular to do that evening, so I thought I might as well take a little walk and get some fresh air.

I'm walking up Market Street, at Powell, when suddenly I hear the newsboys yelling, "Willie Kamm sold to White Sox for a hundred thousand dollars! Willie Kamm sold to White Sox for a hundred thousand dollars!"

So I stop dead in my tracks. What are they saying? Can this be true? Me? I walk over to get one of the papers, and one of the kids looks at me and shouts, "Hey, there he is, it's Willie Kamm. Hey, it's Willie Kamm."

Well, I don't know what got into me, but I panicked. Completely. I started running as fast as I could go up Market Street, charley horse and all, with that pack of newsboys at my heels. "Hey, it's Willie Kamm. Hey, it's Willie Kamm."

Oh, Lord! I ran up two blocks and around a corner and quick ducked in a theater, and there I sat, panting and sweating. I must have sat there for hours. The longer I sat there and thought about it, the more frightened I got. It *can't* be true. I'm not that good. But suppose it is true. It *must* be. What'll I do? I won't go, I'm no Big League player. I won't go, that's all! I don't know how long I sat there. Finally I looked up at the movie. I'd seen the exact same picture the night before, and hadn't even realized it.

Well, then all the hullabaloo started. Record price for a ball player. Hundred Thousand Dollar Beauty. All that. And, of course, I went. I always forced myself to do things. Here's the original check, by the way. The Chicago White Sox gave it to me years later. A hundred thousand dollars for me! What do you think of that?

You know, I don't ever remember a ball game where I

wasn't nervous before it began. But it seemed like once the first pitch went in, my mind would go completely on the game and I'd lose my nervousness. But it never left me before a game, not in all the years I played.

Yes, you can hear the fans when they yell something to you. Or more likely *at* you. Especially if you're playing third base, you hear them all the time. After all, the box seats are only a few feet away. At least they used to be in the ball parks we played in. But a ball player never lets it bother him. Never bothered me, anyway. Just rolls right off your back, like water off a duck.

The worst day I ever had being razzed was one day in Chicago when we were playing the Yankees. It was in 1923 and there had just been all this publicity about the White Sox paying $100,000 for me. I was so terrible that day it was unbelievable. If there was a man on third I struck out, and if there was a man on first I hit into a double play. I did that, and worse, all day long.

Finally, the last time I was up they walked the man ahead of me to get to me, and on the first ball pitched I hit into *another* double play. Well, there must have been about 25,000 people there that day, and I think about 24,999 of them stood up as I walked back to the dugout and told me what a bum I was and that I could go right back to California. Of course, you try to be nonchalant about it. You want to hurry up and get back inside that dugout in the worst way. But you don't want to show them that—so you've got to take your time, yet still hurry, see. Oh, it's a hell of a feeling.

I remember another day, too. We were playing Cleveland a doubleheader at Chicago. Well, a guy in the third-base boxes started in on me early in the first game. He had a foghorn for a voice.

"You bum, why don't you go back to California? You never could play ball and you're getting worse. You're all thumbs. You never hit in the clutch. How stupid can you get? What a fathead!"

He was practically right on top of me in that small park, and with that bellow of his I heard every word loud and clear. He kept it up all during the first game and was still going strong well into the second. It wasn't that he'd let loose a blast once in a while. This guy kept screaming without a stop. He'd hardly stop to take a breath. George Moriarty, the old Detroit infielder, was umpiring at third base, and about the middle of the second game he says, "Lord, how long can this guy keep it up?"

Well, about the sixth inning of the second game he finally started losing steam. His voice got hoarser and hoarser, and pretty soon I almost had to strain to catch the words. I'm watching him out of the corner of my eye, see, and in the top of the eighth inning he finally gets up and makes his way through the stands toward the exit behind home plate. By this time he can hardly even whisper any more.

"Thank God!" I say to myself.

But just as he gets to the exit he turns around one last time and bellows, louder than he had all day long, "YOU PUNK, YOU!"

He sure had lungs, that guy. But no, as far as I was concerned the fans never did bother me very much. Hardly heard them.

FOR DISCUSSION

1. Do you find the poem effective as an introductory device here? Explain.
2. How is Willie Kamm like or unlike players today? How do you think he would react to the Curt Flood situation?
3. Regarding fan reaction, Willie Kamm says he "never heard 'em." What is the irony in this statement? How important do you think fan reaction is as an influence on sporting events in general? Is name-calling at athletic events ever justified? How would you compare and contrast the fans of one sport with those of another in this respect?
4. What details do you find here which suggest that sports management is often impersonal and businesslike toward its players?

INTRODUCTION

The advertising slogan "You've come a long way, baby" has been applied to many forms of female endeavor in recent years—and women's gym classes should not be overlooked. If Phyllis McGinley's reflections are accurate, today's young miss (or ms.) gets more activity in a week than her great-grandms. got in a lifetime. Though delivered in characteristic tongue in cheek fashion, Ms. McGinley's light verse does make a strong case for those who would look back on an earlier age of inactivity with approval, if not downright applause.

Reflections Outside of a Gymnasium

Phyllis McGinley

The belles of the eighties were soft,
   They were ribboned and ruffled and gored,
With bustles built proudly aloft
   And bosoms worn dashingly for'rd.
So, doting on bosoms and bustles, 5
   By fashion and circumstance pent,
They languished, neglecting their muscles,
   Growing flabby and plump and content,
Their most strenuous sport
   A game of croquet 10
On a neat little court
   In the cool of the day,
Or dipping with ladylike motions,
Fully clothed, into decorous oceans.

The eighties surveyed with alarm 15
   A figure long-legged and thinnish;

And they had not discovered the charm
   Of a solid-mahogany finish.
Of suns that could darken or speckle
   Their delicate skins they were wary.   20
They found it distasteful to freckle
   Or brown like a nut or a berry.
So they sat in the shade
   Or they put on a hat
And frequently stayed   25
   Fairly healthy at that
(And never lay nightlong awake
For sunburn and loveliness' sake).

When ladies rode forth, it was news,
   Though sidewise ensconced on the saddle.   30
And when they embarked in canoes
   A gentleman wielded the paddle.
They never felt urged to compete
   With persons excessively agile.
Their slippers were small on their feet   35
   And they thought it no shame to be fragile.
Could they swim? They could not.
Did they dive? They forebore it.
And nobody thought
   The less of them for it.   40

No, none pointed out how their course was absurd,
Though their tennis was feeble, their golf but a word.
When breezes were chilly, they wrapped up in flannels,
They couldn't turn cartwheels, they didn't swim channels,
They seldom climbed mountains, and, what was more
    shocking,   45
Historians doubt that they even went walking.
If unenergetic,
   A demoiselle dared to
Be no more athletic
   Than ever she cared to.   50
Oh, strenuous comrades and maties,
How pleasant was life in the eighties!

FOR DISCUSSION

1. Do you think the poet is serious when she concludes "How pleasant was life in the eighties!"; or do you think she is being ironic—saying one thing, but meaning the opposite? Defend your opinion with references from the poem.
2. The poem is rich in contrast between the "belles of the eighties" and those of today. Go through the poem, stanza by stanza, and enumerate the differences between the "belles" of today and those in the poem.
3. Try your hand at writing a parody of "Reflections Outside of a Gymnasium"—e.g., "The belles of the seventies are tough,/With no ribbons or ruffles and stuff," etc.

The
Way It Is

CHAPTER TWO

Sports are often measured in the past tense—last week's game, the team of '69, ole Smokey Lawrence of the undefeated Liberty Indians. Even after you attend a game, a boxing match, or whatever, you inevitably end up buying a newspaper the next day to read about what you have witnessed. The past, always the past.

Yet some writers attempt to freeze the action, capture the moment, perceive the meaning of an athletic experience as it actually occurs. Through language—the origin of all meaning—you are there: stealing from first to second base; free-falling from an airplane; rowing in an eight-oared shell; taking a punch to the jaw—and more.

By exploring the written "snapshots" which follow, you will satisfy some basic curiosity about what it would be like to swim in a 400-meter freestyle, or to throw a forward pass against some fearsome foursome, or to watch in horror as the intended receiver of an incomplete pass stumbles and dies on his way out of the end zone. It's there: the way it is. And it isn't always pretty.

Sports are often glamorized. Yet beneath this veneer of cheers and champagne there is a professional toughness which is illustrated in the excerpt below. James Dickey, a football player turned poet, advises a struggling quarterback quavering "In the Pocket" to:

                                    throw it hit him in
                        the middle
              Of his enemies   hit move scramble
                Before death and the ground
        Come up   LEAP STAND KILL DIE STRIKE
                      Now.

Hit him in the middle of his enemies? Isn't this poem about
a *moment* in a football game? Why are the members of the opposing team called "enemies"? There seems to be more at stake
here than the mere fact that a quarterback is about to be tackled.
He must throw the pass before "death and the ground/Come up."
What do killing and dying have to do with football? Is the poet
perhaps evoking comparisons to life's larger moments? Read and
decide.

Read, too, the poem "Sky Diving." Feel what it is to "fall;
drop sheer; begin to move/in the breakless void; stretch and turn,
freed/from pressure." This poem is a good example of an author
capturing in words the feeling of an instant. Through the poet's
art, even the most timid of us can experience vicariously that
which we would never try. Again, as in Dickey's poem, parallels
to the rest of life intrude. After the freeing, tumbling, exhilarat-
ing sky-ride is over, we see the people on the ground: "They rise
up, plain people now./Their little sky-time is over."

Both poems describe moments in sports with vivid intensity, yet return us inexorably to the larger issues, to the fact that
each of us has only a little sky-time.

This chapter of *Sports Literature* develops other questions
about the way it is in sports. In "Eight-Oared Crew," a story
about particular oarsmen in a particular shell in a crucial race, we
go beyond the finish line and wonder what "winning" really
means. The story of George Chuvalo likewise explores the question of who wins and who loses in sports. Chuvalo is no longer a
young boxer, and his reasons for continuing in the ring are not
what we might expect. Here we see a man completely absorbed
by his way of life, in spite of the pain, violence, and disappoint-
ment.

Finally, we meet Chuck Hughes, who died of a heart attack
in the middle of a nationally televised football game. (James

Dickey's poem seems to stalk the sidelines here.) Chuck Hughes was not a superstar. He was a man of average talents, who made it to the NFL on desire and hard work but lacked "the great speed" required of those who usually play his position. It would be enough if Chuck Hughes's story made us think of how hard he tried and how much he had to live for. But it asks us to think of ourselves as well—of the fact that we, or our surrogates, were *there* when Chuck Hughes died; of the fact that we always seem to be there on Sunday afternoons, watching people die—whether suddenly or a little at a time.

47

INTRODUCTION

The following poems put you into a particular sports experience. Try, as you read them, to be conscious of how the various poets achieve this goal. Maxine Kumin, in "400-Meter Freestyle," offers one of the most dramatic techniques as she makes you follow the lines of her poem in the same way that swimmers stay in their lanes.

Needless to say, not all the techniques to be found in these poems are so immediately obvious. One common denominator, however, is the effort by each poet to stop the action, to freeze the moment, to take that sense of pastness out of the past. You are asked to examine the way it is in a particular sport; and ultimately you find yourself thinking about the way it is in your own inner experience.

400-Meter Freestyle

Maxine Kumin

The gun full swing the swimmer catapults and cracks
                                                  s
                                                   i
                                                  x
feet away onto that perfect glass he catches at
a
n
d
throws behind him scoop after scoop cunningly moving
                                                  t
                                                h
                                                e
water back to move him forward. Thrift is his wonderful

                    s
          e
              c
ret;   he   has   schooled   out   all   extravagance.   No   muscle
                                                            r
                                                               i
                                                            p
ples   without   compensation   wrist   cock   to   heel   snap   to
h
i
          s
mobile   mouth   that   siphons   in   the   air   that   nurtures
                                                            h
                                                               i
                                                            m
at   half   an   inch   above   sea   level   so   to   speak.
          T
h
          e
astonishing   whites   of   the   soles   of   his   feet   rise
                                                            a
                                                               n
                                                            d
salute   us   on   the   turns.   He   flips,   converts,   and   is   gone
          a
l
          l
in   one.   We   watch   him   for   signs.   His   arms   are   steady   at
                                                            t
                                                               h
                                                            e
catch,   his   cadent   feet   tick   in   the   stretch,   they   know
          t
h
          e
lesson   well.   Lungs   know,   too;   he   does   not   list   for
                                                            a
                                                               i
                                                            r

he   drives   along   on   little   sips   carefully   expended
b
u
t
that   plum   red   heart   pumps   hard   cries   hurt   how   soon

                                                                    i
                                                                      τ
                                                                    s

near one more and makes its final surge   TIME: 4:25:9

In the Pocket

James Dickey

Going backward
All of me and some
Of my friends are forming a shell   my arm is looking
Everywhere and some are breaking
In   breaking down   5
And out   breaking
Across, and one is going deep   deeper
Than my arm.   Where is Number One hooking
Into the violent green alive
With linebackers?   I cannot find him he cannot beat   10
His man   I fall back more
Into the pocket   it is raging and breaking
Number Two has disappeared into the chalk
Of the sideline   Number Three is cutting with half
A step of grace   my friends are crumbling   15
Around me the wrong color
Is looming   hands are coming
Up and over between
My arm and Number Three: throw it hit him in
the middle   20
Of his enemies   hit move scramble
Before death and the ground
Come up   LEAP STAND KILL DIE STRIKE
Now.

50

Sky Diving

Richmond Lattimore

They step from the high plane and begin to tumble
down. Below is the painted ground, above
is bare sky. They do not fumble
with the catch, but only fall; drop sheer; begin to move

in the breakless void; stretch and turn, freed   5
from pressure; stand in weightless air
and softly walk across their own speed;
gather and group, these dropping bundles, where

the neighbor in the sky stands, reach touch
and clasp hands, separate and swim   10
back to station (did swimmer ever shear such
thin water?) falling still. Now at last pull the slim

cord. Parasols bloom in the air, slow
the swift sky fall. Collapsed tents cover
the ground. They rise up, plain people now.   15
Their little sky-time is over.

The Double Play

Robert Wallace

In his sea lit
distance, the pitcher winding
like a clock about to chime comes down with

the ball, hit
sharply, under the artificial   5
banks of arc lights, bounds like a vanishing string

over the green
to the shortstop magically
scoops to his right whirling above his invisible

shadows   10
in the dust redirects
its flight to the running poised second baseman

pirouettes
leaping, above the slide, to throw
from midair, across the colored tightened interval,   15

to the leaning-
out first baseman ends the dance
drawing it disappearing into his long brown glove

stretches. What
is too swift for deception   20
is final, lost, among the loosened figures

jogging off the field
(the pitcher walks), casual
in the space where the poem has happened.

FOR DISCUSSION

1. In each of the poems you have just read, the poet has tried
   to "put you into" the sports experience through language.
   In which of the poems were you placed most convincingly
   into the situation or moment at hand? How did the poet do
   it? (Clue: Count the number of times each poet appeals to
   one or more of your senses. Which of your senses are appealed to, and what is the effect?)

2. What does the last line—"in the space where the poem has
   happened"—refer to in "The Double Play"?

3. Can you suggest another sport that would lend itself to the
   technique employed by Maxine Kumin in "400-Meter

Freestyle"? How would you *show* the event as well as tell about it in words?

4. Write a poem which captures what you think is a beautiful moment in the sport of your choice.

INTRODUCTION

The great majority of us do not choose to drive race cars at speeds in excess of 200 miles per hour. Or dive off the cliffs at Acapulco. Or climb Mount Everest. Or bat against Nolan Ryan, or get tackled by Mean Joe Greene. We choose not to, most likely, because we are afraid. We admire the lack of fear in those who *do* choose to try these things.

But maybe this lack of fear is only an illusion . . . .

The Crucial Part Fear
Plays in Sports

Roger Kahn

A theory that fear is something experienced only by the intelligent has spread almost as fast as strontium 90 during the past ten years. I suspect that the theory was devised by a smart coward in search of prestige, but its precise origin remains unknown and somehow people accept it as tradition and even apply it to such innocent fields as sports.

Do you know why Ralph Branca is now selling insurance near New York City instead of pitching every fourth day for the Los Angeles Dodgers? "It's because he's bright and went to NYU," one NYU man suggests, modestly. "If Ralph were dumber, Bobby Thomson's homer wouldn't have preyed on his mind, because he wouldn't have had the sense to worry. Hell, a dumb Branca would win twenty games every year."

Do you know why Joe Louis was a great champion? "Because he was too slow-witted to be afraid," insists a quick-witted club fighter, who quit just in time to preserve his brain pan. "Joe wasn't sharp enough to know how much he could be hurt. A smarter Louis would have dropped that second fight to Schmeling."

Perhaps two dozen other examples come to mind, but by

now I imagine the concept has come clear. Sports is the one area in which stupidity counts. Smart guys finish last. The good rockhead always beats the good egghead. The trouble with each of these statements is also the trouble with the theory that lies behind them. They withstand everything except analysis.

A few hours after the Dodgers had turned the harvest moon blue by winning the 1955 World Series from the New York Yankees, Pee Wee Reese was idling at the bar in an aged Brooklyn hotel which was the site of the official victory party. Reese had thrown out the final batter on a routine ground ball to shortstop.

"Hey, Pee Wee," said a nearby semidrunk, "what was you thinking with two outs in the ninth?"

Reese smiled benignly. "I was just hoping the next man wouldn't hit the ball to me," he said.

"Shmerf?" said the drunk, in surprise, as his beer asserted itself.

Well, there it was. Honest, intelligent Pee Wee Reese had given an honest, intelligent answer, and anyone within hearing distance could now report that a great professional had known the cold hand of fear in the clutch. But had the drunk asked the same question of a duller ball player, had he picked on a triumphant rockhead, things might very well have been reversed. Pinned against a stein of beer, the rockhead probably would have been the man to say, "Shmerf?"

The quick conclusion, which is that the dull athlete was not touched by fright, is careless and probably incorrect. A dull athlete might have felt far more fear than Reese did, but he could not have put the feeling into intelligible English. Emotion, not words, is the issue, and it's ridiculous to assert that you have to be smart to be afraid. I know a six-year-old shortstop, not especially precocious, who feels exactly as Reese did, every time he sees his pitcher throw the ball.

One day last spring, I was driving down a flat, narrow Florida highway to cover a sports car race at Sebring. It had been raining and water lay in dull, black puddles near the palmettos along the side of the road. The car jerked and hissed through the water as I kept it at 60 miles an hour, and I remember thinking that the men who were trying to do 120 at Sebring must be having a difficult time.

It was night when I reached the race course, and Phil Hill, a slim Californian who is accepted as the best American driver, was pacing near the pits, his driving done, his team's victory all but assured. Hill is a sensitive looking man, who reads a great deal and whose musical taste runs to Beethoven.

"How was it out there?" I said.

"What kind of a question is that?" Hill said, intensely. "Can't you imagine what it was like?"

I had to admit I'd never driven a Ferrari.

"A bloody nightmare," Hill said, his face going pale. "Some courses drain. This one doesn't. Trying to control the car out there for me was like it would be for you trying to drive on ice. I was moving. There must have been five, six, a dozen times, when I thought I was dead. I'd hit a puddle and the car would start to go and I'd be skidding toward somebody and I'd figure this was it. It wasn't, but don't ask me how. Lord, don't ask me how I'm still alive." Hill's hands were shaking. They continued to shake and for a time he was so wound up in tension that he was unable to stop talking.

Two years ago, before the start of an equally dangerous auto race, a reporter asked Juan Manuel Fangio, the former world champion driver, if he was thinking about death.

"Death?" Fangio said. "I only give it a quick, glancing thought."

Fangio is a phlegmatic man who once drove a bus in Argentina and who seems far less imaginative than Hill. Again the outward signs indicate that the egghead, Hill, was frightened, and the duller man, Fangio, was not. But last year, still in his prime and still a champion, Fangio quietly retired from Grand Prix racing. Despite his stolid disposition, he was afraid that matters might turn around, that death might now give quick, glancing thoughts to Juan Manuel Fangio.

Fear strikes athletes without regard to race, creed or intelligence. It also strikes them without regard to the actual peril in their work. For the fear athletes feel is composed of two distinct things. First, there is the fear of physical pain. Here we have auto racers afraid of auto wrecks, jockeys afraid of horses' hooves, halfbacks afraid of linebackers, batters afraid of beanballs and swimmers afraid of the water. Then there is the fear, psychological but still real, of performing badly in front of an audience.

56

Thus we have pitchers afraid to throw change-ups, quarterbacks afraid to call their own plays, golfers afraid of the first tee and girl tennis players afraid that their gold panties won't catch the summer sunlight.

Sometimes an athlete feels such physical fear that he cannot so much as move his head out of the way of an inside pitch. Sometimes he feels such psychological fear he cannot pick up the sort of grounder he has handled 10,000 times before. Sometimes an athlete's fear is a combination of the physical and psychological. But at different times and in different ways, all athletes learn what it is to be afraid.

During the 1952 Olympics, Ingemar Johansson, the Swedish Tiger, was matched against the late Ed Sanders in a heavyweight bout. After a few moments of preliminary sparring, Johansson sized up his opponent and ran. He didn't actually run out of the ring, because the ropes were in the way, but he fled as best he could inside the ring, obviously terrified, until kindly Olympic officials intervened and awarded the fight to Sanders.

"INGEMAR, FOR SHAME!" one Swedish newspaper headlined, unkindly. "He's worse than the British heavies," an American sportswriter said. "They always get knocked out, but at least they take a couple of punches first."

Johansson himself had no comment. Sanders outweighed him by more than 20 pounds and possessed a fierce scowl, but no losing fighter ever pleads fright. The difference between Johansson then and Johansson now is partly craft, but it is also that he has learned to control the fear all fighters feel. When Johansson is frightened these days, he punches or backpedals or clinches or covers up. He no longer does what comes naturally, which is to run.

A jockey, to be successful, must be willing to urge his horse into potentially fatal positions. He must move up between a rival horse and the rail even though the outside horse may lug in at any time, closing the gap. He must move between two other horses, although either may veer and cause an accident.

Some years ago, in spots of this sort, Eddie Arcaro had four spills in ten days. Each time, as he lay in the dirt, horses thundered past, their hooves knifing up clods of dirt and drumming like a charge of cavalry. "For around two weeks," Arcaro said, "I couldn't get to sleep without seeing those hooves around my head." Gradually, the fear waned. "I wouldn't say I'm ever afraid of a horse now," Arcaro insisted recently. "I'm nervous about some, sure, but if I was actually afraid of one, what the hell, I just wouldn't ride him, and that hasn't happened."

Some riders become so involved with fear that they stop taking chances. In the tack room, their colleagues say simply, "He's riding like a married jock." There is no quicker way for a jockey to go out of business. He must either find a way to live with his fear or quit.

Ten days before the Army-Navy football game last fall, Red Blaik, the cool, analytical man who coached Army football for almost two decades, was holding forth on halfbacks he had known. Traditionally, Army halfbacks run with a difference; knees high, head up, driving over, around or through the opposition. "Speed," Blaik was saying, "and feinting and intelligence." He was walking across a practice field where Pete Dawkins and Bob Anderson were running against a scrub line. "Watch them," Blaik said.

The backs ran hard, and after they were hit, they sprang up instantly as if unwilling to give their tacklers any more than the bare minimum of satisfaction. Another Army back was hit and limped slightly.

"All right," Blaik said, "no limping. If you have to limp, don't scrimmage. If you want to scrimmage, don't limp."

The limp disappeared in a hurry.

"Over here," Blaik said, indicating another part of the field, "is a boy with as much physically as Anderson or Dawkins. Maybe he even has more."

A jayvee halfback was plunging, but not in the accepted Army style. He ran well, but just before he was hit, there was a slight but noticeable change in frame. The body tightened, stiffened, tensed, and it was clear that the back was bracing for a fall even before the lineman touched him. When a tackler missed, the back, ready to be tackled, lost a step before regaining full speed.

"Something you have to understand," Blaik said, "is that this isn't a question of courage, pure and simple. The boy could turn out to be a war hero. It's just that he doesn't like body contact. I've seen this hundreds of times and you can nearly always tell from the beginning. Some of them do and some of them don't. A boy who doesn't like contact shouldn't play football, because he isn't going to change."

If fighters change and jockeys change and learn to live with fear, why not college halfbacks? The answer ultimately comes down to time. Johansson was young enough to be a college student when he ran and Arcaro, in his sleepless days, was only slightly older. A college halfback is through at twenty-two.

Dealing with physical fear is a question of gradually accepting hazards, day after day, week after week, until suddenly they no longer seem dangerous. Humans are adaptable, but the adaptations require patience. One simply does not march into a battle area the first time as calmly as one does the second or third. A fighter of twenty-two is likely to be more frightened than he will be three years, or thirty bouts later.

But there is a point where things turn around, where too many years of living with fear break down human drive. Fangio reached that point before he quit. Jersey Joe Walcott fought superbly against Rocky Marciano once, but the second time he sat down promptly after a punch of indeterminate power. Walcott knew Marciano could hit. He took his second purse without a review lesson.

The path of physical fear varies with the athlete, of course, but a general pattern does exist. First, the athlete encounters fear. This may come when he is a child, or when he is older, or only after he has been hurt. Then, for a time, he is at war with himself. Is the fun of the game and the pleasure of victory worth the risk of pain? The good athlete always answers yes, and sets about controlling his fear. Finally, after enough years in sport, it all gets to be too much trouble and he quits. He either sits down in the ring or he retires.

The other fear in sports, fear of failure, is less predictable, more common, less understood, more discussed, and runs into the science of psychiatry. To me it has seemed clearest in terms of poker.

Consider the frightened poker player who is dealt three kings. He blinks, his stomach talks, and he raises like a man who has been dealt a pair of deuces. It isn't purely money, for he plays with the same outrageous caution, regardless of stakes. It's chiefly that fear drives common sense out of his head.

He looks at his three kings and he considers. The man at his right is due for a straight. (No one is ever due for anything in cards. Each deal is independent of the others.) The next man seems confident. Maybe he has a full house. The dealer is smiling. He probably loaded the deck. So it goes and eventually the man with three kings gets about half of what he would have won if he had kept his head.

The nonfrightened poker player knows that three kings will probably be good enough. He bids accordingly and if he loses, he goes ahead and the next time he has three kings he plays exactly the same way. At its worst, fear paralyzes, but rarely in sports does fright assume such proportions. What psychological fear does most frequently is block the normal reasoning process.

When Early Wynn pitches against the Yankees, he glares and knocks hitters down precisely as he would against any other team. But it is not quite the same operation. "Sometimes," he says, "when I get behind to a hitter, I figure I got to do something because here is Mantle coming up and maybe Berra and Skowron. I get behind and I figure I can't walk this guy and I can just feel that fear."

Wynn's solution, arrived at over the years, is to inhale mightily. "After I take that deep breath," he says, "I feel okay." The deep breath doesn't throw strikes, but it enables Wynn to forget what might happen and concentrate on the business at hand.

The best clutch ball player I remember was a man who suffered a nervous collapse during World War II, who jumped a team because he was homesick and who absolutely refused to travel by airplane. His name is Billy Cox, and although there have been many better ball players, I can't think of anyone whose game improved so much under pressure.

Cox was a third baseman, a small, wiry man with big bony wrists, who subdued ground balls with a little scooping motion and was one of the finest fielders of his time. Before ordinary games, Cox often busied himself thinking up excuses for not playing, but whenever the Brooklyn Dodgers were faced with an important series, he was almost eager to go to work.

In the big ones, he was everywhere. He guarded the line, cut in front of the shortstop, and charged topped balls with such agility that Casey Stengel once complained during a World Series, "He ain't a third baseman. He's an unprintable acrobat." Cox was never a great hitter, but he was far better swinging in a clutch than he was when it didn't matter.

"I can't explain it," Cox once said. "My wife says I have 'fearless nerves.' Anyway, before the big ones, I feel my nerves all tightening up, sort of getting ready. You know what I mean?"

"But what about the homesickness?"

Cox's lean face was grim. He did not usually have much to say. "I believe that everybody has some kind of problem," he said. "No matter how good a ball player is, there's something that bothers him. My problem was that I got lonesome on the road. It takes nerve to lick your problem, but you got to have it."

"Well, doesn't it take nerve to play in clutch games?"

"They never bothered me," Cox said. "I never got scared. The thing that bothered me was that I wanted to go home."

Stan Musial insists that no one can be afraid and play baseball well. "If you're worried about what happens when you go bad," Musial says, "you shouldn't even get in the business." Musial is calling this as he sees it, but he forgets his own outlook when he left Donora, Pa., for the great world of baseball, with his wife, whose father owned a grocery.

"I'm not scared," he told a friend, "because if the baseball doesn't work out, I can always get a job in the store."

In the theater, stage fright, a single word, sums up all fear of failure. But in sports, which cover so large an area and employ so varied a jargon, there are a dozen words for what is roughly the same thing. "Choke" is currently most popular.

"When I get out on the field before the opening kickoff I feel it," Randy Duncan, Iowa's great quarterback last season, has remarked. "I can't eat breakfast that day, and when I see the crowd, I guess you could say I'm choked up. Then, on the kickoff, I have to belt someone. As soon as I block a guy hard, the fear disappears. Just body contact once, and I stop choking."

Tennis player Gussie Moran, in her greatest days, found a less taxing solution. "On the pro tour," she says, "I'd get so worried I wouldn't make a good showing, I started taking a slug

The Crucial Part Fear Plays in Sports   61

of Canadian Club before each match. I got so I couldn't play at all without the slug."

The only tie between Phil Hill, trembling after an auto race, and Gussie, downing a shot before the first serve, is the fact of fear, and this drives to the root of the crucial role fear plays in sports. It doesn't matter what there is to be afraid of, whether it's death, or failure, or disgrace, or a double fault. The point is that there is something to cause fear in every avenue of sport, and whatever exists is sufficient. To the athlete, fear is a condition of the job.

Sometimes, after much research, a man announces that fighters or bullfighters, or pitchers who have learned to beat the Yankees are the bravest men in sports. But no one knows the fear someone else feels and so no one can prepare a valid yardstick of athletes' bravery. Only this much is sure: They are all afraid of different things in different ways at different times. It is never possible to conquer fear, but it can be subdued for a time. Watch the great athlete work at his craft and you can see someone who has known fear before and who will know fear again but who goes about his job fearlessly. This is the courage of an athlete and it is towering to behold.

FOR DISCUSSION

1. Make a list of five sports. Rank them according to the degree in which fear influences the players who participate in these sports. Justify your ranking.

2. Roger Kahn says, "There is something to cause fear in every avenue of sport." Can you think of any exceptions? Do *all* sports ultimately come down to some element of fear? Discuss.

3. Sometimes the element of fear in sports goes too far—a player who is gang-tackled limps off the field for a season, or a second baseman, wiped out by a wide slide, misses a crucial series. What would you do to minimize such abuses?

4. Kahn speaks of the role fear plays even in card games. Can

you think of additional contests, not necessarily sports, in which fear plays a role?

5. Apply President Roosevelt's famous remark, "The only thing we have to fear is fear itself," to any sport and develop that thesis with concrete examples.

INTRODUCTION

Consider a university that is rich in tradition. The most prestigious sport is rowing, and men from the "best" families —the families who have put three and four generations through the school—have traditionally manned the varsity shell. Now this tradition is dying.

The junior varsity is comprised of a new breed at the school: men from poor families, men who have won scholarships, men with names like Kowalik and Pivarnik. They are challenging the varsity crew to determine which boat goes to the most important race of the year.

In the midst of this contest is Kip Grant. If the junior varsity wins, the coxswain in their shell on race day will be Kip, whose family has attended the school for generations. Kip Grant has some hard decisions to make.

Eight-Oared Crew

Harry Sylvester

Dusk lay on the river, making all things its own color. Lights had begun to appear in the other boathouses but where Al Leyden—at thirty-eight, the "Old Man"—stood on the landing, there was only the growing shadow, quick-deepening now that the sun had gone out of sight behind the west bank of the Hudson. The shell, moving leisurely toward the landing, was only a darker shadow when it docked. Leyden stood apart from the crew, the mood of the evening heavy in him.

The crew swung the shell out of the water at Kip Grant's command and marched it past Leyden. In the blue light they looked like some giant insect, the shell held over their heads. Kip Grant walked by them, silent now and no longer harrying the crew. Too silent, Leyden thought, but he felt no better for knowing the reason for that silence toward the crew of sophomores.

He touched Kip on the arm and the coxswain turned to him. "How was it?" Leyden said.

In the dusk he could barely see the slight shrug of the other's shoulders. "I don't know. Their form is still good—when they don't have to turn on the heat." He paused and said, again: "What they'll do in the race, I don't know. They learned too quickly . . . ."

Leyden nodded.

"My brothers and some friends are in town for the race," Kip said. "Mind if I run into town for an hour or so?"

"Go ahead," Leyden said. He almost added: "Don't make your going too obvious," but with Grant that wasn't necessary, Leyden knew. These boys from the school's traditional families were mentally precocious. . . .

Leyden watched Kip Grant go into the coaches' room to dress. Grant had begun to do this after Leyden had made the change in the crews. It was not a good thing, Leyden knew, for crew and coxswain to be so sharply divided as they were. Regret stirred in him again at having made that change, but in his mind he knew that he had done the right thing. He came from poor people himself. Even if the university was or had been a "rich man's school," Leyden felt that he himself must be just. His sense of justice lay on him now like a weight. He went wearily up the wooden stairs to his own room.

Two years ago the university had gone out and got some scholarship men to bolster up the football team, which had been bad for three years in a row. They were good boys, the new scholarship men, intelligent enough to get by the stiff entrance exams, but hailing from mine and mill and with names new to the school: Kowalik, Leary and Pivarnik; Granski, Lisbon and Guttman; the Slavs already replacing the Irish among the athletes.

None of them had ever seen a shell; some of them had never seen a river before coming to the school. They came out for crew in the winter of their freshman year and Leyden had watched them that first day in the barge, with the ice still on the river; watched them with pride and with foreboding.

Leyden had two freshman crews that year and the football coach complained that he was keeping the scholarship men from spring practice. So Leyden let them go for spring football practice and they had returned to him after it and said that they still wanted to row. So Leyden had let them row. . . . It was too late to mold them, or some of them, into the freshman crew that would compete at Poughkeepsie that year. So Leyden had let the scholarship men row alone, as a unit . . . and Leyden saw then the thing that might happen.

Leyden had been an athlete and a coach long enough to know that any great team, whether it be a crew or a football eleven, is more than half accident. The unbelievable and precise coordination that made a team great, as a team, was largely beyond the ability of any coach to create. He could develop it once the accident had occurred but he could not create it.

What Leyden had seen was that eight of the scholarship men had or were part of that curious accident of coordination that might make a great crew. He knew, guiltily, that they, for all their crudeness, could beat the freshman crew already formed. And even when that crew was a close second at Poughkeepsie, Leyden still felt that he had been less than just. Rowing was the traditional sport at the university and, partly by accident, partly by design, the crew was almost always composed of names old in the school's history. Leyden wondered just how much this had affected his judgment.

The next spring he had left the scholarship men together as a unit, as the junior varsity, and he had gone about the always difficult business of making a new crew of some of last year's varsity and some of the freshmen. It was not better than an average crew although it had a great coxswain, the senior, Kip Grant. It was a traditional crew in that it had the old names, Carteret, Grant, Morgan, Fairlee. It won one sprint race, was second in two others and last in a longer race.

That spring it took Leyden a long time to do the thing he felt compelled to do. In May, for the first time, he had the varsity and junior varsity meet in a brush along the river. The junior varsity, the scholarship men, won by a little. They won by a bow a week later, despite having lost their form in the middle of the race. Then, they won by two lengths in a three-mile race with the varsity.

Leyden did then the thing he had to do. He called the

varsity together. "The junior varsity," he told them, "has beaten you, decisively. If you want to row at Poughkeepsie as the varsity, go ahead. . . . Knowing you as I do, I don't think you'll want to go to Poughkeepsie that way. The better way is to race the junior varsity the Poughkeepsie distance, four miles . . . and if they beat you, let them go—as the varsity. Tell me tomorrow how you want to go to Poughkeepsie."

So their captain, Jim Fairlee, had come and told Leyden quite gravely that they would go to Poughkeepsie only if they could beat the junior varsity. And they had raced and the junior varsity, stroked by Kowalik, had won by three lengths.

They needed a coxswain and Leyden had asked Kip Grant to go into their boat. And Kip had consented to but he hadn't liked it or them. And so Leyden's varsity was the eight scholarship men and Kip Grant, third generation of his family to sit in one of the university shells.

His dislike for the men he handled the tiller grips for was not unreasonable. They had displaced his friends, had broken a long tradition of which he was a part. Alumni had protested privately and Kip's brothers had even urged him not to sit in the varsity shell. They had done so half humorously, but Kip knew how they felt. He knew, too, how Leyden felt and the weight of the justice that lay heavy on Leyden. . . .

His brothers were waiting for him now in the private dining room they always had the evening before the race. When he opened the door of the room they were yelling at him:

"The kid himself!"

"Say, Kip, is it really true you had to learn to speak Polish?"

In a way he didn't hear them. For he had seen her face. Among the other women there, among the tall Old Blues, it stood out quietly, as Kip expected that it always might. He greeted the others and sat beside her—Mary Adams, his friend since childhood, now the girl he was going to marry. She took his hand under the table and was silent until the others had stopped shouting at Kip.

"Sure," he kept telling them, "we'll win in a breeze."

"They'll blow up in your face under the bridge," Ad Grant said. "I was watching them from the bank this afternoon through glasses."

"They'll row those other crews into the river," Kip said. Their antagonism, however friendly, did something to him. For the first time, and in surprise, he felt as though he were really part of his crew. . . .

They let him alone after a while and he was able to slip out with Mary Adams. The side streets of the town were quiet under the old trees, the wind from the river rich with spring.

"You seem quiet," Mary Adams said. "I had thought you'd be more nervous with the race so close."

"As I get older I suppose I conceal things better," he said. "If the race has made me nervous, something else has made me quiet. Something else besides you." His hand tightened on her arm. "You can always make me quiet. Just being near you."

"It makes me very happy, Kip," she said.

"The other thing," he went on gravely, "is that I've suddenly realized I've been dishonest. I've snooted those men on the crew when I should have tried to know them better. Why I did, I don't know. They're good men."

"I understand," she said quietly. "I suppose it would have been more honest for you to have resigned from the squad or stroked your—own people on the junior varsity."

"My own people," Kip said. There was an edge to his tone. "They rode me tonight. And they're apt to go haywire and fire Al Leyden after the race."

"I think not," she said. "Coming down in the train, they agreed they'd just let him know that they wanted him not to do anything like it again."

"Even if they win," Kip said.

"None of them expect you to win tomorrow," she said.

An old car squeaked to a stop near them. It had Pennsylvania license plates. A head with a battered hat on it poked out one window and spoke unintelligibly to them. Kip went closer to the car and Mary stood on the curb.

"You know where this faller, Pete Kowalik, he stay at? Faller what row in front in bast crew on here?"

From the curb, Mary saw Kip straighten. "I imagine it's a bit late to see him. All the crew men are in bed."

"All day long, most last night, we drive this flivver," the voice went on in a singsong. "Stop every garage on road, by damn. Pete Kowalik, he be worried about us. Couldn't phone him, eider, I bet."

"They wouldn't call him to the phone at this time of night," Kip said. He moved back to the curb. Mary touched his arm. "These people—" she hesitated. "They've come a long way. You could take a message to Kowalik. He's your stroke, isn't he?"

"I suppose," he said, "I'll be a snob until I die." He walked back to the old car, which was refusing to start. "I'll see Kowalik—if not tonight, first thing in the morning. I can take a message to him."

"You just tell him that his brother Joe got here all hokay and that Malie Stefansik, he come too, and we both be there tomorrow, yalling like hell! Say, who are you, mister? Your face, it—"

"I'm one of the managers," Kip said. He turned away.

"I feel better at your having done that," Mary Adams said.

"I feel better myself." They walked a while in silence.

"Something still bothers you," Mary said.

"I know. I don't think we'll win tomorrow. I had to say it in front of the others, but the men are still green for all their power and natural ability."

"No," she said. "It's just the night that makes you think so." She turned to him in the shadow and he kissed her, feeling some old tension in him become lost in another one, renewed. He broke from her. "I have to get back," he said. At the hotel she pressed his hand. "Until after the race," she said.

The boathouse was in darkness when Kip got there. Going up the wooden stairs to the dormitory where the crews slept, the only light he could see was from the crack under the door of Al Leyden's room. Kip was a long time getting to sleep.

After breakfast, Kip said to Kowalik: "I'd like to speak to you on the float." The tall boy looked his surprise but followed Kip outside.

"I ran into your brother last night in town," Kip said. "He had trouble getting here, but he wanted to let you know that he had arrived."

Kowalik looked at once grateful and amused. "Thanks a lot, Grant. I'm glad to hear about my brother getting here all right. But when you called me over here I thought you had something important to say about the race."

"No," Kip said. He turned away, flushing a little. Was he at fault or they? he thought. Was he a snob or were they crude? He had not wanted the others to know that he had spoken even that intimately to Kowalik. Strangely, though, he felt once more his new kinship with the crew, a relation delayed and now hastened by the attitude of his brothers and friends, by the chance meeting with Kowalik's brother, by Mary Adams's quiet words.

A manager came and told Kip that Leyden would like to see him. He found the coach in his room with the crossed oars on the wall. One of them, Kip knew, had been used by Ad Grant six years ago. "Close the door," Leyden said. "Sit down."

"Guess you didn't sleep much," Kip said. "Saw your light on when I came in."

"I never do the night before a race. The crew did, though."

"They all look good," Kip said. His words fell hollowly into a silence created by Leyden's looking away. When he turned to Kip again, Leyden's face showed his weariness.

"They might win," Leyden said, "but probably they won't."

Kip nodded once.

"They have the stuff," Leyden said, "a lot of it. And guts. They just haven't rowed long enough. They'll try too hard and go to pieces."

"It's a touch late to substitute the jayvee for them," Kip said. "I don't mean to be a wise guy," he added quickly.

"I know," Leyden said. "I made my decision and I'm going to stand by it. About the job I don't have to worry. Your brothers and old man Calder of the crew committee phoned me last night while you were away and said that no matter what happened my job was safe. So it's not me. It's those kids. You don't like them. I can see your point even though I come from the same kind of people they do. But I let them win their place, didn't I?"

"You don't have to talk me into anything," Kip said. "I've changed some. It would be hard to tell you why. But I'll do all I can for them. And I want to win myself. It's my last chance. I'm the only one in the family that never sat in a winning boat at least once at Poughkeepsie."

Leyden nodded. "It's not their last chance," he said. "That's why I called you in here. They have two more big years.

70

What I ask you is this. If they win, all right. If they lose, that's all right, too, in a way, although none of us like to lose. But bring them in a crew—an eight-oared varsity crew." He paused and the two men looked at each other. "You know what I mean," Leyden said. "If they go to pieces today they may never get together again, this year or any other. I don't know what you may have to do . . . but bring them in right—for their sake and the school's . . . if not for anyone else's."

The river was like glass, the stake boats hardly moving in it. Kip's crew had the outside lane, the fastest but also the roughest if the river kicked up. Also the nearest to the line of yachts at the finish.

The referee called: "Ready all?" and the California cox raised his hand. Kowalik and Guttman cursed at the delay. "Steady," Kip said. It was the first word he had spoken outside of commands since leaving the boathouse. He looked down the line of them and pride in them and what was left of his vanity of class fought in him. They stared at him and formed a curious fore-shortened design of white on bronze: the sweatbands sharp against their dark faces, the adhesive tape strapped to their bellies, the heavy wool socks.

"Ready all?" the referee said again and no hand was raised. The little cannon boomed and Kip's "Row!" was lost in its echoes, in the sudden rush of waters as the oars bent in the swift, tremendous beat of the racing start. Something had begun to flow in Kip like his blood, but swifter and more subtle, so that he let them come out of the racing start only gradually, his hands beating out the stroke with the tiller grips at 40 before he consciously knew how high the beat was.

Already they had a quarter length on the others and the lead grew rapidly, was over a length before the mile mark.

"Bring it down! Down, you madmen!" Kip yelled. Something in their eyes dismayed him. They were trying too hard, almost as though they were trying to escape something. . . .He felt older than they . . . but kept shouting at them until they dropped their beat. Still open water showed between them and Navy and California, leading the others.

"Leary—you're shooting your slide!" Kip yelled. Under the excitement, he could marvel at the power they were getting in spite of their form, worse than usual. He saw that Navy was coming up and, with the edge of his eyes, caught the flash of orange-tipped oars, Syracuse making an early bid. "We're not getting much run," he thought. "That's where the bad form counts."

"Get together!" he barked. There was blood on the lips of Lisbon and Guttman. "They're trying too hard," he thought. "If I yell too much they'll blow up."

The beat was up again, he realized, and wondered vaguely whether he was taking the stroke from Kowalik or Kowalik from him. This annoyed him as did their passing the two-mile mark without his knowing it.

"Down, down, you lugs!" he yelled. His voice had risen higher than usual. They eyed him fearfully. They still led, but in dropping the beat they lost ground and Navy's bow was almost even with them, and Syracuse and California less than a length behind.

Kip knew that this crew was in no mood for subtleties, whether of thought or action. He saw the bridge ahead and that decided him. "All right," he called. "Bring it up." He felt the thrill of their tremendous power move through the frail boat and he saw, with pride, the lead begin to grow again. They liked that, he saw, letting them go all out.

"Give it to them!" he called. "Give it to them! Break their damned hearts!"

They liked to hear him talk that way. They had never heard him do it before. Some of them were even grinning. They led by open water again. Something like a coldness dropped on Kip and was gone, and the noise of many voices. They had passed the bridge and the third mile.

Kip turned a little. They had over a length on Syracuse. The others were strung out, Navy and California at Syracuse's bow.

Leary was shooting his slide again, Guttman getting his oar out of the water too fast. "Steady," Kip called, afraid to say more. Still the cedar shell fled like a thing alive, still the long oars bit deeply into the river, shoveling the water back.

Seven bombs had gone off on the bridge when they went under it to tell those at the finish that the crew in the seventh lane was leading. So they would be ready for him, Kip knew, on the yacht. And he would be ready for them. He would bring his crew aboard with him and see how his brothers liked that!

Exultation beat up in him. Half a mile now. The crew's bodies, sheeted in sweat, gleamed strangely in the twilight. The line of yachts was opening on either side. They were in, Kip thought. "Pick it up," he called. "Pick it up!"

They drove the blades deep, the great bodies bent. "We're in!" he kept thinking in time with the beat of his tiller grips. "We're in! We're in!" The shell trembled as it tore through the water.

Then they blew. Guttman had taken his oar out of the water too soon, had bothered the No. 6 in front of him and made him catch a crab. Leary, shooting his slide, losing power, almost caught one. What he screamed at them, Kip never knew. But when he saw that the bow oar was catching when Kowalik, the stroke, was taking his blade from the water, he knew that it was all over. What boat first slid by them, he did not know. He saw only the strained faces, the terrible confusion in the waist of the shell, and Kowalik's efforts to keep rowing, to pass the rhythm back to the others. The other shells slipped by like ghosts in the deepening twilight.

"Get together," he said, mechanically. Pathetically, they were trying to. The shell had almost lost headway.

People were yelling on the yachts but one voice, out of a megaphone, pierced to Kip's ears. "Leave those punks by themselves," Ad Grant was yelling from the bow of the yacht. Kip turned. They were abreast his brother's yacht, *Cormorant*. He could see them in the bow, yelling and gesturing to him. "Jump in and swim over here," Ad said.

The full meaning of it all came to Kip in a rush. He should abandon these men before him as a last, contemptuous gesture and sign that they did not belong or deserve to belong to that long tradition of which he and his brothers were a part. In doing so, he would appease his brothers and take some of the edge off their sarcasm tonight. His anger at and scorn of the crew returned to him, strong, and Kip half rose to ease himself over the side of the shell. He remembered what Leyden had asked, with curious foresight, of himself—to bring them in an eight-oared crew, so that they would be fully such in the coming years. To hell with them, he thought, and to hell with Leyden. All of them had humiliated him.

Pathetically, they were still rowing, their oars clashing under the sound of the whistles which were already blowing for the winning crew. From his half-crouch, Kip turned to go over the side. He saw them in the bow of the *Cormorant* again . . . this time saw Mary Adams, a little apart from the others as he always liked to think of her. She was shaking her head, almost sadly. When he turned she waved her hand—for him to go on.

He had sat in the shell again before he knew he had done so. Why? he thought and felt stupid. This is silly, he tried to tell himself, but he saw the years that were to come, for them, and some strong, nameless excitement passed over him and left him weak and clearheaded. Sarcasm could never hurt him as much as he had the power to hurt these men before him.

"Way enough!" he called. They looked at him, startled. "Way enough!" His voice bit. The oars came out of the water, hung poised for his command. He made his voice as casual, as even as he could. "Now get together," he said, as though they were just out for a practice paddle. "You've been going like a bunch of washwomen."

"Ready—" he said. Their faces had grown almost composed. He felt pleasantly the sense of his own power, heard Ad Grant's voice through the megaphone, but did not hear Ad's words. . . ."Row!" Kip said. The eight oars took the water like a machine.

Ahead the whistles were screaming for a Navy crew that had come up in the dusk to beat Syracuse and California. And that dusk filled the river, turning the shells into shadows. But those who happened to be looking saw a curious sight—last by almost an eighth of a mile, but moving with a rhythm precise and sure, with unbelievable power; last now, but rich with great promise, an eight-oared varsity shell came home.

FOR DISCUSSION

1. We tend to think of the terms "winning" and "losing" in fairly simplistic terms. Referring to "Eight-Oared Crew,"

try to write extended definitions of each word. What did the boys in Kip's shell win? What did they lose?

2. The world loves a loser, but it doesn't like a sorehead. When does a loser become a sorehead? What sort of behavior have we come to expect of the defeated team, the losing coach, and so on? Do these rules and rituals exist only in particular sports? Discuss.

3. The old maxim goes: It doesn't matter whether you win or lose. It's how you play the game that counts. Is this still valid today?

INTRODUCTION

Lacrosse is a game as old as the American Indian. It is as rough and demanding as its younger cousin—football. Nevertheless, football commands stadiums crammed with cheering crowds while lacrosse is lucky to survive in oblivion. In spite of this neglect, Bud Jenkins learns that lacrosse offers something which football fails to provide.

I'm a Dedicated Man, Son

Stewart Pierce Brown

Even Harry the Horse was silent at the prospect of another bad year for the lacrosse team, and when Harry was silent, the outlook was grim.

Both teams came charging up on the ball at the same time. Scrubs and varsity met, helmets thumped, sticks clattered, and the sound of groaning was heard in our land. And in the middle of it all, Brittle Baker slumped to the ground like an unstrung puppet.

This time it was his ankle. Baker's bones are so brittle you can give him a fracture just by walking past him in heavy shoes. He was carted off to the campus infirmary, and with him went the last hope of the university's having even a mildly successful lacrosse season.

In fact, my roommate, Red Benson, varsity goalie, sighed and said, "There goes the last hope of the university's having even a mildly successful lacrosse season."

"True," said Tex Kelly, our fun-loving center. "Unless we win a lot of games, we'll never be able to lure such luminaries of the lacrosse world as Maryland and Army and Johns Hopkins onto our schedule."

"We are destined," said Harry (the Horse) Humboldt,

"to continue laboring in the vineyard of athletic obscurity."

Those may not have been our exact words, but they give you an idea of what we were all thinking. For years the university lacrosse players have been thinking such thoughts. Lacrosse is kind of a stepchild around here. Football gets the big play. It draws the crowds, it pays the bills, it puts the university's name in the headlines. Football is played in the new stadium across the river; lacrosse is played on old Nelson Field. Football is watched by sixty thousand cheering fans every autumn Saturday; lacrosse is watched by Coach Franks—and even he looks restless every once in a while. The grounds department hasn't seeded Nelson Field since the football boys left, and all the maintenance department has done to the field house has been to cut down the hot water supply in the showers. The university does furnish our uniforms, but the Indians who invented the game were better dressed.

You want to know something funny? We don't care. But what we *do* care about is our schedule. We play lacrosse because we like it. We get a terrific charge from being out there on a spring afternoon with a bunch of good guys, whipping the ball around. It's wonderful exercise and it's a lot of fun, but we'd like to play some of the good teams. We're tired of State Teachers and National Institute. We'd like to play Navy, or maybe Maryland—some of the really hot clubs. Even when you play a game for the fun of it you like to play the big boys.

Now when I say "the *fun* of it," don't get the wrong idea. Lacrosse is a rugged game. Basically, the idea is for one team of ten men to toss a rubber ball between the other team's goal posts, which are about 6 feet apart and 6 feet high, with a net behind them. This ball is somewhat smaller than a baseball and harder than a freshman's skull. To move it from one end of the field to the other—110 of the longest, most lung-collapsing yards you ever ran—you carry it with a stick that's a cross between a tennis racket and a snowshoe. It has a long wooden handle with a scoop on the end, woven of leather thongs. You simply cradle the ball in the pocket of your stick and run down the field and flip it between the posts. You get a point every time you do this, and all that prevents you from doing it as often as you want is the other team.

And they can prevent you by any means short of dropping dynamite down the front of your jersey. They can body check you, they can hit you with their sticks, they can knock you down and jump on you—or at least that's the way it feels sometimes. Technically it isn't quite that bad. Body checking is okay, but no flying blocks, like they used to have in football. You can try to knock the ball out of a man's stick with your stick, but you draw a penalty if you hit him on the head. And there's a rule that says no one but the goalie can touch the ball with his hands. Other than that, it's kitty-kick-the-door-down and heaven help the man who bruises easily and mends slowly.

They tell me the Indians used to play with a human skull instead of a ball, and I've seen many a day on Nelson Field when it looked as though we were about to give the game back to the Indians literally. The other afternoon somebody's helmet rolled off during a scrimmage. Somebody else picked it up and asked, "Whose is this?"

"I don't know," Red said. "Whose head is in it?" The point is, the guy looked to see.

But there's a lot of finesse to the game, too, a lot of technique, and a lot of speed. It's really something to watch a couple of good stick handlers sling that ball around, and you haven't seen the ballet in its purest form until you've seen Navy's forward line go passing downfield at top speed in the face of tough opposition. The intricate plays some teams have worked out would make a chess player quit in envy. So what you've got is a body-contact sport that requires speed and intelligence too.

What we *haven't* got here at the university is a chance to play any of the better clubs. We never have had. Practically generations of lacrosse teams at the university have been trying to make the big leagues. Their lack of success has been spectacular.

But with this year's squad, it looked as if we might do it. Hopes among the old lacrosse alumni began to rise, and in the athletic office they told us the big teams were ready to be scheduled as soon as we got one good season under our belt. As I say, it looked as though this were going to be the season.

Then wham! Brittle breaks his ankle and our dreams of glory faded slowly away again.

After Brittle had been taken down to the infirmary, we

called it a day and clumped into the field house. It was a cold-water mausoleum. Even the Horse was quiet, and when you don't hear that picture-rattling laugh of his, you know the situation is grim.

"Well, it looks like Taxidermist Tech again next year," Tex said finally.

"Cheer up," I said. "Tomorrow's another day," and they threw me in the shower.

But I was right; tomorrow *was* another day and, as it turned out, quite a day. The jayvees scrimmaged us all over the field. Usually we drub them, but soundly; this time, though, they really gave it to us. The big difference was one man: their first attack, a kid we'd never seen before.

This was a real lacrosse player, this boy. He went through the varsity as though we weren't there. He had speed and power and when it came to broken-field running he made Pete Curlow, who got all the football headlines last fall, look like a hippopotamus on ice. Red was arm-weary from batting down his shots at the crease—and Red didn't stop them all. This kid was really hot.

"This kid is really hot," said Red, who has a way with a phrase. The rest of us were so tired we could only nod.

Red motioned to the kid and he came over to our little circle of asthmatics. There was a friendly smile showing through the wire mask on the front of his helmet. He was tall and rangy and he wasn't even puffing. His legs came out of his shorts like a couple of small oak trees, and he had a pair of hands on him that made the big leather lacrosse gauntlets look like pigskin dress gloves. I figured he weighed about 190 pounds—189 of it muscle and bone.

His name was Bud Jenkins and he was a sophomore transfer. This was the first time he'd been out to practice when the jayvees scrimmaged with the varsity. He was a quiet guy, kind of modest and retiring, yet he had a sort of basic confidence. We pirated him off the jayvee squad right then and there. On the varsity we moved Dick Herren from attack back to cover point and put Bud in his place at first attack.

It was the fuse we'd been needing. We exploded all over the place. When State Teachers came to town to open the season on Saturday, they were halfway home in the bus before they knew they'd been hit. And State Teachers, as a rule, gave us trouble. I mean, we had a lacrosse team! Nelson Field became the scene of great rejoicing; the Horse was laughing practically incessantly. In fact, the only man on the squad who wasn't doing handsprings was Dick Herren, but even he had to admit we had a better club.

On the second Saturday we clobbered St. Martin's, and we really rolled up the counters too. Jenkins scored six times.

He was a joy to watch out there. He'd whip straight down the field until he ran into trouble, and then he'd suddenly start hopping and sidestepping. The defense men would be left pounding one another over the head. And if they tried to gang up on him, he'd go blasting right through the middle, like a jet-propelled tank. His stick seemed to grow right out of his arm. He kept that ball in there as though it were tacked, tied, and trussed with twine. His goal shots traveled slightly faster than the speed of light, yet he could hang a pass out in front of you as lazily as a marshmallow.

And the best part of it all was, he was no prima donna. He was in there every minute, working hard and fast, and he'd laugh almost as loud as the Horse when anyone else scored. He got a big kick out of just playing lacrosse.

Our third game was with Eastern Military. The Cadets were always tough for us, and this year they were supposed to be really hot.

The two centers faced each other, with the ball between the backs of their sticks. At the whistle they pulled the sticks back smartly and went scuffling for the ball. It rolled off to the right, and Bud scooped it up and shot it over to Tex.

From there on, it was a battle fit for the Colosseum; but no matter how well we played, the Cadets played better. In fact, they began to look a little too hot for us to handle.

But just about then our Mr. Jenkins began to catch fire and the picture changed abruptly. He slammed in two scores, and that started the rest of us going. We finally won 10–4.

So we had three in a row: the Teachers, St. Martin's, and Eastern Military. We were warming up just before the National Institute game when Red tapped me on the arm and nodded toward the stands. "Who are those characters in the bleachers, daddy?"

"Why, son," I said, steadying myself against him, "those are spectators."

They were, too—about thirty or forty students, strung out along the splintery boards, watching the warming up in a kind of amused way. But they were *watching*.

"How did they know there was a lacrosse game here?" Tex asked. "Somebody been indulging in loose talk?"

"I'm not used to playing with people watching," the Horse said. "I'll probably go all to pieces."

Dick Herren shrugged. "The glamour boy's family, probably," he said and walked away.

Whoever the people in the stands were, we gave them quite a show. We walloped the whey out of the Institute 17–2. We didn't even care about not having hot water in the field house after that game.

And that was only the beginning.

The next home Saturday, there was an even larger turnout. And that night we were all in Tex's room when suddenly the Horse came bursting in, waving the town newspaper and yelling, "We made it! We're in! We made it!" It took five of us to tear the paper out of his hand. We smoothed it out, and down at the bottom of the third column of the second page of the sports section we found the tiny headline: UNIVERSITY LACROSSE TEAM RIPS ACADEMY 11–4. In stunned and reverent silence we read every word of the few brief lines. It was the first time the paper had ever printed anything more than the results of a lacrosse game.

It wasn't the last time, though. We got a story every weekend after that. And the crowds continued to grow. They even took to cheering, and after the initial shock we got to like that.

After the Tech game Andy Anderrsen came into the locker room and shook hands with every man on the team. He had played back in '31, when our teams were *really* bad; yet in the two worst seasons the school ever had, he made the All-America second team. He was a legend around the campus.

"Well, boys," he said, "it looks like you're going to put the old school on the lacrosse map at last. I guess we've finally made it. Keep on like this and there won't be a college in the country that'll refuse to play you." He picked up Red's jersey and shook it in our faces. "Just remember that every guy who ever wore this uniform is in there rooting for you!"

Even if he meant only the men who had worn that particular jersey, it would have been a sizable cheering section. But corny or not, it was mighty quiet in that locker room after he left.

On the following Monday, Brittle Baker reported that the athletic office was trying to schedule Army for us next year, and maybe Maryland too. We were really looking up.

Nobody was kidding anybody. We owed it all to Bud Jenkins and we knew it. Maybe he did too, but he never showed it. He kept right on being the same modest guy he'd been that first day. The only change was that he played better every Saturday, which meant the team played better too.

Then one balmy spring afternoon, with the flowers nodding in the fields, the birds on the wing, and the varsity shining brighter than a chromium-plated dime, fate hauled off and kicked us in the seat of our collective pants.

On that particular day, Hector Granitson, the university's illustrious football coach, and two of his assistants showed up to watch practice. They stood on the sidelines and didn't look at anybody all afternoon but Bud Jenkins.

"We have pirates in the bottom of our garden," Red called to me as we lined up to meet the jayvee attack.

"Maybe Bud'll look bad today," I said hopefully, but I couldn't have been more wrong. The kid was sensational, and after practice, as he headed for the field house, Granny and his men cut him out of the herd and stood talking to him while we went on to the showers.

I could pretty well guess what they were saying to him. Granny Granitson's speech to a boy on why he should play football for the university is practically irresistible. It's a cross between an Arthur Godfrey commercial and a finance company pitch. He explains that football is just a plain smart investment. The university takes good care of you: bed, board, and a job, over and above your scholarship. When you graduate, there is professional ball, where you can earn yourself a bag of dust in just a few seasons. With that, and what you've saved from your undergraduate salary, you're all set. No dreary years of working your way up; no skimping and saving. You're off to a flying start.

When Bud finally came into the locker room, Tex asked, "What did the body snatchers want, as if I couldn't guess?"

Bud nodded. "They want me to come out for football."

"When?"

"Right now," Bud said. "For spring practice."

For a moment nobody spoke. Finally Red asked, "What did you tell them?"

"I told them I'd think it over tonight," Bud said quietly and went in to shower.

Granny knows talent when he sees it. He had Bud in at tailback, and the kid was running wild before the week was out.

Our first game without him, as luck would have it, was against the toughest team on the slate: Rutgers, the only name school we met. Needless to say, they took us apart.

The final score was 16–3.

A couple of days later I bumped into Bud and asked him if he wanted to go have a Coke.

"I'm glad to see you're still speaking to me, Mac," he said. "I thought maybe I was *persona non grata* with you lacrosse men."

"Watch your language."

"I'm sorry it worked out the way it did," Bud said. "Granny's offer just seemed too good to pass up."

"Sure. He makes it sound like a lifetime subscription to Fort Knox. How's it working out?"

He hesitated a second and then said heartily, "Oh, fine—just fine." I didn't say anything and he went on telling me how great it was. "Of course," he said, "they keep you on the go; you don't get much chance to relax. Granny wants to win ball games."

"He's *got* to."

"Yeah, I suppose so," he said, staring into his Coke. "He's been wonderful to me, though. Got me a job and all my meals. And next fall he says I'll have a scholarship. Everything's going fine, really." He looked at me quickly, but I kept drinking my Coke. He asked, "How are you guys making out?"

"Oh great. What we lack in power, we make up in sheer inability."

He drained his glass and looked at his watch. "I've got to run. I've got a three o'clock at Bailey's."

I looked up in surprise. Bailey's is the campus tutoring outfit. "Since when is this?"

"Since football," he replied, with a funny smile. "Can't let classes interfere with football, y'know."

We wound up the lacrosse season with one more loss and a tie. The paper didn't carry any more stories on us, and by the last game the crowd had dwindled away to just Brittle Baker and his girl. Andy Anderrsen, that grand old man of lacrosse, we never did see again.

"Probably cut his throat," Dick said. "We might have been able to deliver if the glamour boy had stuck around."

"Well, money talks," the Horse said, not laughing.

"Now wait a minute," I said. "Any one of us would have done the same—" I stopped; I knew I was wrong. And then Coach Franks came in. He gave his end-of-the-season wait-till-next-year speech, and when he finished, everybody dressed and left.

That fall the university had a terrific football team, and Bud was hotter than a mouthful of curry powder. But I wondered about his scholarship. Somebody told me he was still doing time with Bailey's.

One afternoon I stopped by to watch the salaried football heroes practice. The number-one boys were taking five, and Bud came over to where I was standing. It was getting dark and there was a nip in the air and somewhere I could smell burning leaves. Across the river the lights of the town winked busily.

Bud sighed. "Nice time of day."

"Nice time of year," I added.

He nodded. "I like fall."

"We've got a hay ride tonight with the Pi Phis. Want to come along?"

He looked at me hard. "You mean it? I mean, I understand the guys don't—"

"I'm one of those guys and I'm asking you."

"Gosh, I'd like to, Mac, but I don't see how I can. Anyhow, I'm usually too bushed by nine o'clock to go anywhere."

A whistle shrilled and the floodlights came on. "Into the den, Daniel," I said. "I'll see you soon."

Bud walked slowly out into the bright lights, buckling on his helmet.

A couple of months later, when the lacrosse schedule for next spring came out, Army was on it but none of the other big leaguers.

"Well, that's not so bad," the Horse said, as we crowded around the bulletin board to read it. "We just beat Army and then *all* the big boys will want to play us."

We started practice early. Most of the varsity was back and we got right to work. In fact, about the second or third week out we began to look pretty fair. Not mid-season form or anything like that, but not bad, either. We spent most of the time on ball handling, and passing and basic fundamentals, but late each afternoon, just before we quit, we ran a few plays and took a couple of shots.

One day in particular we were really charged up. We kept Red on the hop knocking down goal shots—*everybody* was winging them in there. He began to clown it up, and pretty soon we were all skylarking around, mugging and shouting and taking crazy shots and generally having a ball. You could hear the Horse halfway across the river. Coach Franks didn't try to stop us; he just let us get it out of our systems.

I had just tried a really weird shot: a twisting hooker on the dead run that made me look like an eel with a bad tic. Tex trotted up beside me. "Gently, Nijinsky," he said. "That way lies rupture."

"That shot'll make lacrosse history, son," I told him.

"Well, you're being scouted," he said, nodding toward the gate at the end of the field. Bud Jenkins was standing there, half in the shadow, watching the practice.

"What's he doing, spying?" Dick said, as he raced by after a loose ball.

"Nah," Red said, "he just wants to see how the other half lives."

"Lay off," I said. "Maybe he's just curious."

"Okay, let's move it around out there!" Coach Franks called and we forgot about Bud. Later, when I looked back at the gate, he was gone.

We opened the season against State Teachers again. The Teachers looked bigger this year, and when the whistle blew they lost no time in gobbling up the ball and thundering down on Red like a herd of buffalo. He grew four extra arms and blocked three quick shots in a row, but finally they slammed one past him. Later they got two more and then they scored again in the second quarter. We managed to sneak one in, meanwhile, so that at the half we were down 4–1.

In the second half it started to drizzle. Fortunately the rain slowed the Teachers down more than it did us, and we managed to win 5–4. We were lucky.

The next Saturday we managed to beat Eastern Military 6–2, which doesn't look too bad, except that we should have beaten them 60–2. We just couldn't seem to get going. We missed passes, we missed checks, we missed a dozen chances to score. None of us looked good. "Gentlemen," Franks said afterwards, "it's my painful duty to remind you that Army is on our schedule this year. Each of you please be sure the athletic office has the name and address of your next of kin."

There was no doubt about it, the university's lacrosse fortunes were at a low ebb.

"There is no doubt about it," Red began that night up in the room, but I told him to knock it off. He knocked it off and we sat there in a sub-zero silence for the rest of the evening.

After those terrible taffy pulls with the Teachers and the Cadets our crowds vanished: Brittle's girl wouldn't come any more. The paper ignored us completely.

Army was only three weeks away, and I got the grippe.

It hit me the Monday before the game with good old National Institute. The doctor slapped me into the infirmary, where I had nothing to do but drink orange juice and have nightmares about fire-breathing giants from West Point who handled lacrosse sticks as though they were lead pencils.

After practice each day some of the guys would stop by to read my magazines and eat the fruit my mother sent me. I was always glad to see them, but at the same time I was a little irked too. I'd lie there brooding about the team all day, sweating it out, and then they'd come trooping in at night as carefree as the Bobbsey twins on a picnic. Every time I brought up the game on Saturday with National Institute, they'd just kind of drift off onto something else.

Finally, Thursday night I flipped. I asked them point-blank: "Listen, aren't you guys just a *little* worried about Saturday?"

Red took a big bite out of an apple that I was saving for my dessert. "No," he said blandly, "not particularly."

"Well, you ought to be!" I shouted. They looked up from their various magazines in surprise. "Do you think we're good or something?" I went on. "Listen, these Institute boys took the Teachers fifteen to eight. We haven't scored fifteen points in two games. I'm telling you, you better quit goofing off or you're going to get your tails trimmed."

They looked at me, then at one another. Tex silently formed the word "fever," and Red nodded wisely. The Horse said soothingly, "Take it easy, boy, you'll be all right."

"I *am* all right!" I shouted.

"There, there, now, you're tired," Red said. "Come on, everybody, we'll let him rest." They tiptoed out of the room in lock step.

Saturday I was still in bed, and I drove the head nurse crazy asking her every ten minutes or so if she knew what the lacrosse score was. She never did. She didn't even know there was a game, but finally, around four-thirty, when I figured it must be over, I asked her if she'd call the athletic office and find out what happened.

"It's all right," she said, coming back from the telephone, "we won, thirteen to two."

"Thirteen to two?" I shouted at her. "You're nuts!"

She glared at me and slammed the door with a bang.

That night the whole team came over. They crowded into the room and stood there blocking the door, grinning at me.

"Okay, what got into you guys?" I asked. "Where did you suddenly find thirteen points?"

"Abracadabra!" Red said.

They all stepped aside and there was Bud Jenkins, with a fresh strip of adhesive across his nose and the biggest grin of all.

I stared at him blankly.

"Smile, you germ-ridden misanthrope," the Horse said. "Our boy here has reformed."

"Yes," Tex said. "He was once drunk with football glory,

but now he's become a brother member of A.A.—Athletes Anonymous."

Bud's grin was practically pushing his ears off his head. Everybody was grinning except me.

"You mean you gave up football for lacrosse?" I asked Bud. He nodded. Everybody nodded.

"He was once drunk with football glory, but now he's—" Red started to say, but he went down under a pile of protesting teammates. He shouted for help, and the head nurse came in and threw them all out for making so much noise. Bud sneaked back and sat in the chair with his feet propped up on the bed.

"How come?" I asked him.

He shrugged. "I like lacrosse."

"You like football too," I reminded him. "I thought you had it made. A scholarship, All-America, the pros. . .what happened?"

"Nothing, really, Mac. It's just that they've taken all the fun out of football around here. You've *got* to win ball games."

"Well, we like to win too, y'know."

"Sure, but it isn't the only reason you play. That's the difference."

"Then you were at practice all week?"

"Since Tuesday. The guys didn't tell you because we wanted to surprise you, Mac."

"I was surprised all right," I said and we both grinned.

Then we sat in silence for a while. A nurse's rubber soles squeaked along the corridor outside, and off across the campus I heard the bell in Hollins Hall. It had begun to rain, a soft spring sound on the window.

"You know what really did it, Mac?" Bud asked as the bell stopped tolling.

I shook my head.

"The Horse," he said simply.

"The Horse?"

He laughed. "I was watching you guys at practice one day. You were really having a great time of it. And right in the middle of it the Horse laughed all over the place. That did it for me. I'd forgotten you could have fun at practice. I'd forgotten you could

88

play a game for the fun of it. So I figured it was time for me to come back home."

And that's how Bud Jenkins wound up playing lacrosse for the university. I'd like to be able to tell you that with him in there we went on to beat Army, but we didn't. It was a good game, though, and the Army guys all shook hands with us afterwards. They're playing us again next year too, and on the strength of that game—and the fact that we went the rest of the season undefeated—we've lined up Johns Hopkins and Maryland. Yes, sir, it's going to be quite a spring next year. I only hope old Andy Anderrsen comes down for a couple of games. He'll have nothing to be ashamed of.

FOR DISCUSSION

1. How does the author make the character of Harry the Horse amusing? Why is this character so essential to the story?
2. How would you compare the lacrosse team and the football team at the university? Why did Bud choose one over the other?
3. How does the theme of this story relate to those of the two previous selections? Defend your answer with quotations from each selection.

INTRODUCTION

In order to win in football, you must "get up" for the big game. For Hal, captain of Highland's football team, there was no better way to psych himself up than to hate someone on the opposing squad. Hal always equated this murderous hate with winning, and everyone agreed that winning was what counted. But after his fatal meeting with Dave Cronk, he wondered . . .

The Only Way To Win

Charles Mercer

He got up late that Saturday. Ruby, the cook, served him breakfast in the dining room. He was reading the sports section of the morning paper at the table when he heard his mother come into the house.

But he pretended not to hear her. Sometimes, particularly in the morning, she annoyed him. Sometimes, when the old man wasn't around, she treated him like a baby. It was annoying to be treated that way when you were eighteen years old.

"Hal," she said cheerfully as she came toward him. "Sleep well, dear?" She ran a hand across his blond hair, which was short and bristled hard as a brush when rubbed the wrong way.

"Oh, sure."

His mother gazed at him fondly. He was a big kid, tall and wide shouldered, with even features.

"The last game of the season today." She sounded glad. But before she could tell him how glad she was, the telephone rang and she left the room.

He stared out a window. The sky was blue and the sun shafted down brightly, laying the precise shadows of bare maples on the big yard. It was a perfect day for football.

"Carol for you," his mother called.

He took his time going to the telephone. Carol would wait, he knew. She was the best-looking girl in Highland High, but she'd wait indefinitely for him.

He was, after all, the captain of Highland's football team and the class president and on the honor roll. He was going to college next year, and his old man was J. D. Caldwell, who really was somebody around the suburb of Highland and in the city, too.

Those were some of the reasons why Carol Kirsh went steady with him.

He picked up the phone and said, "Yeah." His tone did not ape toughness; it simply was flat, sure. It was the tone he used with practically everyone he knew. It was the old man's tone. It got results.

"Hi," Carol said. She always sounded relaxed.

"What d'you know?"

"Think I'll have a little party tonight," she said. "The usuals. Okay?"

"Sure."

"Okay." She paused as if waiting for him to say more, and when he didn't she said, "Give it to Glenfield today."

"Natch."

"So old Grummick isn't letting Buzz play. What a graut!"

"Yeah." He took a deep breath. "We'll do okay without him. See you later, kid." And he hung up.

He wished then that he'd prolonged the conversation awhile. He often felt there was something he should say to Carol or she to him, but it seemed they never could.

Grummick the graut, he thought as he wandered into the den and sprawled on the sofa. He wasn't sure what the word "graut" meant. It was a word the gang used to describe a certain—well, it described a guy like Grummick, the high school principal, who didn't care about having a winning football team, a vague character who would rather generalize than be specific.

Just last Monday when Hal had gone into his office to try to argue him into letting Buzz Strathmeyer play in the Glenfield game despite his low grades, Grummick had done it again. He'd gone off on a tangent.

"Tell me, Hal," he'd said suddenly, "what's happened to

you and all that gang you run around with? You've always got to win! Did it ever occur to you that it might be good for you to lose a little? Someday you'll wake up and feel you missed something. You know what you'll miss? Your youth."

Grummick had smiled and pushed his hair off his forehead. "No, Hal, I won't let Buzz play on Saturday. I'll be out there cheering for you. But I won't feel too bad if we lose."

A graut, Hal thought disgustedly. He picked up a magazine as the old man clumped in, his face flushed from playing golf.

"What d'ya say, J. D.?"

"Oke." His father grinned. He liked Hal to call him J. D. It showed, he'd boasted, that this, his only child, was a mature man at eighteen.

But it just went to show you, Hal thought, that you never could satisfy the older generation. Grummick wanted you young. The old man wanted you mature. You never could please everybody.

Mother appeared in the door behind the old man, gazing at him worriedly.

The old man winked. "Take it easy, kid, and then," he drove a fist through the air, "give Glenfield the works!"

Hal suddenly wanted to follow them to the dining room. For an incredible moment he wanted to be a little boy again. But he didn't follow them. He sat still, wondering what was wrong with him.

Maybe the trouble was that this was his last high school game today. And, most important, it was the Glenfield game, which really was supposed to be something this year because each team had dropped only one.

Besides, there was a tradition around Highland that the team could lose every game up to the Glenfield contest, but if they won that one it was a successful season. There was a tradition that Glenfield, the suburb on the plain, was jealous of Highland, the suburb on the hill, where the people were supposed to be richer and the houses bigger.

So it was essential to beat Glenfield, to uphold the tradition, to keep the bums in their place.

The bums? He was thinking suddenly of Jean Kenyon. She'd be a senior at Glenfield High School this year. She was

—well, she was so easy to remember. He'd met her last summer at the lake. He'd met her on the far raft.

He was surprised to learn that she came from Glenfield, for he hadn't supposed that anyone so lovely would live in that town. But he was more surprised to learn she was working as a waitress that summer at a hotel where her aunt was a housekeeper.

She never stopped surprising him from the first day to the last. She disagreed with him amusedly on so much of his—well, his attitude. And she showed such amazing contradictions.

She was so ambitious that she worked as a waitress in the hope of going to college; yet she told him that she thought too much ambition was a bad thing. She was extraordinarily shy about coming home with him one evening to meet Mother and the old man; yet, once there, she wasn't a bit afraid to disagree with the old man or to tell Mother she was a waitress.

But her biggest surprise she saved for one day late in the summer. They were lying on the raft talking that afternoon.

That is, he was being positive about something—about the rightness of a mighty man who was much in the news. That was the sort of thing they often found themselves talking about. And she, as usual, was good-humoredly disagreeing, not so much with his opinion as with his positiveness.

"How can you be so sure, Hal?" she was always laughingly asking him.

Suddenly there was a great splashing, and Bolo Godwaite pulled himself onto the raft, yakking loudly. Bolo was a skinny kid who worked for the boat club that summer. He was all right at times, but Hal didn't want him around just then and told him to scram.

Bolo asked plaintively if Hal thought he owned the darned raft, and Hal got up leisurely and threw Bolo into the lake. Bolo climbed back angrily and Hal pushed him off again.

"Hal!" Jean rose, her eyes smoldering. "Don't do that!"

"I told that two-bit boatman to leave us alone," he said.

"But it's not your raft," Jean said.

Bolo clambered onto the raft again, gasping for breath, and again Hal flung him off. Then Jean pulled on her bathing cap, dived off the raft, and swam toward shore. He watched her go with bewilderment, before diving and swimming fast after her. Behind him he heard Bolo, who had struggled onto the raft again, yah-yah-yahhing derisively.

He caught up with Jean in the shallow water and tried to talk to her. She didn't answer until they reached the beach. Then she turned and said, "So long, Hal. It's been fun." She walked away fast.

He was hurt and then he was angry and eventually he was terribly lonely. He went around to the hotel where she worked and finally cornered her.

When he started to speak she said, "It just won't work, Hal." She extended a hand and he took it automatically. And then she hurried away, but not before he saw the tears in her eyes.

Well, it was lucky that Carol came back from Europe with her family just then, and they picked up where they'd left off in June. Of course it was lucky. It had to be or none of this would make sense.

Sense. That was the important thing. He hadn't showed much sense after he returned from the lake and phoned Jean. He'd just wanted to give her the chance to change her mind if she saw things differently then. He'd just wanted—well, dog-gone it, to see her.

But not any more. Not after she was so polite on the telephone but firmly refused to date him. After that the green and blue summer days, the silver and velvet nights on the lake—all that was past.

Now in the cold season he was going out to the last game —and win. He'd show her he was a winner. He'd show her what she'd missed. For she undoubtedly would be there. Yes, he'd show her today.

He felt fine when he trotted onto the field at the head of the squad and the Highland stands cheered and the band played "On to Victory."

There was a welcoming yell from the Glenfield stands as the enemy came onto the field. He always thought of the opposition as the enemy. He had to hate the opposing team; he had to work himself into a cold, calculated hatred in order to do his best.

Once last season, in the Red Oak game, he'd played against Minty Balch, an old friend from days at the lake. In that game

Minty had helped him up when he was down and he'd helped Minty up. He just couldn't work up any hatred against Red Oak and so Highland had lost.

But he'd learned his lesson. He must not stop hating.

He saw the old man and Mother on the fifty-yard line. Then he glimpsed Carol. She sat in the midst of the gang. She wasn't so corny as to wave to him, of course, though he rather wished she would. And while he saw her face, he felt she really wasn't there at all.

Warming up, he slowly worked his way across the cold November field. He looked over the Glenfield stands frequently, wondering if he'd see Jean, telling himself he didn't care but wondering anyway.

He thought that the people from that town certainly had no tone. A lot of them looked pretty seedy. Of course, Jean had tone, but—

The warm-up ended then and the first string clustered around Coach Ford at the bench. Ford played him at fullback —that lonely position where you had to make like the all-American boy most of the time.

It began in all-American-boy style all right. He won the toss and Highland spread into receiving position. Here was the perfect football day. There were his parents and his girl watching him as was always the way in football stories. A drum rolled as Glenfield swept forward following a beautiful kick.

The ball came in a flat trajectory straight toward him. He tucked it in an arm easily, almost tenderly, and swept after his grouping defense. But Drew Taylor was moving too slowly in front of him, and suddenly it seemed that there was no defense. Then the truck hit him.

He was lying on the ground, dreaming about the all-American boy. He heard the whistle. And he didn't have the ball. His fingers clawed at the turf as if to dig a place to hide. But he knew he couldn't hide, and he squirmed over to find and kill the man who had the ball.

The guy lay beside him. He was a little guy and under his big helmet he looked like a baby in a bonnet. He was hugging the ball and grinning.

"Hi," he said to Hal.

"You'd better get out of the game," Hal said slowly. "You'd

better quit right now or your own mother won't recognize you."

The little guy stared at him in amazement and then he started to laugh. The referee took the ball and the little guy got up, laughing. It was Glenfield's ball on Highland's twenty-six-yard line. The Glenfield stands were wild; the Highland stands stunned.

Hal called for time. He knelt on the ground with the team around him and used tough language. Then he said, "Who is he? Who is that runt?"

"That's Cronk," somebody said. "You know."

Now he knew. He'd only heard before. The papers had touted Dave Cronk in their high school sports columns, and Coach Ford had yakked about watching Cronk, a junior, a new kid who'd just come to Glenfield.

I'll kill that runt, he thought. I'll get him. It's the only sure way to win. He told the team they had to hold.

And they did. Hal yearned to get at Cronk but he didn't have a chance.

When it was Highland's ball on its own eighteen-yard line, Hal downed the impulse to try to run it out. He did the conservative thing and kicked out.

Cronk gathered in the ball away up near his own twenty-five-yard line and came down the field, not terribly fast but balanced, like a ballet dancer. He seemed to move in a rhythm all his own, offbeat from the rhythm of anyone on that field, sprinting and slowing and weaving unpredictably.

It was a difficult rhythm to follow, like a strange and beautiful dance. But Hal sensed it and moved in slowly, stalking him. Cronk came through Brown and Stansyck and Harrison, and then he sprinted, angling away from Hal. They streaked toward an inevitable point on the Glenfield side of Highland's thirty-yard line. But as the point of impact seemed impossible to avoid, as Hal's arms swung forward to seize and fling down and crush the small body, Cronk seemed to stop dead. It was an almost impossible halt in his sprint, a kind of blurred optical illusion. Yet Hal, in his quick study of Cronk's rhythm, had expected it. His cleats dug at the ground, but the momentum of his heavier body carried him past the angle of Cronk's break. His right hand flailed at Cronk but Cronk twisted from his grasp.

Somehow Hal managed to pivot. His legs churned, his heart seemed to coil and spring him forward. There was the goal line, there was Cronk, there was he. The distances between took an eternity to narrow.

And suddenly the three were bunched in one. That was how it must look to all the world. Only the runners knew differently. Dave Cronk knew he was across the line, for he began to turn his head.

Certainly Hal Caldwell knew. He could not stop this score now, but maybe he could stop Cronk. The sure way to win was to forget this score and stop Cronk.

He tackled him at the waist. His arms went around the slight, hard body under the loose jersey, and he tipped off on his right toe in a shallow dive. And in that instant he saw Cronk's face, surprised, wondering why he was tackled now that he was across the goal. Hal flattened his weight along Cronk's back, driving his thick padded shoulder into the loose helmet as they went down, driving his weight hard as Cronk flattened under him.

He rolled on over Cronk and got to his feet slowly, hearing the ecstatic screaming from the Glenfield stands.

But Cronk didn't get up. He lay there on the grass. He certainly was a little guy.

Hal kept wiping his hands on his pants, trying vainly to get the sweat off his palms. He looked down at Cronk. His eyes were closed, his mouth open and curled at the corners in a kind of smile, like a kid playing dead. Hal kept wiping his hands on his pants.

The Glenfield doctor appeared and Hal went back to his team. Somewhere an airplane droned in the fall sky, but down here the people were silent, staring at the motionless body of Dave Cronk.

After a while some students trotted out from the Glenfield bench with a stretcher. They moved Dave Cronk onto it and carried him off the field.

As they reached the edge of the field somebody cried, "Dave!" A small dark girl darted from the stands. Behind her came Jean.

Hal started forward and stopped, gaping at Jean. Why, out

of all the thousands in the stands, must it be Jean who ran to Cronk's stretcher?

Then he saw her hold the smaller girl back from the stretcher. Maybe the small dark one was Dave Cronk's girl. That was the way it had to be.

Please, he thought as he turned away, don't let Jean be Cronk's girl. But if she is, he thought, Cronk has made a good choice. You had to give him credit. You had to give Dave Cronk credit for a lot of things.

Brown said, "Well, we got rid of our competition."

Nobody spoke. Nobody even looked at Brown except Hal, who said, "He'll be all right. He'll be back next quarter and running right through you—and through me too."

They looked at him in surprise and he realized he'd never said anything like that before. He was being a lousy captain. But he wanted Cronk back.

"Yes, sir," he said to them, "Cronk'll be back."

But Cronk didn't come back and without him it wasn't much of a game. Glenfield kicked the ball wide of the posts in the try for the extra point. Highland should have romped for a touchdown after that, but Highland seemed as weakened as Glenfield.

Hal wondered if anyone except himself knew why. For it was his fault. He was playing sloppily. He didn't care who won. He was just waiting for Dave Cronk to come back into the game. When Cronk did come back he would go up to him and shake his hand. Not for the grandstands. Just for himself. He wanted to shake the hand of the best player he'd ever seen.

He was still anxiously waiting for Cronk to come back early in the second quarter when Ford sent in Harris to replace him. As he trotted toward the bench, the Highland stands gave him a hand. It wasn't an ovation, just a polite hand. But even that was better than he felt he deserved.

Ford and Grummick and a stranger stood at the end of the bench, staring at him.

"Look, kid—" Ford placed an arm around his shoulders. "There's been an accident. Cronk, he—he—"

"Hal," Grummick looked at him gravely, "Dave Cronk's neck was broken. He has only a slim chance."

The world grew blurred. He heard their voices but he couldn't make out what they were saying.

Finally he heard his own voice. "Call the game. Glenfield won. Dave Cronk won the game."

At dinner that evening his throat constricted at the first taste of food, and he left the table. His father followed him into the den.

"Look, Son," he said at last, "I used to play football myself."

"Did you ever kill anybody?" asked Hal.

His father grimaced. "Now look here." He made his voice loud. "You cut that out. An accident is an accident."

"It wasn't an accident." He raised his gaze to his father's. "Don't you see? I was so mad at Cronk I wanted to kill him. So maybe I have."

"Don't talk foolish." His father repeated the words measuredly, almost shouting. "Everybody gets mad sometimes when they're playing football. It just happened. It's one of those things. Reminds me of the plant. You remember when I absorbed Faber's outfit. Well, I—he—I thought he could take care of himself on a deal, but he was overtrusting. I mean—"

"You mean," Hal said, "you tricked him. And now you're trying to justify what happened as something like the natural risks of business. Just like you're trying to justify this as the natural risks of football. All because we were doing our best to win. Well, it doesn't seem right."

Then, knowing he'd hurt him, he muttered, "I'm sorry, Dad," and he realized it was the first time he'd called him dad in a long while.

"That's okay, Hal." The voice was low, persuasive. "When you come into the plant with me—"

He didn't listen. In the past whenever he'd thought about the future he'd assumed he'd go into the plant with his father after college. But now he knew he wouldn't. He was going his own way. He hadn't the vaguest idea yet where it would lead him, but at least it would be his own way.

He stood up. "I'm going down to the Cronks' house."

His father gaped at him. Then he made his tone judicious. "All right, Hal, all right. Pick up some of the fellows and—"

The Only Way To Win   99

"No," Hal said, "I'm going alone."

As he went through the hall his mother came up, her face taut. "Carol called you, Hal. She said some of the gang were at her house and you hadn't showed up yet."

"Does the dizzy dame think I'm going there *tonight?*" he shouted. "I'm going down to the Cronks'."

Her eyes widened. She might be going to cry. Suddenly she pulled his face down to hers and kissed his forehead. "I'm glad," she said. "I'm awfully glad."

The Cronks lived on a side street lined with old small houses crowded in tiny yards. As he drove along he remembered that Jean had told him she lived on this street. But he tried not to think about her.

He stopped his car in front of the Cronks' house and hunched behind the wheel for awhile, thinking that he couldn't go in. But he did.

A girl opened the door. In the sudden light he blinked at her in surprise. Jean!

"Come in," she said in a low voice. She stepped ahead of him into the small living room. "Mr. Cronk, this is Hal Caldwell."

A slight man wearing a dark suit sat in a chair, dragging on a dead pipe and staring straight before him. His eyes met Hal's. They were faded eyes, expressing nothing. Slowly he got to his feet and came to Hal and shook hands limply.

"You were very decent to come," he said. "I'm sorry, my wife, she—she's upstairs resting." He turned. "This is my other son—this is my son Jack."

Jack Cronk was about fourteen years old, big for his age. He sat, hands stuffed in his pockets, and glowered at Hal.

"Glad to meet you, Jack," Hal mumbled and started toward him. But Jack simply stared at Hal with hatred.

"And this," said Mr. Cronk, turning to the dining room archway, "Dave's sister—my daughter, Marilyn."

She was the small dark girl who had rushed from the stands when Dave was carried from the field. She looked at him through a film of tears, and suddenly she whirled and fled through the darkened dining room.

"Hal," Jean said quickly, "my brother, Dick." He had come

from the hall behind them, a big kid possibly a year or two older than Jack, fifteen or so. He lounged against an old upright piano and stared hard at Hal.

"Jean's told me a lot about you, Dick," Hal said.

"Yeah?" He was a not-so-tough kid trying to act tough. "That's a hot one. I never heard about you."

"Mr. Cronk," Jean said, "won't you let me get you some coffee now?"

"No. No, thank you, Jean." He looked at Hal. "Take a chair. Jean's been—well, she's sort of been helping us here. We're neighbors, I guess you know. Friends. Jean and Marilyn. Jack and Dick. They've made it nice for us coming into this new town. The other fellows—the Glenfield fellows, the ones on Dave's team—they just left."

Hal sank into the sofa, trying to ignore the stares of Jack Cronk and Dick Kenyon. They hated him and he did not blame them. He hated himself. How could he start again and be different?

He cleared his throat. "I came to say, Mr. Cronk, that I—" His hands clenched in the futility of saying anything, "that Dave is the best football player I ever played against. He—he is a great little guy. I—I'm sorry."

Mr. Cronk dragged hard at his dead pipe. Finally he said, "He sure liked football. He is pretty light, only a junior, but he sure liked the game."

Then, the terrible silence. Dave would be sitting here now if it hadn't been for this afternoon.

Mr. Cronk lowered his pipe. "It was an accident," he said dully. "It was—one of those things that happens when you—go hard at something."

Supposing he told them it wasn't an accident? But it would only make things worse for them instead of better.

Dimly he felt that it might make things better for him if he told them. But it no longer mattered how he felt. Now it only mattered how they felt. He wanted to do something. Words, even the sincere words that were ready to tumble from his lips, were too weak.

"Mr. Cronk. Mr. Cronk, at a time like this—I mean, because of what's happened, you—you suddenly find yourself loaded with expenses you didn't expect. And I wondered if—I'd like to do something toward—"

"No!" Mr. Cronk got up and scowled down at him. "Thank you for calling, young man."

Jean rose too. Jack and Dick sneered at him.

He got to his feet and backed into the hall, mumbling incoherently. Jean opened the front door for him and suddenly stepped out after him.

"I'm sorry," he said.

"You're a fool," she answered. "Just because— You needn't think— Coming here trying to buy something with your father's money!"

"I'm not trying to buy anything." His voice rose unhappily. "And it's not my father's money. I've got five hundred dollars in savings bonds in my own name, and I just wanted to do something—" The words trailed off as he saw her expression of misery.

Impulsively, she reached out and touched his arm. "I know," she said. "I feel as sorry for you as for—them. Hal, you didn't have to hit Dave so hard, did you?"

He shook his head. "That's the awful thing," he said slowly. "At the time I hated him so much that I wanted to kill him."

She stared at him for a moment. Then she swung around and went inside and slammed the door shut behind her.

Monday was the most difficult day of his life. He didn't want to go to school. But he went, of course. He knew he had to go. It was like being thrown from a horse; you were always supposed to get up and ride again. Yet once he was in school he found that everyone was as friendly as always and that no one blamed him for what had happened.

The city's Sunday newspaper had set the mood with its front-page story about Dave Cronk's accident. It had reported that his neck was broken "in a goal-line tackle," making it sound as if the whole Highland team had piled on him. There were even a few lines about Captain Hal Caldwell's insisting that the game be called. He sounded good in the newspaper. Dave Cronk might not live, but he, Hal Caldwell, sounded good.

Carol walked from chemistry to history class with him, chattering about the Christmas dance. She didn't mention Dave

Cronk or Hal's failure to attend the party Saturday night. Nothing had really changed. He could go right on as he had been.

He went home dazedly. His mother came in a few minutes later. They sat in the living room as the dark afternoon waned, and finally he told her about the Dave Cronk incident in detail.

"Perhaps he'll pull through," she said. And then after a long time, "I won't tell you to try to forget it, Hal. You'll forget the worst of it eventually. But I hope you can remember the best of it. Because there could be just a little good in it for you.

"It may—" She hesitated and looked around the large, expensively furnished living room. "It may make you see that there's a penalty in trying too hard for some things that don't count at all. In a sense, you know, your father and I are more to blame than you for what happened. We must have taught you that the important thing is to win, no matter how. That's what's wrong, Hal. If you could learn that, some good could come out of this for you."

In the following days he thought about what his mother had said. Dave Cronk's condition improved, but Hal lived in a kind of solitary confinement of his own construction. He went around school with Carol and the rest of the gang, but after school he didn't go to the drugstore with them or date Carol in the evenings. He went home alone and read or merely sat. And he seldom stopped thinking about Jean.

Finally, on a gray afternoon in December, Carol stopped him as he hurried toward his car in the school parking lot.

"Listen, Hal." She looked at him coldly. "It doesn't take a house to fall on me. Everybody gets the idea that you want to be left alone. There's just one question. Are you taking me to the Christmas dance next week?"

He looked at her for several seconds. "You'd better get another date," he said and walked to his car.

Then he did what he'd wanted to do for a long time. He drove down to Glenfield and looked for Jean among the crowds of homeward-bound students.

At last he saw her. But she was walking with Marilyn Cronk, and he didn't have the nerve to stop and speak to them. It was the one thing in the world he wanted to do, but he didn't have the nerve.

The next day he left his car at home, not wanting to ride up to Jean in the sleek convertible. After school he walked to Glenfield, but he didn't see her.

On the third day, when the first light snow of the season covered the ground, he walked to Glenfield again. And then at last he saw her, walking alone in the gathering darkness of late afternoon. Again he was afraid to speak to her, but he had to know what she truly thought.

He caught up with her and said quietly, "Hi, Jean."

It seemed to take her forever to say "Hi."

"May I carry your books?" It didn't seem a corny question, not now, not with her.

"All right," she said after another pause and gave him the stack of schoolbooks.

He had imagined himself saying many fine things to her, but now he could only say, "You want a soda or something?"

"No, thanks."

His heart seemed to hesitate in its heavy hammering. "Everything going okay?"

"Oh, yes," she said. "Just fine. And you?"

"Fine." His tone was unconvincing.

He did not speak for some time, for he was content just to be walking along her street with her, the light snow scrunching underfoot, the bare branches of the elms tossing overhead in the northern wind. Lights from the windows of the old houses cast faint yellow paths on the new snow. A man's voice rang across the street. Somewhere a shovel scraped a path.

He breathed deeply. "Jean, I've been wanting to ask you, could—would you go to our Christmas dance with me?"

Her lips parted. For an instant he was sure she'd agree. But she shook her head slowly. "Thanks, Hal, I'd like to. But I can't."

He looked at her closely. "Just tell me one thing, Jean. Are you Dave's girl? Because if you are, I understand. I know it wouldn't be, well, right for me to try to see you any more. I mean—see, I've got to be punished for what I did. I know that. And it would sort of be just what I deserve if you were his girl and that's why you didn't want to see me."

She looked at him gravely. "No, Hal, I'm not Dave's girl."

"Then why—" He paused. "I guess I don't need to ask you why you don't want to see me. It's because of the way I am. That day on the raft, the day I kept pushing Bolo off, it was just like the way I set out to fix Dave's wagon, wasn't it? You saw then just what I'm like. I've got to be the big shot. I've got to have my way. I've got to win."

He shook his head. "I don't trust a guy who tells you he's going to turn over a new leaf. I know I'd like to change, but, well, words don't mean anything. It's how you are inside and how the inside makes you act outside—"

She halted suddenly at the path to her house and looked up at him as his voice trailed off. Her face was troubled.

"Maybe I'm the one who's being superior," she said. "Maybe I'm being the smug one now instead of you. But I want time to think over things, Hal."

Suddenly, instinctively, he knew that you couldn't force the most important things. And this was the most important thing of his life.

He interrupted her quickly, "Let's not talk about it right now, Jean. Let's see what happens. Maybe someday I'll walk down here again."

Her mittened hand squeezed his as she took her books from him. "I'll see you, Hal." Then she was running up the path to her house.

He walked on slowly. For a moment he was tempted to look back, but he was certain she wouldn't be watching him. He was sure that she wanted to forget the attraction of last summer.

On the Cronk steps he noticed Jack holding a shovel and Dick Kenyon balancing a broom. Talking with Jean, he had not seen them come out to clean the walks. They stood motionless as cats and stared at him across the snow.

"Hi." His despondent voice was so indistinct that it probably didn't carry to them. He didn't care now. He never could change the fact they were his enemies. He walked on, head lowered.

The sharp blow on his back staggered him. He stumbled and wheeled. Jack Cronk faced him, shovel raised to hit him again. Beside him stood Dick Kenyon, his face pale and determined.

"That's for you, hot stuff." Jack's face was contorted savagely. "You stay away from here!"

"And stay away from my sister," Dick cried shrilly.

The crazy guys! And then he thought that the expressions on their faces must be what his own had been when he had looked at Dave Cronk that Saturday. That was what Dave must have thought about him: The crazy guy!

"Jack," he said, "Dick, look—"

Dick swung the broom at him. Hal ducked and snatched it from him and flung it aside. He could beat these kids to a pulp. But he wouldn't, no matter what they did to him.

Together they drove in at him, butting and swinging fiercely. He slipped and fell backward. He fended instinctively, but he didn't try to hit them as they fell on him. He saw the shovel swinging at him and he tried to duck.

In the deep darkness and numbing pain he heard Jean crying, "Dick! Jack!" And in the darkness he knew she *had* stood and watched him.

He was lying on the sidewalk and she was crouched beside him. "You crazy kids! He didn't even try to defend himself," she said. "Suppose you've killed him!"

"I didn't mean to kill him!" Jack cried.

He could see her beside him, he could hear her. His head throbbed painfully.

"I'm okay," he said. "You hear me, Jack, Dick? I really am okay. Things are going to be all right."

FOR DISCUSSION

1. In the story "The Only Way To Win," Hal changes his attitude about a lot of issues and individuals. Discuss specific ways in which Hal grows.

2. What role does Jean play in the story? How does she affect Hal?

3. Kip Grant and Hal Caldwell are essentially wrestling with the same problem. Define their struggle and discuss each boy's solution.

INTRODUCTION

Athletic events are often touchstones in our lives. We remember where we were the day the Mets won the pennant. We remember what we were doing when someone said that Ali had defeated Frazier. We treat our memories of events much as we would treat a valued shoe box filled with old photographs. Each photo captures a slice of time and crystallizes it forever.

The "Snapshot" that follows is a poet's remembrance of a tiny, isolated event. Using language as though it were an Instamatic up in the stands, Robert Wallace snaps a scene for his memory album.

A Snapshot for Miss Bricka Who Lost in the Semi-Final Round of the Pennsylvania Lawn Tennis Tournament at Haverford, July, 1960

Robert Wallace

Applause flutters onto the open air
like starlings bursting from a frightened elm,
and swings away across the lawns
in the sun's green continuous calm

of far July. Coming off the court,   5
you drop your racket by the judge's tower

and towel your face, alone, looking off,
while someone whispers to the giggling winner,

and the crowd rustles, awning'd in tiers
or under umbrellas at court-end tables,   10
glittering like a carnival
against the mute distance of maples

along their strumming street beyond
the walls of afternoon. Bluely, loss
hurts in your eyes—not loss merely,   15
but seeing how everything is less

that seemed so much, how life moves on
past either defeat or victory,
how, too old to cry, you shall find steps
to turn away. Now others volley   20

behind you in the steady glare;
the crowd waits in its lazy revel,
holding whiskey sours, talking, pointing,
whose lives (like yours) will not unravel

to a backhand, a poem, or a sunrise,   25
though they may wish for it. The sun
brandishes softly his swords of light
on faces, grass, and sky. You'll win

hereafter, other days, when time
is kinder than this worn July   30
that keeps you like a snapshot: losing,
your eyes, once, made you beautiful.

FOR DISCUSSION

1. The title of the poem is "A Snapshot . . . ." How skillful is
    the poet in creating his word picture? What does he particu-
    larly want us to see?

2. The poem is more than the re-creation of a moment. How does the poet ask us to think of matters beyond the tennis match that has just been lost?
3. What is the crowd's attitude toward Miss Bricka here? How does it compare with the poet's attitude toward his subject?

INTRODUCTION

George Chuvalo has lost a few fights, but he is respected as one of the toughest men in boxing. He has fought the best of the heavyweights, and now he is getting ready to fight Muhammad Ali. He is not given much of a chance in this bout.

One wonders why George Chuvalo continues. If he ever had any dreams of being heavyweight champion, by now they must have dimmed to a pinpoint. The portrait of Chuvalo that follows suggests some reasons why he fights on. This is the way it is as he gets ready for Ali.

George Chuvalo: Pain & Violence as a Way of Life

Leonard Gardner

In the Eagles Gym on the second floor of an old green building in a residential part of Vancouver overlooking the bay, there were so many spectators they had to be cajoled into giving the man they had come to see space enough to punch the bag. They scurried after him for autographs on his way to the shower, and, barred from joining him in the stall, they waited until he emerged in his terrycloth robe and surged with him to his dressing room. Locked out, they milled restlessly, gazing at posters of past fights covering the walls and at advertisements for the Muhammad Ali wristwatch on sale behind a counter. All the cameramen were leaving and the reporters that still remained were clustered around Ali's buoyant trainer, Angelo Dundee, a short man with dark protruding eyes, modish clothes, and hair combed artfully forward, who was giving his consideration to a theory that Muhammad Ali was the greatest athlete of all time.

"He could have been a great track man or a baseball player, and he's tall enough for basketball," said a newsman in a green plaid suit and a homburg graced with a band of exotic feathers.

Dundee contributed a little help: "He would have been great at football, too. Can't you see him as a tight end?"

When Ali came out in his street clothes—a blue warm-up outfit—his face bored and still boyish at thirty, he paused to comb his hair before accepting the pens and paper. With Dundee and his entourage he was pushing slowly toward the stairway when someone said, "George is here." At this cue Muhammad's face came alive. His eyes widened; his head, up above most of the other heads, turned from side to side.

"George? George is here? Where is he? Where's George? George, where you hiding?"

George Chuvalo's dressing room was at the head of the stairs, and Ali began to beat on the door. "George, you in there?" He leaned in and winked at Chuvalo, who was sitting in the crowded room in a pair of pale lavender undershorts. "George, I'm coming in to get you." He winked again, as if to make sure George understood it was a game or to persuade him to play too, but George just sat there.

"Don't let him in," prompted Dundee.

"I'm coming in!"

And then Ted McWhorter, Chuvalo's trainer, a frail, taciturn black man in old clothes and worn-out suede shoes, on whose face every worry of forty years of boxing seemed to have left its mark, dutifully came forward. "Go on. Get away. You can't come in here. George in here," he said sadly.

But Muhammad pushed his way in and locked the door. Grinning, he screamed threats, grunted in imaginary struggle, pounded a wall, kicked the door. Then he opened it and let McWhorter shove him out to his delighted fans. George remained in his chair, unamused.

"He doesn't bother me," he said. "But he seems kind of like a kid, you know? It's unprofessional."

Now a timid knock sounded on the door, and two give-away color photos of Ali were passed in.

"Guy want to know will you sign these," said McWhorter. It seemed a rather insensitive request of one whom the sports pages were calling the forgotten man in the coming bout, but George obligingly scrawled "Keep punching" and his large, elaborate, illegible signature over them. Whatever vanity he may once have had seemed to have been burned out of him in the combustion of millions of calories and the fire of eighty-six battles. Known for his stoicism, he combined extremes of energy and repose. It was a quality peculiar to the ring, demanded by it, and seemed now the heart of Chuvalo's personality, as if profession and character had become one. It had served him well for sixteen years, but now it was being suggested that stoicism might be all he had left. He was approaching thirty-five. The subject of retirement had been opened in 1967 when a beating by Joe Frazier hospitalized him with a fractured eye socket. In 1970 a battering by George Foreman appeared to convince both his critics and his fans that the long rugged career had come to an end. But it didn't convince George. No one yet had ever knocked him down. Eleven days after the Foreman match he was fighting in Yugoslavia, his parents' birthplace; and now, two years later, his refusal to quit had become a part of his image.

Chuvalo's broad body dominated the center of the cubicle and required the other men in it to range themselves along the walls, which were covered with pictures of boxing's greats. While McWhorter wrapped his hands, George conversed with everyone in the room, periodically plunging into loud, rapid exchanges in Croatian, his first language, with two Yugoslavian friends. He sat very straight, with the easy bearing of a man perhaps even unaware of his pride. His thighs, buttocks, biceps and shoulders bulged, but he had the heavy frame to carry all that muscle in good proportion. His wrists and ankles were thick, his rib cage enormous, his skull large, and his face of a remarkable breadth. His nose, which he said had only been broken once but grew wider every year, was so wide at the bridge it was like an abutment, a shield for his eyes, which were dark and alert. It was a face with a violent history he later read for me before a mirror, moving his finger from the fresh pink scar tissue on the side of his nose and on his high jutting cheekbones to the paler scars over his eyes, saying: "That's Cleveland Williams, and that's Williams—he really opened me up—that's Mel Turnbow, that's Quarry, that's Frazier, that's Buster Mathis. . . ."

McWhorter secured the hand-wraps and adhesive tape and we all stood up.

"Are there many people out there?" George asked.

Half the crowd and all the newsmen had gone. Chuvalo had the whole gym floor for his spirited shadowboxing. His stablemate, Clyde Gray, warmed up with him. Gray was scheduled to fight Manny Gonzolez on the coming card. A leading contender for the world welterweight title, he would normally have been a substantial favorite over an aging Gonzolez, who had once been near the top but now had the dismal look of impending defeat; but this would be Clyde's first contest since the death of his brother, Stewart Gray, from injuries sustained in a bout in Winnipeg several weeks before. Clyde was now a somber presence in the Chuvalo camp. He admitted he had no more zest for boxing and was going on only for the big money that seemed at last to be near his grasp.

McWhorter was laying out the headguard, Vaseline, mouthpiece, cup and gloves for George's sparring. He had come out of Alabama, trained fighters for many years in Detroit, and lived now in a Toronto hotel across the street from the Lansdown Gym. He was a bachelor of fifty-seven and wore a small mustache. Serious, circumspect, shifty-eyed, he had little tolerance for questions and distractions and seemed at times to brood, as if the tensions of his fighters were being deposited in him and in his ritualistic care of the details of training. He had the concentration of one fending off disturbing influences, and even put up an alarmed struggle against a girl who tried to coax and then drag him into posing for a photo with George. She had to settle for a picture without him. His mind was on bringing George into the fight at the peak of readiness; and after seven weeks of training the two said as one that George was in the best shape of his life. McWhorter was not talking retirement.

"When George wants to retire he'll retire. Why should he retire now? It'd be different if he was walking on his heels and fighting for nothing, but he's making $150,000 a year. He's always training. He keeps himself fit. He don't drink or smoke. He's got a wife and five kids. He stays home and gets his rest. Why should he quit? Patterson is thirty-seven. He's worth $3 million and he's still fighting."

Bill Drover, Canada's No. 2 heavyweight, who was training with George for a fight of his own, didn't think Chuvalo was through either. A right hand to the chin was more evidence than he needed. McWhorter stopped the sparring to allow him to recover, but Drover seemed to have lost his strength. George carried him through the rest of the session and Drover left the ring saying George still had a chance for the title. An impressive speaker, Drover had recently completed a broadcasting course and his enunciation was as impeccable as ever, though his eyes still showed signs of the punch. "You can't believe it until you're in there," he said. "You can't believe his strength. There's no way to stop him. He just keeps coming and coming. The only way you can stop him is with a stick of dynamite."

The next morning the two men were running in the park on a narrow path along the edge of the bay, under redwoods, firs and flowering dogwood, past totem poles and floating ducks, past a group of young white-clad runners going the other way, George setting a brisk pace, a look of exhilaration on his face, his mouth open to the cool air that had a sharpness and purity suggestive of the snow on the mountains just across the water. Drover ran a few yards behind, partly bald, with a little fat shaking at the waist, his nose prominent and askew, his face slightly quizzical, as if at twenty-eight he faced questions the older man ahead of him could ignore.

"I told one guy I was going to retire in ten years," Chuvalo said over lunch. He had come from a television interview and the usual question had been raised. "It's always the same thing —when are you going to retire? I'm not so old."

"I guess they think you're taking too many punches," I said. That was another subject he had to contend with. Some sportswriters called him a catcher and he was sensitive about it.

"They never see the ones I block. What do they want me to be, a stick-and-move guy with my reach? I bob and weave and slip. I'm not a catcher. I don't just stand in the middle of the ring and get hit with everything a guy throws at me."

"I'm not going to write that kind of thing," I said. "I'm not going to say you ought to quit, either."

"You know, I feel I'm just the same as I always was. I'll fight another year or two, but I'm going to play it by ear. When I think I can't function as well as I used to and when I don't enjoy it anymore, I'll quit."

114

I asked if his wife, Lynn, was still pressuring him to retire. She had become something of a sports page personality with her tears and her pleas of "Stop it!" when George went through some of his more difficult evenings. I had heard of scenes in dressing rooms where she begged for a promise that the fight about to begin would be his last—perhaps the reason she was home in Toronto now with the children.

"She's pretty well over that. She says whatever I want to do I should do. She doesn't go to my fights anymore. She stopped going after Foreman. She gets herself all worked up and then she gets me worked up. She's like a thunderstorm and a nice peaceful day all rolled into one. It's better if she's not around when I'm fighting."

"Did she ever like boxing?"

"She likes fights. She just doesn't like my fights. She says she likes *good* fights," he said with a smile. "Foreman caught me with a really good hook. It knocked me across the ring, but it was just the force of the punch. I wasn't hurt. I knew what I was doing. I was just getting ready to put my fight together when the referee stopped it."

"You weren't dazed?"

"No. I've never been dazed."

"Well, what do you feel when you take a really hard punch right on the button?"

"I just feel the punch. I don't feel rubber legged or dazed. I just feel the impact—the momentary impact."

He commented on the eye Frazier had injured, which was now held in place with a silicone shield. "I think it's stronger than it was before. What it's called is a blowout fracture. The optic floor caved in. Half my eyeball was sticking out. I just refer to the silicone as a piece of plywood to mend a floor that fell through. I had double vision for a few weeks, but it's okay now. I've never had any more trouble. I never think about it. I never worry about personal injury—except cuts—I just worry about losing."

He had just come from the hotel barber shop. So his hair wouldn't fly dramatically when Ali hit him, he had had it cut, but it had taken some time for the barber to become bold enough to take much off. Though prepared to take punches, George was optimistic. He thought he had a better chance now than when he fought Ali for the championship six years ago. Muhammad had been at his peak then, and Chuvalo, pressing doggedly for fifteen rounds, had given him his hardest fight. Belittled going in —called a punching bag by the press and an old washerwoman by Ali—he came out with the reputation as the toughest man in boxing. He was also said by one correspondent to be the most maligned. George thought the years since then had taken more from Ali than from himself. He had been in condition for the last ten years. He took a week off after a bout and then went back into training. He liked the demanding routine, liked making the money that had been a long time coming, and he liked the fights. He said it was the challenge of boxing that kept him going. He had a need to put out a hard effort. "I like to feel I've earned my shower."

He had money now and was getting some businesses going, but admitted he couldn't imagine himself running them. He confessed he had never had any ambition for anything except boxing since he was seven years old. "I used to hang around a newsstand looking at *Ring* magazines and I wanted to be like those guys in the pictures, and I never did want to be anything else after that. I've never had any jobs. I've hardly worked at all. I never liked working."

Open and animated, he spoke without self-consciousness, the words coming so rapidly they sometimes ran together in the way he spoke Croatian. Not long before he was reading *The Ring* he had learned his English in the streets of The Junction district of Toronto, and now he began telling about those days and about his parents.

Before his father's immigration the family name had been Cuvalo—watcher—a name from the days when Croatia was ruled by the Turks and his ancestors, serfs, had been herders, sheep watchers. The generations of Cuvalos that followed remained poor country people. George's father grew up on a farm. At ten he suffered a broken arm that his uncle advised against setting so the boy might avoid military service. He grew up with an arm he was never able to straighten and was drafted anyway. Back from the army, he married, and six months later left for the opportunities of Canada with the intention of saving the money for his bride's passage. It took him ten years. He cut wood in Northern

Ontario, labored on road gangs. A year after his wife finally arrived, George was born in Toronto. He spoke of his mother now with fondness and appreciation, describing her as having been extremely warm and loving, a woman 5 feet, 8 inches tall and weighing 200 pounds, yet not fat, structured with his own thickness of bone and muscle, who during her noon hour would run the mile from her job as a chicken plucker to his school in order to give him a kiss and a bag of potato chips. His father was of a different nature, rough and stern, a man of sixty-eight now, who walks over 10 miles a day and who George still kisses good night.

At ten George had four amateur fights and thought he was too thin. When he returned to the ring at fifteen he was a heavyweight. He left school that year for the packing house where his father worked. After a year he had had enough of butchering and returned to high school, where he felt his classmates were snobs and was self-conscious about his clothes. He kept to himself, lifted weights and boxed, and at seventeen was Canadian AAU champion. At nineteen he was a professional, living restlessly in a basement apartment with a fifteen-year-old wife. In his debut he had entered a novice heavyweight tournament in Toronto and won it with four knockouts in one night. That established him as a hometown attraction, but it wasn't conducive to an unhurried development of skills. His handlers appeared to think they had a born champion; in his next appearance George was thrown into the main event with the champion of South Africa, Johnny Arthur. Though it was Arthur's thirty-fifth fight, Chuvalo came out with the decision. Nine bouts later he was in over his head against Bob Baker. At twenty-one he was ranked tenth in the world, and at twenty-four he was desperate. He had lost half of his last ten bouts. He had four children, no job, no money, a mortgage he couldn't meet on a house he called a matchbox; he was borrowing from his mother-in-law, at odds with his manager, dissatisfied with his trainer, discouraged with his style and unable to get a fight. When he failed as a used car salesman, he borrowed $5,000, bought up his contract and went to McWhorter in Detroit. Durability could compensate for crudeness only so far. McWhorter gave him the tools suitable for his strength—a bobbing, weaving attack, short punches, counters, combinations.

George Chuvalo   *117*

"That's when I really got determination," said George. "I only had two shirts in Detroit. I remember one day I was down in Battle Creek trying to get a fight and I was wrestling with Jack Selfridge, just playing—he was the promoter. And he tore off one of my buttons and the tears just started coming to my eyes over the whole situation. I realized I had nothing for my kids. I'd made $600 in my last three fights. We didn't have a thing. And right then I got determination."

After a few more fights under his own management, George went to Irving Ungerman, who could give him the backing he needed. Their partnership took him through ten popular years as a top contender.

Ungerman, a poultry processor whose father had employed George's mother, was waiting now in his suite in the Vancouver Hotel for George to appear with him in a television interview. He was short, a former amateur flyweight, hyperactive, excitable, dressed in stripes, wearing sideburns, smoking a cigar. Chuvalo called him "The Noise." He was his first fighter and Ungerman relished the role of manager. He had not collected a percentage of George's earnings since 1969, when they had agreed that year was to be George's final one in boxing and so he should take with him out of the sport all that he could. The arrangement had persisted, said Ungerman—who by repute had no financial worries anyway—because he had kept thinking that each additional fight was going to be George's last. He made no secret about wanting him to retire.

"Win, lose, or draw," he said now to the camera, "I just hope for a fine showing." The cigar went back into his mouth and George leaned toward the microphone.

"Well, while Irving is hoping for a fine showing, I'm hoping for a fine win."

Irving hastily corrected himself. "I'm hoping for a fine win, too!"

George lay down on the bed after the interview and opened a boxing magazine. "What's this? They got Ali rated over me?"

Now somebody wanted a still photo and George got up and locked Ungerman in a strangle hold.

That evening George and I struck out for Chinatown as if

pursued by McWhorter, who lacked George's liberal views on diet. We walked at a pace close to a run, and it was clear that to Canadians on the street George was no forgotten man. People kept turning to look at him: a number of men wished him luck; one managed to keep up with him long enough to grasp his hand.

He came to a stop finally in front of a policeman astride a motorcycle. "Excuse me, are we anywhere near a Chinese restaurant that's not fancy but where the food's good?"

"Are you who I think I am?" the confused policeman asked.

When we arrived as directed at a place called the Ho-Ho, the policeman was parked in front of it. He tore some sheets from his citation book. "Would you mind? I have two sons who'd really appreciate it."

As George was writing "Keep punching," another officer, evidently alerted by radio, roared up and dismounted with his pad.

The first policeman escorted us into the restaurant and led the way to the table he decided should be ours.

"You know," said Chuvalo over duck and fish and almond chicken and beef with greens, "my mother's uncle is maybe going to be a saint. He was a priest in Yugoslavia. His name was Peter Barbaric. He died when he was a young man and five years later they dug up the cemetery and he was perfectly preserved. So the Catholic church is discussing canonizing him."

As the fight approached, the desire for Chinese food began to take George over. After dinner he would go for a walk with Drover and Gray and return sometimes wet from a sudden rain to his room to sit in his shorts and talk until after midnight. His T-shirts—one with a picture of Donald Duck on the chest—and sweat pants hung over the backs of chairs to dry. A pair of hand grips, jars of vitamins and honey were on the dresser. On the bedside table was a copy of *Boxing Illustrated* and a magazine called *For Men Only*. He called room service for orange juice and tea, commented on their exorbitant prices but added that the promoter was paying for them.

At Ali's hotel, the Georgia, where a nightly promotional party was in session, one heard that Chuvalo didn't have a chance. One reporter suggested he be retired with a lifetime supply of Empirin. It provoked a dispute about the state of George's head.

"He's not punchy," I said. "He's an intelligent guy."

"Well," said the reporter, who had just got to town and hadn't talked with George, "what do you mean by intelligent? Intelligent for a boxer or an intelligent person? I mean, sure, maybe he talks all right, but is he capable of, say, carrying on an intelligent conversation about radial tires?"

The reporter was a specialist in auto racing. I lacked the knowledge for a discussion of radial tires, so the conversation dwindled to silence over the carcass of one of Irving Ungerman's turkeys.

Maybe Ali knew about radial tires. He drove to the gym in a bronze Ferrari and talked about everything else. He said he was stepping up his training fight by fight so that he would hit a peak in his return match with Frazier, which Dundee had been saying was as good as set. He said he was the resurrection of boxing, that he wanted to cross the Alps on elephants, that his enforced layoff was the best thing that had happened to him, because it got him friends all over the world, and that he was going to be the first man to put Chuvalo down. Then he scuffled with Ungerman, whose mock punches, all low, seemed to betray a desire to fight the man himself; and he beat on George's dressing room door as usual. The door was divided in the middle into two sections, with a shelf over the lower half. The top half flew open and George came diving out over the lower half, his face wild with rage. The shelf broke as his ribs came down on it; his legs shot up and if McWhorter and others hadn't caught him he would have tumbled head first to the floor at Ali's retreating feet.

"I can make myself think I'm mad in a second," he said, touching his ribs.

"How do you know you're not?" I asked.

"Maybe I am."

He went out and broke the steel swivel on the speed bag.

At the weigh-in on the day of the fight both men were so subdued that the most colorful character at the ceremony turned out to be a preliminary fighter named Jimmy Nobody from Nowhere, who announced to anyone who cared to listen that he would rather be a nobody going somewhere than somebody getting nowhere. The promoter, Murray Pezim, told the crowd of newsmen gathered around the scales that he was happy to bring this great fight to Vancouver, a statement received as an admirable show of gameness. This was Pezim's first venture into boxing and had required guarantees of $200,000 to Ali and $65,000 to Chuvalo—the largest purse of George's career. Pezim, whose previous experience had been in securities, had said earlier that Ungerman got him drunk one morning and talked him into this bold enterprise. But he said he might even do it again. This kind of gracious resignation with which he faced what everyone seemed to agree was going to be a loss of at least $100,000 had given him a poignant charm. The Georgia Hotel had been filling with men of a peculiar sameness of appearance, who stood in the lobby in doubleknit sport coats, patterned shirts and zippered boots, looking jaded, mysteriously affluent, cynical and exhausted; and they were upstairs now in the hallway outside the room where the weigh-in and the medical exams were taking place. Pezim spent much of his day in the lobby.

"How was the weigh-in?" he asked with concern. "Was it all right? I mean from a professional point of view?"

Another man out of his element at the weigh-in but who seemed to be enjoying it more was Dr. Joe Greenberg, just in from Toronto—the Chuvalo family doctor for many years and, more recently, George's cut man. A gentle, patient, gray-haired general practitioner with an elegant weariness, he discussed George from a medical point of view.

"His durability simply comes from a super-tough constitution that he got from his mother," he said, but added that the ability to take a punch didn't necessarily make a man less likely to be hurt; though George showed no ill effects from his years in the ring, damage from boxing could be insidious and he wished he would quit. "We've had a lot of discussions about it over the years. George is a very reflective man, but he's totally committed to boxing. He thinks of himself as a boxer and can't think of himself as anything else."

We went out into the morning rain behind Ungerman and McWhorter and some of George's friends, and as we trailed them around the street, the doctor explained his presence in boxing as a response to a need. "Take a nosebleed. To stop a nosebleed you apply pressure." He grasped the bridge of his nose. "Yet I've seen seconds poke swab sticks up nostrils and stir them around. Somebody once showed me Whitey Bimstein's secret formula for cuts. You couldn't even clean it out afterwards." Then he revealed his own treatment for cuts—Whitehead's varnish, used many years ago in surgery.

We followed Ungerman into an airlines office, where a mix-up over a ticket was compounded by ten minutes of explication. Then we all went back to the room where George was in bed watching a word game on television, and he was engaged in a number of intense conversations until it was remembered that he was resting. We left the hotel, went around the corner, passed through a doorway and suddenly it seemed it was midnight. We were in a din of drums and guitars in darkness relieved only by a spotlight on a nearly nude girl dancing for no one discernible. The group stood for a confused moment and came out smaller in number. "What are they doing in there?" Dr. Greenberg wanted to know. "I thought we were going to a drug store."

While McWhorter moodily selected gauze pads and a 16-ounce jar of Vaseline, the doctor criticized the use of smelling salts in sports.

"What if something was to happen tonight?" asked McWhorter. "You wouldn't want no smelling salts?"

Dr. Greenberg smiled tolerantly. "Nature knows best. Why revive a guy just to send him out for more punishment?"

Chuvalo entered the ring in purple trunks and robe, followed by McWhorter in his run-down suede shoes. The Pacific Coliseum was filled only to half capacity, but the cheering was loud and excited and it rose again as Ali came down the aisle a moment later. The day before, Ali had run 3½ miles and worked ten rounds in the gym, most of them tirelessly circling the ring, and now at the bell he went back into that same bounding dance, one way, then the other, his arms dangling at his sides, presenting that wide-open but unreachable target that gave his fights their fascinating tension and his opponents so much frustration. George, walking after him, trying to cut the ring off and corner him in accordance with the pattern of his own training, held his guard high and blocked most of the few jabs Ali threw. He even landed some of his own. He appeared confident, and in the second round landed a hard right cross to the side of Ali's head as he was pulling away, but the jabs were thumping him more frequently now and he was beginning to swell. George was pacing himself, wasting no punches, and though Ali was conscious of pace too, his legs seemed exempt from the laws of fatigue. He danced on and on, up on his toes, shifting, fading back, always in motion and going with the punches, his muscles soft and relaxed, his left snapping out from the hip, swift and accurate, yet with a look of negligent ease. George blocked it when he could. He bobbed and weaved—not always enough to satisfy Ungerman, who constantly shouted defensive advice from the corner. He ducked, but his ducks were forward leans that he tended to hold a little long, and Ali had been practicing uppercuts.

George was taking punches, but he was conducting a disciplined fight against as fast and elusive a heavyweight as the sport has possibly ever known. And though behind all the way as he had to be, he did at times trap Ali on the ropes and explode with the combinations to body and head that the distance between the two men had been forcing him to keep in check. But in the open ring his fleeting opportunities reduced him mostly to single punches, and he threw too few of these. And always that long left was thumping his face. He cornered Ali in the fifth and jolted him with hard blows to the head, but the advantage slipped from his control: Ali lay back on the ropes, beckoned him in and dropped his arms. While the crowd yelled for George to go in and Ungerman yelled at him to stay out, George balked. It was a moment that seemed to go on and on. Ali even stretched his arms out on the ropes, and George's refusal of this dream opportunity, clearly a trap, but dangerous for Ali as well, was like a psychological turning point, establishing each man's degree of confidence. George knew Ali could beat him to the punch, and Ungerman knew it too. Later Ungerman was to say: "I just didn't want him to get hurt. He shouldn't be looking to get in the big one because he wasn't going to anyway." And so George backed off, only to go on with his pursuit as soon as Ali went back into motion.

In the next round he was battered by a torrent of combinations and emerged with a deep vertical cut over his eye that provided more than an ample test of the staunching qualities of

Whitehead's varnish. After that the fight was Ali's. George walked into the stream of jabs and hooks with no less courage or resolve, but soon Ungerman was shouting to him just to last it out. In his far corner after the eighth round, the pressure showing on his face, George bellowed an enraged curse at his seconds because, he said later, they were all yelling at him at once. It seemed also the curse of a thwarted will.

At the final bell Chuvalo was still trying. Though he had lost nearly all twelve rounds, the crowd rose in ovation and the aisle behind his corner was jammed with frenzied Yugoslavians shouting "Bravo, Jure!"

At the press conference Ali said it was a lie that Chuvalo was washed up. He said he had hit George with his best shots, and George said he enjoyed the fight.

In the dressing room while George took a long steaming shower, McWhorter drained the plastic flask of emergency brandy from the medical kit.

Wearing a pink knit shirt and a soiled suede jacket, George rode with friends to a hospital for stitches, stopped at a pharmacy for pills to reduce swelling, and went on to a party at Ungerman's suite, where the television was on for the fight news, McWhorter kept his hat on, and Ungerman urged his guests to eat more turkey.

"It wasn't a hard fight," said George. "But you get dizzy chasing him. My nose hurts, that's all. I got hit less this time than in our first fight. I landed more body punches in that one, but I got better head shots in this one. I know I hurt him."

"Did you see the film it put over that cut?" asked Dr. Greenberg. "That cut was hit 150 times if it was hit once. But did you see how that stuff closed it?"

"So the fight's over," someone said.

"My last fight'll be with my wife," replied George.

"I raise 175,000 turkeys a year," said Ungerman.

Ungerman flew home the next day. George stayed on with McWhorter, who was transformed into an expansive man in a new red check sport coat, new hat and pressed grey slacks, talking about a vacation in Acapulco.

"I'm still partying," he said in the hotel bar. "George's fight was beautiful. Beautiful. He hit some good licks. Now I can have my fun. You understand? Now I can talk. Now's my time to relax. Now I got time for me. I could tell you some stories now—*good* stories. You know about Chuck Davey, don't you? You know who he is? He's known all over the world. And I did it. Chuck Spicer, Johnny Summerlin, and that boy, that boy that got killed. I know his name as well as my own. Sonny Banks. Got knocked out and never regained consciousness. George knew him. They used to spar together. Me and George went to his funeral. They a lot of stories I could tell you now the fight's over. Now maybe we going to Acapulco for a couple weeks, just me and George. He my man. I'm going down where it's nice and warm and lay in the sun all day."

He went with George and his friends to a night club that evening, but they never got around to discussing Acapulco. George spent most of the time at another table, talking to a promoter about a fight.

FOR DISCUSSION

1. Judging from the article, what idea of George Chuvalo does Leonard Gardner want you to have? What details does he include that lead you to answer as you do?
2. What has sport—boxing—done to Chuvalo?
3. How has Chuvalo's participation in boxing affected his way of life? Try to think of instances in which participation in a particular sport leads to specific consequences in other areas of one's life.
4. It is sometimes said that a man should marry his job first, then marry his wife. Do you think this advice is especially important for an athlete to follow? Why or why not?
5. Refer back to Peck's poem in the first chapter. Are any of the attitudes toward boxing revealed there similar to those seen in this article?

INTRODUCTION

The story that follows is in many ways larger than the man at its center, for Chuck Hughes is a hero by default. He was a remarkable man, but, in football at least, he is remembered more vividly for the way he left the game than the way he played it.

Ultimately, though, it is not just a story about Chuck Hughes, but a reminder that millions of us—TV viewers—were there when he died. The author asks us to consider our reaction.

On Chuck Hughes, Dying Young

Barnard Collier

In the fourth quarter of the Sunday-afternoon pro-football game on TV, a twenty-eight-year-old Detroit Lion named Chuck Hughes dropped dead of a heart attack on the fifteen-yard line in front of the gathering of millions of Americans.

You did not know right away he was dead, but you knew something was very wrong. The cameras showed a close-up of Dick Butkus of the Chicago Bears standing over him and waving in a scared and frantic way for the referees and then for the doctors on the Lions bench. A player must wave for the referees before the doctors can come out on the field or it is a violation of the National Football League rules. A player might be lying there faking an injury to stop the clock. The Lions were behind by five points and they needed a touchdown before the clock ran out in order to win. But an incomplete pass had already stopped the clock, so Chuck Hughes had no reason to fake. He must have looked very bad off to Dick Butkus, because you knew that Butkus is mean and ornery when he is out there on the football field and doesn't normally come to the aid of an injured man who is not on his team.

126

The doctors ran out and started moving around too fast. You knew from looking at it on TV that this wasn't just a man with the wind knocked out of him. He was too still. Nothing of him moved. The doctors were working too hard. Instead of just loosening his pants like they do when a man is down with the wind knocked out, they went for his chest and mouth.

One doctor was pounding on Chuck's chest with his fist, and the other gave mouth-to-mouth breathing. This football player was not going to get bravely to his feet and walk off the field under his own steam, hanging from the shoulders of the trainers and dragging a leg. This man was not just injured. You knew from watching on TV that this man was badly hurt. In fact, you could tell by that funny feeling you get inside when death comes that there was a dead football player on the field. It was like the feeling the Indians must have gotten when they watched the spirits of their dead braves and chiefs rise out of the bodies and float up the chimney to fly away into the other world. Somehow, on TV, you could practically see the spirit leaving the body.

Chuck's wife Sharon was in the stands. She did not know that he was dead. She thought maybe he had swallowed his mouthpiece, or his tongue, which is something football players sometimes do. When they do, it looks very bad as they gag and choke for air. But if the doctor gets out there in time with the little gadget he carries in his back pocket to pull the tongue back out, there usually is no problem. The man can breathe again and he gets back into the game. But Chuck was so motionless. Then Sharon knew that her husband was very bad off, and she started screaming.

It seemed to her like ten minutes before Butkus stopped waving at the referees and the doctors got out there.

The doctors told some newspapermen later that in our society a man is dead only when he is pronounced dead. Chuck was pronounced dead at a hospital forty-five minutes after he fell down. But a doctor said, "In my heart I know he was dead out there on the field about ten seconds after I got to him."

They waved Sharon down from the stands, and she climbed into the ambulance with Chuck. Now she was sure he was dead. But maybe they could revive him. They seemed to be trying so hard. But the ambulance drivers: "Where is the key?" "I don't know. You got the key." "No I don't, you got it." "Maybe it's in the back." "I thought you had it." She wanted to scream, "For God's sake, one of you find the key and let's get going!"

She stared at what the doctors were doing and she watched as Chuck's ear turned slowly black and blue. Now it did not make that much difference to her when the ambulance got to the hospital. Now she knew Chuck was beyond reviving. After that, time slowed down so much that hurrying did not matter.

She kept thinking about their marriage and how much Chuck was in love with football.

When Chuck was a little boy in Breckenridge, Texas, he carried a football around with him nearly all the time. He started playing football with his brother Johnny when they were in the third and fifth grades of the elementary school. Johnny was ahead. They played competitive football very young in Texas: in the grade schools a boy with the talent and the gifts could learn the fundamentals and grow up to make Texas proud of its football crop.

Chuck was a little blond kid. His father was a small, tough Irishman who went off to World War II as one of those flying sergeants in the Air Force. He flew planes over the Hump in Burma and crashed a couple of times but came away okay. Then he cracked one up in Labrador, and it mashed him up so badly inside that the Air Force gave him a one-hundred-percent disability rating and retirement. But Chuck's father said, "If I can't fly a plane, I'll fly a desk." He was never the same though, and his heart gave out one night in his sleep four years later.

Chuck's mother was a sweet, delicate, small lady who bore sixteen children. She loved each one as well as the other. One little girl died when she was only two. The rest were all alive when Mother Hughes died at age fifty-two from what the doctors said was a worn-out heart. Chuck was fifteen years old then, in the summer of 1958. Johnny and Chuck went to a farm to live with a relative until the end of the school year in Breckenridge before they went to live with Tom, their big brother, and his wife in Abilene.

For brothers, Chuck and Johnny were good buddies. Except that Johnny liked to pick on his little brother. For some reason bees did not sting Johnny. So he used to catch bees and wasps in his hands and slap them on Chuck. The bees would sting Chuck good, and Chuck would get roaring mad and start to cry and to fight wildly. But he never could get a solid lick in on his bigger brother. Perhaps Johnny gave Chuck so many handfuls of bees because he was angry inside that his little brother was better at football. Chuck was a very good athlete.

He had a pair of the quickest hands anyone in that part of Texas had seen in a long time. If you have any sense for it, you can spot quick hands in a boy without looking too long. But in Texas people seem to have some extra sensitivity to it. Maybe it is a little leftover skill from the old days when Texas men wore pistols and had to sense whether a stranger was quicker before seeing him draw.

Chuck also had good moves. He could fake a defender out so badly that the man would stand there looking stupid while Chuck was taking off four or five steps in the clear behind him.

Chuck loved to catch the football. He loved to catch it and feel it in his hands and then run. He was too small and skinny to catch the ball and run over people, so his coaches all told him: "Chuck, you must never, never try to run over people. You get the ball in your good hands and run *away* from them." Chuck would get the ball in his good hands if it was flying by anywhere in his vicinity and run away.

He also had something else. He was never the kind of receiver who would do what they call "listening to the footsteps." That means that when the defense man is running at you from behind like a mad steer, and the ground is thumping, and you know you are going to get creamed as soon as your fingers even brush the football, you don't listen. You don't listen to the footsteps.

Chuck never listened to the footsteps and in college he was a star receiver and a record-maker for Texas Western, where he went on a scholarship. Chuck was chosen to be an All-American.

He was small and he was skinny—at best he was 6 feet tall and 170 pounds when he was a sophomore on the team—but he worked himself harder than anybody to get into shape. He ran pass patterns time and time again. He always made sure he started out on the right foot every time and he got the timing down to the split second in his head.

He had decided he was going to be a pro, and now he carried a football everywhere. Once a coach told him that a great pass receiver has got to know the feel of a football. You've got to know it like you know your own body. You've got to know how it feels when it's right and when it's wrong. The only way to know it is by carrying it, by touching it, feeling it, getting used to it, rubbing it. Chuck's brother Tom, who raised Chuck and six other children after their mother died, says that Chuck could tell exactly where the seams of the football were even if the ball was handed him behind his back. Chuck carried the football to the dinner table with him and put it in his lap; he touched it first thing in the morning when he woke up and last thing before bed at night.

He met Sharon in his sophomore year. She was Homecoming Queen, a short, pretty girl with long hair. Chuck was just the most beautiful man she had seen. He wasn't a big brute like the other football players, and only just a little too sure of himself for her taste. And his muscles were magnificent. She told her girl friends that his muscles were just what the doctor ordered for her. She wanted to get married right away; all the other sophomore girls were getting married.

Chuck said no. He couldn't get married right away if he was going to be a pro. And he was going to be a pro. He would marry her when he signed a pro contract. He carried the football the whole time. When they studied together it was there; it rested between them on the seat of the car at the drive-in movies. When Chuck signed a pro contract with the Philadelphia Eagles in February of his senior year, they got married. Sharon was twenty-one years old.

The rookie year is the toughest year in the pros, especially if you don't have a no-cut contract. Without the no-cut clause they can cut you from the team right up to the last day of training camp with no questions asked. Chuck and Harry Jones were both rookies the same year and they roomed together in the college dormitory the Eagles used to house their players during the eight weeks of camp. Harry had a no-cut contract and he was safe, but Chuck didn't and he went through hell.

All day on the field he tortured his body to make it do just that much more than any of the coaches thought it could. Some days he was spectacular, and all of his extra effort, the straining, the extra wind sprints, the extra concentration paid off with some wonderful catches. But some days he called up everything extra he had and it still was not enough to make him stand out as the best. Both Chuck and the coaches knew it.

Athletes and coaches are extremely critical. In pro football no player gets away with anything for very long. Coaches and players watch the game films and run them back and forth looking for the weaknesses in themselves and their opponents. The opposing side is also looking at the game films and the scouting reports hunting for weaknesses. Now there are computer programs that pick out statistical weaknesses in a team that human minds cannot always spot. A team must take advantage of every knowable percentage to win over the long haul.

The "game" we see every Sunday in the pro-football part of the year is actually an incredibly complicated one of advanced military-style strategy and tactics between two teams who are probably better equipped and informed and sophisticated about the battle they are fighting than any army in the world. When they find a weakness, they are completely ruthless about exploiting it. You don't say in pro football, "Well, let's not take unsportsmanlike advantage of their left defensive tackle because he's pretty banged up and slower than usual." You run right over him. You punish him with contact early. If he shows any signs of weakening you call your plays to his side. In the pros you know the difference between victory and defeat, and if a man is weak in any way, nobody is too polite or too kind or too sorry to let him know it.

Chuck had a weakness. It was a glaring, uncorrectable, inherited weakness for a wide receiver. As they say, "He didn't have 'the great speed.' "

To be a starting wide receiver on a winning team in the pros you must have "the great speed." You must be able to take off away from your defender with the kind of acceleration that leaves him panting just out of reach. That is the kind of runner that gets the break-away play and makes the catch for the big touchdown when you need it. Coaches look always for "the great speed" and they program it into the team's offensive plays.

Chuck did not have it, or as they said, "Chuck wasn't blessed with 'the great speed.' "

Still, Chuck made the cut for the Eagles on the last day in

training camp and the night he found out they made him drink whiskey with beer chasers and he got drunk and sick because he was not accustomed to hard liquor. But he said it was the best sickness of his whole life.

The Eagles kept Chuck because of his good hands and the fakes. They kept him to use in the emergency, when the number-one wide receiver is hurt and you need a man in there with a good chance to hang on to something if he's really hot that day. Of course you can't start him because of the weakness. If you have a man who has good hands and fakes and "great speed" too, you have to play him ahead of a man like Chuck who has only two out of three. Otherwise it would be like playing five-card stud with just four cards.

On the Eagles, Chuck sat on the bench. But, really, Chuck never sat *down* on the bench during a game. He was always standing up as close to the coach as he could get, with his helmet in his hand, yelling for the team, making funny jokes, ready to run in there whenever the coach needed him. He figured that if he put himself in the coach's line of vision often enough, the coach would recognize him and send him in. But on the Eagles Chuck was behind two fast wide receivers. They could run the hundred in nine-four and nine-six. Maybe, at his best, Chuck could do the hundred in ten flat. Those tiny parts of a second make and break careers in pro football.

In the summers, Chuck and Harry Jones used to follow each other in different cars from Texas to the Eagles training camp. Chuck would insist that they stop at a motel at five o'clock so that he could put himself through a hard workout before the sun went down. He would run wind sprints, and then his precise pass patterns. He and Harry would play catch. When Chuck got to training camp he wanted to be in shape. He wanted them to know that he had the makings of a star wide receiver if they'd only let him start.

A kind of unexplainable thing for nonathletes happens to pro-football players in training camp. Harry Jones says the closest he can come to describing it is to remember how he and Chuck, who was his roommate, used to lie in bed so sore they couldn't move and talk about *everything* until they finally fell asleep at two or three o'clock in the morning. For eight weeks, without any wives or girl friends, it was kind of like being married to somebody who could really understand what you went through. Somebody who could say the things that got your confidence up for the next day.

One night Chuck said he was thinking about how his father and his mother and his brother Pat, who was just thirty-four, had all died of heart attacks. Chuck said he sometimes worried about that, and he hoped the same thing wasn't in store for him.

It was one of those things you put out of your head when a friend confides in you about it. Harry Jones nearly forgot it. Chuck never bothered to tell Sharon about it.

Chuck got traded to the Lions after three years and he was happy about it. He hoped he would get a better chance to play. He liked it in Detroit, and the Lions and their fans liked old "Coyote," as they called him. It was a nickname he picked up on the Eagles because his nose was long and sharp like the coyote that chased the roadrunner in the "Roadrunner" cartoons on TV. The nickname went well with his west Texas drawl and the handmade alligator or turtle cowboy boots, and his western suits and his Texas hats.

But it was not much better for him on the Lions. He did get to play more often than on the Eagles, and the Lions were a winning team with good spirit. But Chuck had the bad luck to be behind two more wide receivers with "the great speed," and they had to get hurt before he got in. He could not get a start no matter how hard he tried. On Thanksgiving Day in 1970, in a play that his brother Johnny remembers they reran on instant replay six times, Chuck made a turn-in catch where he threw himself straight out into the air about 3 feet off the ground and flew like a human arrow for about 5 feet to snag a football with his fingertips. And he held on to it when he crashed into the cold hard ground. It had to be an extraordinary catch to be rerun six times on instant replay: the film stands as a record of the kind of effort Chuck could make.

Last fall, he'd come home to Sharon and their two-year-old son, Brandon Shane, and Sharon would ask him how practice went. He did not like to talk what he called "business" at home. He would say, "I had a rotten day." Or, "I had a great day. I can't understand why I'm not in the lineup, but I had a great day."

And that's all he would say to Sharon about business. She wanted to massage his sore feet, his sore legs, his aching Achilles tendons, and rub his head. But seldom would he let her. He told her that she couldn't understand how it was with pro-football players.

His favorite record was a country-western song by Tammy Wynette called *Stand By Your Man*. Chuck would play it over and over for Sharon and other Lions wives when the Lions and their wives went to each other's houses. The song said that a woman should stand by her man no matter what, even though she doesn't understand. He would sing it in a twangy, flat voice: "Sometimes it's hard to be a woman . . . giving all your love to just one man. You'll have bad times . . . and he'll have good times . . . Doin' things that you don't understand. Stand by your man. . . And tell the world you love him. . . . Keep giving all the love you can . . . Stand by your man."

Sharon and the other wives hated it. They didn't understand and they were close friends with each other because of their lack of understanding. They would fume and sulk about how the men got off practice at two-thirty and spent the next two hours in a tavern drinking beer together and patting the behinds of their playmates. But Sharon knew Chuck was under tremendous pressure because he wasn't playing. Playing was the only thing he wanted to do—had ever wanted to do. So Sharon made less and less fuss, and they seemed happy.

The only odd thing Sharon noticed that last week before the Bears game was that whenever she came back from the grocery store Chuck would ask her if she had bought Alka-Seltzer. Sharon never remembered his using much Alka-Seltzer before. Other than that he looked very well. He had gotten sandwiched between two tacklers in a preseason exhibition game with Buffalo and that put him in the hospital twice with terrible pains in his chest. The doctors gave him every test they could think of in case it was a heart condition that caused the pain, but none of the tests showed anything wrong. And the pain eventually went away.

So on the Sunday of the Bears game Chuck was in his usual laughing, happy mood, standing down there near the coach when one of the Lions' wide receivers got hurt. The coach recognized Chuck and sent him into the game. It was the moment he had been waiting for. It was already late in October and it was only the second time they had put him in a game since the official football season opened.

Nobody in the press box knew Chuck had come on the field. Somebody yelled "Who the hell is that?" when Chuck ran a post pattern downfield and made a spectacular leaping, third-down clutch catch of the football for a 32-yard gain.

"It's Chuck Hughes," somebody called out after looking up the number.

They ran the great catch back on instant replay.

Then the press and the TV talent knew Hughes was in there and they were going to keep an eye on him when he went deep. They would put an isolated camera on him, too.

The next two plays went deep, but to the other side of the field. Chuck had run perfect patterns and had faked his man out and was open down in the end zone all by himself. But the plays went the other way.

Chuck walked out of the end zone after the second play and trotted slowly back to the huddle down the middle of the grid-iron. At the fifteen-yard line he looked as if he had tripped. Then somebody in the press box saw him pile up flat on his face in the grass.

They turned the TV cameras on him for us until the spirit left him, and then they turned away. For millions of Americans to intrude on the unfortunate death of a football player was no longer appropriate.

FOR DISCUSSION

1. Chuck Hughes was not a superstar in the mold of a Dick Butkus or an O. J. Simpson. Why do you think Barnard Collier chooses to tell his story? What is it about Chuck Hughes, the man, that Collier finds significant?

2. Collier seems to think it important that we were all present at Hughes's death. What does his article say about televised sports? About us?

3. Is the camera at a televised sports event ever an invasion of privacy? Are there some things that you believe the camera should *not* show the viewer? If so, what?
4. Which sport do you think TV transmits best? The worst? Why?

The
Way I Am

CHAPTER THREE

Elsewhere in *Sports Literature*—notably in the profiles of George Chuvalo and Ernie Banks—we have dealt with the effects specific sports have on individual athletes. In this chapter, we would like to give this question our full attention.

In our discussion we return to an idea that we touched on earlier. No matter how a sport shapes a person, the actual period of shaping is, oftentimes, very brief. Brian Piccolo had a very short season. Like Chuck Hughes, his football skills were comparatively modest, yet he possessed the courage and drive necessary to reach the top in a relatively short time. He emerged a driving, bursting halfback whose main purpose in life—playing football—was thwarted only by the onset of cancer. And Brian Piccolo's personality, shaped by his brief tenure in sports, served him well in his fight for his life. If, as we suggested in our general introduction, sports bring out the best and the worst in us, one of the clearest examples of the best is Brian Piccolo.

Another young man who has not had many years in sports, and who perhaps has even less time left, is the consumptive fictional hero of "John Sobieski Runs." Slight of build, forever coughing, a shy talker, he discovers that he can run. He pays a high price for this discovery by taxing his limited physical resources, but nonetheless John Sobieski runs. Running is life itself. It becomes impossible to identify John without speaking of what he does: John Sobieski *runs*.

Elsewhere we see other human beings for whom sports have provided life's ultimate meaning. This meaning varies; it can be a memory, as it is to Flick Webb, the "Ex-Basketball Player" who once scored 38 points in a game, and whose "hands were like wild birds." Now, years later, Flick works in a filling station or sits and plays the pinball machine at a local café.

> ... just sits and nods
> Beyond her face toward bright applauding tiers
> Of Necco Wafers, Nibs, and Juju Beads.

What are we to think? Updike is ambiguous; he says that Flick's "hands are fine and nervous on the lug wrench," and that he sits "Grease-gray and kind of coiled"; and we see that he "Sips lemon cokes, and smokes those thin cigars." Sports, he suggests, can leave a residue of animal grace in those it has touched and left behind.

Another poem, by Peter Meinke, suggests that sports can create a life philosophy which survives even after an athlete leaves his sport for other duties in life. James Dickey was a football player, a linebacker who played with intensity. In Meinke's "To an Athlete Turned Poet" we see him writing with the same ferocity that he gave to football.

In "The Old Pro's Lament" we glimpse a vision of what many of us would probably like to become through the games we play. When all our skills have deserted us, we would like to dream of

> an old man
> playing in an empty court
> under the dim floodlights
> of the moon
> with a racket gone in the strings—
> no net, no ball, no game—
> and still playing
> to win.

INTRODUCTION

What does the sports experience mean? You will see some clues in the studies of George Chuvalo, Chuck Hughes, Brian Piccolo, and other athletes.

John Sobieski, in the story below, is much younger. He couldn't be expected to answer such a weighty question.

All John Sobieski knows is that he has to run.

John Sobieski Runs

James Buechler

One September afternoon the door of the cross-country team room at an upstate New York high school opened a little way and then closed again, admitting in that instant a very short boy who looked a little underfed even for his size. Nobody paid him the least attention. In the first place, there were only three people in the locker room. One was a member of the varsity, a dark, Italian-looking boy dressed ready to go out in sweat pants and a sweat shirt with a picture of a winged spiked shoe printed in red on its breast. He sat tying on his lightweight cross-country shoes in front of a star-spangled locker, sky blue in color and covered with white stars, with a red-and-white stripe running around the edges of its door. Most of the lockers were dark green, but there were a half dozen or so such splashy ones. The dark boy sat on one of two wooden benches running the length of the room, about two feet out from the lockers. On the opposite bench a boy in track shorts lay stomach down, his head to one side, his arms hanging, while a serious-faced man, an assistant coach, picked with his fingers very fast at the backs of the other's legs, snick-snick-snick-snick-snick. The liniment he was using smelled sharply above the prevailing, long-accumulated odor of sweat.

Turning from the door, the short boy stepped over one of the benches in a motion remarkably easy, considering his size.

With his face in the corner made by the last locker and the wall, he began to undress. He had a blue looseleaf notebook with the name of the school on it, and he laid it on the bench. Then he took off a brown knit sweater, which he folded up on top of the notebook. Under that he wore a white shirt starched so stiffly that when he took it off it held the creases of his wearing and would only fold brokenly in a high springy pile. Now he simply stood for a moment in his undershirt, with slender shoulders and brown hair about the color of his sweater, wearing a pair of darker brown pants. He looked like a boy who had been sent to the corner for something he ought to be ashamed of. He had been trying to get something out of his pocket that didn't want to come, but all at once, as he stood tugging, the thing gave, flew out—an ordinary piece of blue cloth—with a sweep and flourish that seemed to disconcert him. Immediately he loosened his belt and let his trousers fall to his ankles. He stepped out of them and into the blue cloth thing, a cheap pair of gym shorts with a string pull at the waist. These on, he was uniformed. The brown pants he rolled up with his little pile, bent and tightened the strings of his shoes, and, fixing his eyes on the door at the far end of the room, walked toward it between the lockers, a very thin boy who might have been called lanky if he had been a foot taller. He opened the door, looked out, and finding that it led to the playing field, disappeared through it, running.

In the locker room the varsity member, his dark hair hanging over his face in long Vaselined strands, had finished with his running shoes. With a shake he laid his hair back on his head in orderly lines and, at the same time, gave one single, sophisticated glance across at the coach.

Still picking away, the man said, "He could grow."

John Sobieski—this was the short boy's name—found himself running out of the school building's shadow into the warm sunlight, over hard, even ground covered with short grass which stretched away, from beneath his own thin legs, into the biggest flat field he had ever seen. Moving across it, he passed over gleaming lines of white lime powder and, except for them, did not feel he was moving at all, running though he was across the big green field in the sun. He saw, far away on his left, the football players, tiny, bright-colored people, hunching and waiting, rising and moving and entangling all together in waves, heard whistles, and saw before him, past many lines and various goalposts, more boys—the running team. Many were lying all about on the ground, but many were standing up too, all upright together in a tight kind of pack that vibrated and moved around like a thing in itself, something very bright, red and white, spinning there in the sunshine on top of uncountable bare legs. As he came nearer he saw that the people on the ground were only discarded sweat suits with nobody in them; the runners were all up and gathered around a very tall man who was waving a clipboard of papers in the air above his head as he spoke. The runners had on bright red shirts with lettering across the chest and white shorts edged in red, and they shifted and pranced on their slight little running shoes as on hooves, their bright uniforms blended and mingled to make up that whirling bright-colored thing which, idling nervous and impatient in place up to now, suddenly lurched and flexed and strained within, before extending itself loosely and easily away as, on its many legs, it began trotting off over the field. John Sobieski ran as hard as he knew how; as he pounded up, the big man flagged him on with the paper-fluttering clipboard, boomed, "Right there . . . after those men!" and John Sobieski was past and pounding after the pack of runners that stretched away loose and red and white in the sunlight toward a far fence bordering the field.

So they were running, and John Sobieski was with them. But already his legs felt heavy, and he was breathing faster than he had ever breathed in his life. He had come running all the way across the big green field, only to find that they had started already. The unfairness of it made him hot and sick. He had come out for cross-country knowing he would have to run miles, but they had started before he was ready. His throat ached; his feet he raised up and clapped down like flatirons. As he ran he thought to himself, "It's not my fault, they started before I was ready . . . . I'll stop right here, somewhere."

They had come to the end of the field and passed through a gate; they were running on a sidewalk past houses. A boy in a red shirt was running not far in front of him. John Sobieski could see his own shoes hitting the sidewalk one after the other, while he himself seemed to ride above somewhere as on some funny kind of running machine. Bumping along in this way he was interested to find, after a while, that his machine seemed to be moving a little faster than the other boy's machine. Fascinated, with curiosity and detachment mixed, he watched the increasing nearness of the other boy's white pants—for some reason that was all he could see—until gradually he came alongside the other. Both of them were bouncing up and down furiously, but the other boy seemed to bounce up and down in the same spot, while John Sobieski was very slowly moving, until, gradually again, he couldn't see the other boy anymore. But it didn't make any difference; there was another boy in front of him.

And this one approached and went by, and another one sprang up. Regular as telephone poles they went slowly by him until there had been six. He counted them because he didn't have anything else to do. Then everything grew dark, and though it was only because they had entered a park and were running on a path through woods, John Sobieski didn't know it. All he knew was that he was running after a strange white flag that moved before him in the dim. Fluttering and twinkling, always ahead, it dipped and wound with the path, and John Sobieski behind. At last, after a long time, they broke out into the light. There was the fence around the shadowed green playing field and, inside it, the football players, looking weary in their dirtied uniforms, and beyond them, far across the field, the high school building. John Sobieski's heart lifted. He saw that the white flag was nothing but another pair of the white shorts edged with red. The boy running in them was only strides in front, and, though he was tired, he set himself to beat this one boy at least. As he sprinted around the fence toward the school—which burned at its edges like a coal, blocking off the sun—it seemed to him he had just started, he was virtually flying, he would pass them all. And he did overtake the boy in the twinkling white pants, and another.

Standing up against the bricks of the school building, the assistant coach, who had just finished a rubdown in the locker room, watched the line of long-distance runners coming around the fence. They toiled with incredible slowness and suffering, each one preserving only the formal attitude of running. Long ago they had lost the speed the attitude is supposed to produce. He watched them toiling, one by one, and as he watched, one moving slightly faster than the rest strained painfully closer to the next man, painfully abreast, and in time came up behind the next runner, whom he would probably pass before reaching the school. The coach turned and walked swiftly toward a corner of the building.

Now the leaders had reached a gate by the school. There something halted them, making them run into one another in their weariness. As John Sobieski came up he stumbled and fell against the slippery neck of the boy in front of him. The boy's sweat came away on his lips, and as they passed through the gate a man shouted something at each one. John Sobieski felt his shoulder grabbed and squeezed.

"Thirteen!" the man said to him. It was the assistant coach.

Nobody was running anymore. They all walked around in circles. So did John Sobieski. He felt sick again. His chest and throat exploded every time he tried to breathe, and he was terribly hot. What he wanted most was just to be unconscious, but he couldn't bear to sit or lie down. He saw a boy crouching on the ground, retching onto the grass between his hands. Somebody had brought in the sweat clothes off the playing field, and boys were picking their own out of a pile. They hung their sweat shirts over their shoulders like capes and tied the arms in front. After a while John Sobieski began to feel better. He walked toward the locker room, more or less with five other runners. Just in front walked the boy who had vomited, with a friend supporting him on either side. A sweat shirt was thrown on John Sobieski's back; the arms came dangling down in front of him. He never saw who did it, because nobody seemed to look at him or pay much attention to him.

Back in the locker room it was strangely quiet, considering the place was filling with runners, who sat down on the benches or tinkered quietly at their locker doors. John Sobieski went to his own pile of things, turned his back, and let his blue shorts slide down to his shoes. Then, holding his brown pants open, he stepped into them, stuffed the shorts into his pocket, pulled the crackling white shirt over his undershirt and the sweater over that; and leaving the sweat shirt neatly folded on the bench, he turned around and stood, his back to the entrance door, surveying the room. It was as if he had only just come in and was

John Sobieski Runs 145

looking for something. Now he smelled the perspiration smell fresh and strong and moist, mingling with the steam that clouded out from the top of the shower-room door, and mingling, too, with all the hubbub that had come up in the short time he was changing. Everybody in the steamy room seemed naked, and they all seemed unnaturally up above him, but that was only because nearly all the runners by now were standing on the two benches, which were two parallel pedestals for their sweating, moving nude bodies. John Sobieski moved between them in his brown sweater, looking very intently for something, and having no attention paid him. He even walked a little way into the shower room, clothes and shoes on and all, and peered through the steam at the runners there. But nobody seemed to notice this either.

Finally he went out by the same door he had first come in, passed through a few halls, and left the building.

"Thirty-four," he thought to himself as he stepped outside into the cold afternoon air. "I beat twenty-one at least."

He walked home. The night passed, and then the next day—but John Sobieski couldn't have said how. He was a small, thin boy sitting at back desks in various classrooms with a blue notebook open in front of him, but what he was seeing was not a teacher or a blackboard, but four or five boys in twinkling white pants running before him, and he himself coming up behind, planning how he was going to take them.

By four in the afternoon he was on the field again. The runners were warming up. Some were doing pushups; some were lying on their backs on the damp ground and springing up in quick little sitting motions; some just stood around with serious faces, paying no attention to others; some were rotating their torsos, with hands on hips. John Sobieski looked around carefully and did some of the same things. The tall man of the day before was nowhere to be seen, but after a few minutes the assistant coach came walking out toward them with a boy on either side. His face was hard and dark, but his eyes were large and white and serious, and appeared to be considering other things even as he said something brief and imperative to the boy next to him. This boy gave one single vigorous nod and without warning whirled, and was away. Instantly the others took after him and John Sobieski, who hadn't been ready for it to happen so fast, was left doing pushups on the ground.

He jumped up and ran after them, though he knew it was hopeless; he was already 50 yards behind the pack and at least 100 behind the leaders. For the second time, they had started before he was ready. Before they had even left the playing field, he felt sicker than he had at any time the previous day. His body was a misery to him. He ran along beside the endless steel wire fence crying to himself, "Why did I think I could run! I can't! I'm not any good!" He ran another hundred yards and he prayed, "Please let me just finish. I don't want to beat anybody. All I want to do is just finish!" Because somewhere inside him was the idea that if he could endure it just this one time, then maybe he would get his fair chance, when he could really do something, tomorrow.

His father had warned him. At the end of summer, when John Sobieski came home one night and told his mother and father he wasn't going back to St. Stephen's anymore but was going up to the big city high school, his father had asked him: "What do you think you're going to get by going up there?"

"Everything," said the boy. "They got everything up there, so you can do what you want, when you get out. You can be whatever you want."

His father was smoking. At first he said something, muttering only to himself, while he shook out a long wooden match. "Nah—you can't do what you want, John Sobieski," he said then, and blew out smoke. "You just try it and you'll find out. You better stay around here. We'll teach you everything you need to know."

"No, I'm going up there."

His father looked straight at him over the table, with something ugly in his look. "Do you know who you are? D'you even know your own name?"

"Sure. Everybody knows who they are."

"No they don't. But you, you're John Sobieski. That was my father's name too. He came over here when he wasn't any bigger than you are. He was one of the ones that helped put up St. Stephen's in the first place. I went there myself and so did my brothers. That's where we belong—and you're just the same as we are. No use trying to be any different, because you belong around here. You ain't ever going to be any different from that."

"Yes I am," said John Sobieski. "Oh, yes I am."

And they looked at each other, the two of them almost exactly the same size except that the father was older, and so everything about him was somehow thicker, and more unwieldy. John Sobieski's mother kept out of it, away at the stove. The two looked at each other from opposing chairs until the father's expression broke, and he turned away.

"You think you can do what you want," he said, quite differently. "You start out all right with it too. You leave the house every morning and you only come back at night. You get pretty far away. After a while you think you don't have to come back at all. Then one day you get caught out there all by yourself—and you get licked, good."

"No," said John Sobieski.

"Stay where you are," his father pleaded. "It ain't so bad down around here."

"No, you talk like that because you're old. Well, I'm not old. I'm not going to listen to it!" He got up and went into his bedroom, where he could be by himself.

Struggling, spreading out, the runners pounded along upon a hard city sidewalk. They strained and reached, with knees and toes and shoulders; each step had only one job—to slide over as much ground as possible. Most of them could not see, and none paid any attention to the big car that followed along in the street keeping pace, but inside it the head coach, the tall man who usually carried the clipboard thick with papers, hovered just beyond the toil of the runners. Ahead of him, in the next block, he watched an indistinct cluster of legs and a flash of color separate themselves, as he came closer, into a runner in blue shorts and white top trailing a line of three abreast in the red-and-white uniforms. As blue-and-white closed with the red, the legs became entangled and inextricable again, until suddenly somebody got stepped on. A boy in red shirt and white pants reeled to the side, off the curb and into the road, where he fought to recover himself, climbing back to the sidewalk only to drop rapidly to the rear, his pace broken. Meantime blue-and-white had moved up between the other two, so that the three of them, bouncing up and down, remained for a long moment like a slot machine come to rest after changing, red-blue-red, until gradually blue-and-white disengaged himself again and moved out in front.

The coach accelerated and passed on, but John Sobieski didn't notice him. He had hardly even seen the three runners. His eyes were wet and partly closed as he ran, and all at once he knew that something was in front of him, preventing him. More or less, he saw them. But there wasn't anything he could do except keep running, because he knew if he were checked at all he would have to stop altogether. Then after a moment he was clear and by himself again. He ran on. No vision of the school building raised him. It was a gray, damp day. He didn't know how far they still had to go. He passed more runners, singles or straggling twos, without any struggle. He couldn't think about taking them, or of anything; they were just going slower than he was, and he moved by.

It was over abruptly. They passed through the same gate as yesterday, freely, without being stopped, the runners all streaming in and dispersing, and as soon as John Sobieski realized where they were and stopped trying to run he collapsed.

"Walk him around!" somebody shouted. It was the tall head coach. He had parked his car and now stood just inside the gate, wearing a long raincoat. "What's the trouble?"

Two runners had already lifted John Sobieski to his feet, but he was fighting them off, and they couldn't hold him; they were tired themselves.

"I don't know . . . he's talking to himself," one answered between breaths. "He's trying to say numbers."

"Walk him around," the tall man repeated. "That's the way to finish a run. There isn't a one of you should have anything left at all!"

The two of them took John Sobieski's arms across their shoulders and together they walked him around on the grass. After a while they had their own wind back, but as soon as John Sobieski got breath enough, he began to cough. The afternoon was chilly and damp. He took several wheezing breaths and then coughed again, badly. By the time the others had walked off the effects of their run, he was coughing steadily for long stretches.

The two boys took him into the locker room. They sat him on a bench in front of their own lockers and got his clothes off, while he continued coughing. They walked him with care through the jostling, sweating, strong-smelling runners into the steamy shower room, and one readied a shower while the other held John Sobieski. Then they put him under it and left him.

Later, when the two runners were dressed and ready to leave, they turned to find the small thin boy standing naked across the bench from them, dripping onto the floor.

"Feel better now?" the bigger one asked. "What's the matter, forget your towel?" He drew his own heavy damp one from his gym bag and took the one that his friend was carrying rolled up under one arm and hung them both over John Sobieski's shoulder. The small boy opened his mouth as if to say something, but instead he was overcome by a fit of coughing.

The two had to go. "Give them to us tomorrow," said the one, pausing in the locker-room door. He was a big, strong-looking boy with a very large head. "Ernest Borkmann and Joe Felice." Still John Sobieski stood, just looking at the two boys; he was fighting a rising cough, and the door had already closed before he called after them:

"John Sobieski!"

He went back to the bench with his towels. All the runners had left. He wiped himself, put on his clothes, and put his running shorts in his pocket. But he didn't leave the two towels behind; he took them along home with him. His second day's running was over.

When he reached his own street it was dark, and a cold, foggy rain was drifting down. By the light of street lights the wooden two-family houses rose high all around him, their thrusting, peaked roofs shoulder to shoulder, the mist falling from the darkness above upon their wet slate backs. Inside they were warmly lighted behind curtains.

John Sobieski went straight to his own bedroom. His mother and father, eating already, could hear him coughing behind the door. Finally he came out and sat down. A fire was going in the kitchen stove, since it was still too early in the year to light the furnace, and in the sudden, close warmth John Sobieski began to perspire and then to cough and cough. His eyes would become fixed, his face red and then contorted as he tried to stop himself, at least long enough to eat; but the thing would burst out at last and leave him shaking, his eyes watering. He drank cups and cups of coffee, which his mother poured out for him. His father read a newspaper on the other side of the table and glanced at John Sobieski when he coughed, but said nothing.

Later, as he sat on the sofa in the living room, wearing his heavy sweater, the cough subsided. His mother and father sat across from him on either side in upholstered chairs; his mother's fingers were crocheting something nimbly, and his father still had his paper. John Sobieski sat by himself on the sofa doing nothing, thinking about nothing, just sitting still under a lamp and gazing blankly at his parents. At one point, as his father folded over his paper to study the lower corner, he caught his son gazing at him.

"What now?" he demanded.

"Nothing. Can't I look?" said John Sobieski.

His mother, too, raised her head, worried-looking and sorrowful. She reminded John Sobieski of those old women with kerchiefs around their heads whom he used to see when he had been an altar boy serving early mass. They knelt and prayed, holding their beads, with a look upon their faces and in their eyes as though the whole world were filled with sorrow; and John Sobieski hated sorrow; he couldn't stand it.

"Oh, I don't like that coughing," said his mother, shaking her head.

But John Sobieski didn't mind even sorrow, now. All he wanted was to sit, just as he was, in his own house, doing nothing, thinking about nothing at all.

Then morning came again, and John Sobieski must go up to the high school. He took the two towels plus a third one for himself that he got from his mother, his running shorts, his notebook, his lunch bag, and a black umbrella of his father's, because the morning was dark and threatening rain again. By the time he reached the school his arms ached from carrying so many things, and when he thought of the running he would have to do that day he felt sorry for himself and thought, "No wonder I can't run. Nobody else has to wear themselves out just getting here!"

The rain in clinging drops or running down the panes of the windows, the shifting light and dark places in the sky—all were watched apprehensively by John Sobieski as he sat in the classrooms' dim electric light that could barely establish itself all day against the bleak light from outside. After his last class, as he walked among crowds of others through the dim and noisy corridors, Ernest Borkmann found him.

The big boy took him down to the wing of the school where the lockers were, past the door of the cross-country room and on to a further door where he left him. For one moment John Sobieski hesitated, but then he let himself inside quickly and faced the room.

In front of him, behind a desk, sat the tall man of the clipboard—a large and handsome-appearing man with long white hair combed back, seen now for the first time indoors, without his coat and hat. Leaning back with folded hands, he was talking to the smaller, darker, bony-looking young man who sat on the windowsill with his back to the rain, his knees drawn up high and his feet on the radiator.

"Is that him?" the tall man asked. "The one that runs in the blue pants?"

The other coach only nodded gloomily, watching John Sobieski, the whites of his eyes showing in his dark face.

"What do they call him, anyway?"

A little smile seemed always to be hanging at the corners of the white-haired man's eyes and lips, as though to him things were always cheerful and a bit funny somehow.

"John Sobieski," responded the boy himself.

"John Sobieski . . . I hear that John Sobieski's a pretty good runner, Stan."

"He does the best he can."

"No, sir," said the white-haired man, "he's good, because he likes to run. He likes to go out there and beat those other boys. He likes to take 'em. Now, how's he going to do it the way he's been, Stanley? That isn't right. We have to give John Sobieski a chance, the same as everybody else. You come here, John Sobieski!"

The tall man reached forward and pointed to a box at the front of his desk. Of course it had been there all along, but for John Sobieski it only came into being at that moment. The boy opened it. Inside, under tissue paper, his hands grasped a pair of the spikeless cross-country shoes.

He lifted them out. They were small in size, for his own little feet, narrow and light and pointed, with hard and sharp rubber bottoms for digging in and starting; and he could see himself already, as from some distance away, the black shoes slashing like hoofs, slashing and slashing in arcs, the shoes of John Sobieski!

"John Sobieski's going to Utica with us," said the head coach, grinning. "John Sobieski's going to run at Syracuse—John Sobieski's going to New York City!"

"Well, you get a uniform and sweat suit from the manager, John Sobieski," the younger man told him more soberly. "Put a towel around your neck when you go outside and don't try to run very hard today. It's too cold for it."

The runners jogged across the field and gathered together under the drizzling clouds. Neither coach was anywhere around. John Sobieski had been one of the first ones out, and for once, at least, he was ready. Imperceptibly this time, without a signal of any kind, the runners began their run. They went off slowly without making any sound, all the move and flash of their bright uniforms muffled within the heavy gray sweat suits. They moved at a shuffle just over a walk, then at a trot, and then a little better. In the beginning they ran very close to one another in a tight pack, and yet in rigid silence, as though pushing together against some enormous burden, one so heavy that it might never be moved at all without an effort from each so intense as to isolate him from all the others.

Once outside the fence, John Sobieski found the pack lengthening. As it stretched out gradually, it seemed to snap in two. He was the last of the line that was moving ahead, and there were nine runners in front of him. He stayed where he was without working very hard. Then all at once, when he was scarcely tired, he spied the school building ahead of him, and he pulled out and ran as fast as he could. He passed the others easily, every one—not so fast as if they were standing still, but as if he were moving about twice as fast—and entered the gate first by a long interval.

Instead of stopping, he kept running straight on into the locker room. There he took a hurried shower and had already dried himself by the time the others began to come in, talking quietly, in twos and threes. John Sobieski dressed as fast as he could, his face buried in the new locker that had been assigned to him. He was afraid to turn around because they might all be looking at him, because he had come in first. He felt as though he were charged with electricity, and the figure 1 were shining out upon his back.

He was sweating again by the time he reached home. His coughing was so continuous that he knew he would not be able to stop it, or even halt it for a few minutes, until he had something to drink. But even so he went directly to his bedroom and carefully spread out on the bed his new running things, which were now all wrinkled and damp. The unfamiliar bright-colored things attracted his mother and father, and they came in to look.

"Where can I put these to dry . . ." John Sobieski demanded. But then he closed his eyes, grasping the long bar at the foot of his bed; his upper body leaned forward, the tears pressed at his shut eyes, and the cough came rolling out of him. " . . . where nobody will touch them?"

"Touch them," said his father angrily. "What are we going to touch them for?" And he left the room.

"We can hang them up over the stove," his mother assured him with bright, grieving eyes that only made the boy furious. "Come and eat with us."

"I'll be there!" he told her. "I have to see about this stuff first."

It was a Friday night. John Sobieski had the whole weekend to dry his running things, and on Monday he went to the school equipped just like all the rest—except that he had come in first the last time they had run. But that same day the figure 1, which he could almost feel burning upon his back once he was among the runners again, faded out. Nobody paid any attention to it.

Now every day was bright and blue. The cold air burned like alcohol on the skin of his arms and legs when he took off his sweat clothes and began to run in the afternoons. He was happy just to run with the others, keeping up with them along different streets of the city that he had not known anything about before. In the first time trials he finished twelfth.

The coaches took fifteen boys to run at Utica the following Saturday. They drove a few hours in cars, got out to warm up behind a strange and brand-new high school, gathered on a line in a bunch—one of a dozen such, each in its own bright colors —and then a gun was fired, a cloud of white smoke rose above the man who had fired it, and the bunches all sprang into a forward wave to cross the field together. John Sobieski was left behind, exhausted, right at the start. He decided he would just finish the race, this one last time, and then he would never run again. He felt that way all through the unfamiliar woods and as he came down out of them onto the field again, into the mouth of the bullpen between funneling ropes that crowded him against boys in front and on both sides until he stood still with one of the coarse-fibered ropes in either hand. Somebody wrote something on his back—a piece of paper with a number on it had been pinned to his red shirt—and then he staggered away, to walk around and begin coughing.

Riding home in the head coach's car, he learned their team had won the meet. Their first five men had come in second, fourth, fifth, seventh, and eighth for a score of 26. John Sobieski found the number 24 written in pencil underneath the big printed number on the paper he had torn from his back. Besides that, he had a blue satin ribbon. Two hundred boys had run, but only the first twenty-five received ribbons.

Monday his name appeared in the city newspaper. "A freshman, John Sobieski, was the Red and White's tenth finisher." Ernest Borkmann had cut the story out of the paper and showed it to him in the locker room before practice.

"Where did you come in?" John Sobieski asked him.

The big boy folded the clipping carefully with large strong fingers and put it away in his wallet. "I got sick," he answered, frowning. "I didn't finish."

Saturday they ran at Syracuse, and there were twice as

many runners. The high school placed second. John Sobieski, their seventh man in, finished thirty-ninth. It meant he had improved about nine places. And he beat three of their own runners who had finished ahead of him the week before.

This time he rode home with the younger coach. The other runners were subdued; John Sobieski's continual coughing was louder than all their quiet talk. It filled the car, though he strained to suppress it by sitting motionless with all the air breathed out of him, so that he would have nothing to cough with. But he had to breathe again sometime, and then the air would rush into his lungs, explode, and be thrown out once more. "Roll up your windows," the coach told the runners. Twice they stopped at gas stations to let him drink water, but even so he would only start coughing again in a few minutes.

Now John Sobieski began to notice that boys on the running team nodded or spoke to him when he saw them in the school's halls, and even a few others seemed to know who he was. He lived only for running. He got up in the morning and walked to the school for it, waiting all day for that living half hour when he emerged on the playing field and ran, suffering, until he swore he would never do it again, and at last finished somehow and returned to the locker room. His life was running. It was different now than ever before. "I only eat and sleep at home," he thought to himself as he sat and watched his father and mother in the evening. "They see me go away, and they see me come back—but they don't know what I do!"

It was five o'clock in the morning. New York City, the biggest city in America, lay more than 150 miles away to the east and south. The head coach had already driven off with five boys, and now the other coach and two remaining runners and a manager all got into a little car that stood by itself at the curb in front of the school. John Sobieski had the front seat. He hunched down inert and from there watched the dark houses, the peaking rooftops, roll by. Nobody said anything. The manager and the runner in the back seat were both trying to sleep. Once they were well into the country, John Sobieski sat up and looked out. It was just getting light. The sky was gray, as though cloudy. In the open fields there was light, but everything else remained shadowy. Buildings that they passed stood gray and chill-appearing, except for yellow windows distinct and square in a few isolated houses. The boy was glad to see them. It struck him as cheerful somehow, for it meant that people were awake within and beginning their work for the day. Something in him yearned toward them, but he was going to New York City; and he was glad to be going to New York, but he didn't want to run there.

The next time he looked out it was fully light; the day would clear. They were driving on a parkway now, twin concrete highways that seemed to descend endlessly taking huge dips and turns. As the little car rose up with engine roaring to meet each new crest, John Sobieski waited to see if the city were ahead, but the road on the other side only plunged them downhill again, twisting out of sight among hills and woods.

He couldn't sleep, but he closed his eyes for a long, long time, hoping that when he opened them again they would be there, and he would at least have rested a little.

What made him sit up again finally was a loud whining of tires. Then outside, all around, he saw more cars, a great many of them and all going to the same place. The young coach, sitting next to him, was very busy driving. John Sobieski saw that the man's face was now intent, his eyes fiercely concentrated ahead. He was passing the other cars as though they were runners. They went between some fairly high buildings and then ran downhill across a bridge; the coach paid money out his window, they went on down the ramp, blue water came around on the right, and immediately up in front of them, very high, a suspension bridge swung across to the other side. They drove underneath it, and there were the tall buildings of New York standing out ahead as he had thought they would be—except that they weren't down close to the water, but were built on top of a steep hill rising on the left.

Just then the runner in the back seat—it was the same dark-haired boy who had been sitting on the bench when John Sobieski first entered the locker room—called out, "Hey, we're on the island!"

The older runner knew they should be running at a park somewhere back in the Bronx. The coach knew it too—he had run there himself when he had been a cross-country runner—but coming into the city he had missed his turn and was still looking for it when he had been caught among the cars rushing into Manhattan. He got off the parkway now and they ran steeply uphill between buildings, all of them bigger than John Sobieski had ever seen, but not what he had expected of New York either. They were big dirty boxes with innumerable windows in which, it looked like, people lived. It gave him a pang to think that.

They kept turning into different streets, driving fast, and then they were out of Manhattan again. All at once the coach turned off the highway and drove straight across a flat athletic field. Right where he stopped the car the runners were massed—bright-colored, moving and shifting by the hundreds, tightening up—and just as they went to get out, a shot was fired. The pack jolted, loosened, and stretched away like an expanding accordion, the farther edge moving rapidly over the field, while the near edge remained on the starting line playing out runners in waves. The coach swore aloud as he helped rip jackets and sweat clothes from John Sobieski and the other runner. Then the two of them were on the field running, before some had even left the starting line.

And if ever they had started before John Sobieski was ready, it was this time. Next to him, in front of him, behind him, shoving him, were runners; and he himself, short and thin, unable even to see above them. He felt as though he were dying, and as a drowning person sees his whole life, he saw his running. Then he knew he couldn't run at all; he was always sick, he only beat others by tormenting himself. And he hated it, because he cared only about beating the others and not all of them either, but just those on his own team, for of the rest there were so many as to make his own struggles seem feeble, indistinguishable.

Yet even now, as though it were a thing quite separate from himself, his small body was pressing forward through the thick of the runners. His eye was caught by the flash of a red shirt that he knew must be from his own school. Slowly, he was coming up to it. He made his way sideways between two larger boys, and when another boy just ahead stumbled, sighing, and gave up, John Sobieski dodged around him and into the free pocket, darting forward unhindered until he was running behind the familiar

158

red shirt. When it found openings, he followed after. When it forced a way, shoving runners aside, he went through as though he had done it for himself.

They had passed over the parkway on a bridge of stone arches and now they were running on a bridle path that turned and climbed upward under trees, around the bulk of a great hill on the other side. The stream of the pack had narrowed until it was only four to five runners wide, and at one edge the hillside fell away steeply—down to John Sobieski couldn't see what, though he was running on that side himself, just within the pack.

Twisting slowly uphill, flashing gay-colored, the pack surged over the crest of the hill and slid downward again, winding around, faster and faster. Somewhere John Sobieski had left the red shirt behind and now that the race was downhill, he tried to break out and pass runners, but he couldn't. It was impossible, with the runners pounding on all sides of him; he couldn't move from his place. He stood it until he couldn't any longer; then he pulled abreast of the boy immediately in front of him and went through diagonally to the right. He saw he was free. He let himself out, his feet smashing into the ground in long downhill strides. But while he was passing, exposed out there, an impulse that originated in an obscure movement somewhere deep inside the pack suddenly reached him and struck him through the elbow of the boy beside him. For an instant he continued to run wildly along the edge of the hill, with his arms waving and snatching for balance, but he was being toppled inexorably, and he was over.

John Sobieski went down running, but he couldn't keep on his feet. A young tree caught him by the arm, spun him around and threw him, rolling, down the slope. He hit things; but the pain wasn't so great as the exhaustion and sickness that came on immediately as he ceased running. He lay on his side on dry leaves at the bottom, his body jackknifed and heaving. Overhead was the thunder of the passing pack, the rustle of their feet among fallen leaves, the muffled reverberations of the shocks of a thousand galloping legs all shod in the sharp-pointed running shoes like hoofs—passing by, pounding, and gone; a pause—a scattered hurry of stragglers—now one, now several; their breathing like the furious labor of bicycle pumps, their feet clumping—dying away; now all gone altogether—passed on.

He was left alone. Everything was quiet. A hot sickness, separate from the ache of lungs and throat, went back and forth over him, for the first time unmixed with the bustle of others walking around feeling the same way. He hated himself, he hated his body that gasped and gasped for breath among the crisp leaves. He could not bear to think that even though he had lost, he must still suffer for trying. For a while he did nothing; he didn't even try to get up, because there wasn't any use in it. But he started to feel the cold on his arms and legs and through his thin uniform. When he finally got to his feet he was so weak and listless he could hardly climb the steep bank. He pulled himself up from one young tree to another, and then clung to them on the uphill side, resting.

Up on the bridle path again, his coughing came over him. It began loud and wet, and would get worse, he knew, harsher and drier, as his running sickness improved, but now it was all the same to him. He walked downhill weakly, without purpose, staggering and coughing. As he came out of the woods, the dark-haired runner, recovered from his run, his sweat suit on, met him in the middle of the stone bridge over the parkway. Beneath them, the bright automobiles whined in both directions. John Sobieski leaned on the boy, and together they went down to the field, an enormous one big enough for twenty football games. On the far side of it the young coach's tiny car stood by itself, and, as they were crossing, the man got out and came toward them.

"Somebody pushed me . . . I fell over," John Sobieski tried to explain, between fits of coughing, but the man only scowled, glanced briefly into the face of the other runner, and didn't answer.

They got him into his sweat clothes and inside the car. They rolled up the windows and laid him by himself on the backseat, with the coats of all three boys thrown over him. The coach and the other two rode up front, mostly in silence, while John Sobieski coughed with a horrible crouping dry sound all the way back to their own city.

From where he lay he could see it growing dark outside. The shapes of roofs were sharp in the cold sky. He was aware of the fits and starts of the automobile and the traffic sounds of the city outside; of the rush of cold air entering and the voices of the two boys briefly saying good-bye; finally of the emptiness of the car with only himself and the coach remaining—when at last the car stopped for good.

"Is this where you live, John Sobieski?" the man asked from out on the sidewalk. He looked up at the gray two-family house, while the boy was climbing out over the front seat.

"You listen to me now. I want you to get into that house and not come out of it for a month. You're sick. You belong in bed, for God's sake, and not out killing yourself running. It isn't running anymore, when you have to trade on your health just to get a place. That doesn't do us any good—it isn't reliable. You go in there and get better. Forget all about running, for a while."

The man spoke angrily. He held the car door open against the wind with his back and watched John Sobieski, but the boy just stood before him saying nothing. He got back into his car and drove away.

John Sobieski made his way upstairs. He went right to his room and to bed. His mother saw at once that he was sick and looked after him.

He stayed in bed three weeks. Most of the time he slept. There was nothing he wanted to get up for. After the first week he didn't cough anymore; as long as he didn't run it would be all right. His father came in to see him after supper. The older man seemed a little embarrassed. He would bring a kitchen chair and set it just inside the bedroom door, and talk across the space at his son, who would be watching him, lying deep in his bed, his brown head on a big pillow.

"How do you feel tonight?"

"All right."

The father nodded. He wouldn't smoke in the bedroom. He sat for a while. "The one time I was in New York," he said, "I went on the train with my father. When we got there we just stood up in some place and ate sauerkraut and frankfurts. That's all I remember about it."

John Sobieski listened, but didn't say anything. After a bit his father got up to go out. "Well, stay where you are now. Rest up a while. That's the only thing."

"Listen," John Sobieski called after him, "I'm still going back there, after I get better."

His father looked down at the linoleum. "They still want you, after you got licked like that?"

"I don't know. It doesn't matter if they want me, though—I'm going to go."

His father went away.

In the dark bedroom, John Sobieski closed his eyes. He could hear the wind blowing outside between his house and the house next door. A boy moved before him in the dark; John Sobieski was coming up closer, from behind. . . . He caught himself and swore, and thrashed in the bed with regret. He couldn't remember running without remembering his failure. Yet in twenty minutes more, going off to sleep, he would see before him a boy dressed in white shorts and red shirt, and he himself, coming up behind, planning how he was going to take him.

FOR DISCUSSION

1. Why does John Sobieski run?
2. From your answer to the above question, generalize about the meaning of sports in the lives of Gale Sayers, Chuck Hughes; about the meaning of sports in your own life.

INTRODUCTION

Much has been written about the relationship between Brian Piccolo and Gale Sayers, teammates on the Chicago Bears before Piccolo's death and Sayers's eventual retirement from football. Sayers wore number 40 on his uniform; Piccolo, number 41. In view of their warm relationship, this numerical closeness is very appropriate.

"Pick" is Gale Sayers's account of their relationship. Here we see the way two men develop in the game they play together, and in the way they feel about each other. Was the sport responsible? Would the qualities of the two men, and their affection for each other, have been the same if they had dedicated their lives to some profession other than football? You decide.

Pick

Gale Sayers

Brian Piccolo and I began rooming together in 1967 and we became close friends. It's easy to make a big deal out of the fact that he was white and I'm black and to wonder how we got along. But there was nothing to it, although I admit at first we did feel each other out. I had never had a close relationship with a white person before, except maybe George Halas, and Pick had never really known a black person. I remember him telling me that he wondered at first, "Are they really different? Do they sleep in chandeliers, or what?"

The best thing about our relationship as it developed was that we could kid each other all the time about race, do our thing in perfect ease. It was a way, I guess, of easing into each man's world. It helped take the strangeness out of it.

Like, before that 1969 exhibition game in Washington, a writer came into our room to interview me, and Pick really laid it on.

"How do you get along?" the writer asked.

Pick said, "We're O.K. as long as he doesn't use the bathroom."

"What do you fellows talk about?"

"Mostly race relations," I said.

"Nothing but the normal racist stuff," he said.

"If you had your choice," the writer went on, ignoring all the digs, "who would you want as your roommate?"

I was very tactful. "If you're asking me what white Italian fullback from Wake Forest, I'd say Pick."

Piccolo was born in Massachusetts and raised in Fort Lauderdale, Florida—by way of He-Hung-High, Mississippi, I always said. At Wake Forest he was the campus honcho. He made All-America running back. He led the country in rushing and scoring in his senior year, but he wasn't drafted. They claimed he didn't have too much size or too much speed, but the Bears took him as a free agent. Like all free agents, he was a long shot to make it in the pros. But he hung in there with determination and guts and he turned out to be a helluva football player.

How good was he? Well, he was always proudest of the fact that one year he graded higher than I did. At the end of the season the coaches review all the game films and grade each player. And in 1968 Pick graded about 98 and I graded like 74. "If I do something," Pick said, "I do it. If I'm told to block the linebacker, I do it. I'm a ball player's ball player. They got to go with me."

I first met Pick at the All-America game in Buffalo, New York, after my senior year. There were four of us in that game who were going on to the Bears' camp—Dick Butkus, Jimmy Jones, Pick, and myself. And Butkus and I never said a thing to any of the others, or to each other. "You were so bad then," Pick once said to me. "You were a real hotshot."

The thing is I was very shy then. I'm not outgoing, anyway. I don't try to push myself on people. And I was really quiet. I was always listening—I still am a very good listener, which I think is a good trait—but I was no talker. While the other Bear rookies socialized among themselves, said, "Hey, how you doing? We'll see you in training camp," Butkus and I didn't have one word to say to anyone, including ourselves. Piccolo claims we both changed amazingly over the years, and I guess that's true.

Anyway, I did give Pick a glancing hello that first time in Buffalo and that was it. We were on different teams in the All-America game and he didn't play because he had a pulled hamstring. Every year we have a ten-day rookie camp at Soldier's Field, and he wasn't in there because of the pull. The hamstring really ruined his rookie season.

The next year, 1966, we got a little closer. We lockered next to each other, his number being 41 and mine 40. ("I had Dick Gordon on my left," he once said, "Sayers on my right. I felt like an Oreo cookie.") And we got to know each other a little better. We became friendlier and friendlier.

I had to get friendly with him because he was my backup man and I needed him. When I was tired I depended on him for a blow. He always said, "I have the distinction of never being put into a game by a coach." We always worked it between ourselves. Mr. Halas was head coach then and he never liked to take me out of a game. But there were times when I just ran and ran and ran and I was completely whipped. And Piccolo knew it, but he would have to engage in a lengthy charade before they'd take me out.

First Pick would ask me, "Gale, are you tired, do you want a blow?" If I said yes, he'd go to Ed Cody, our backfield coach, and say, "Gale's tired, he wants to take a blow." And then Ed would come back to me and say, "Gale, are you tired?" Just to make sure, you know. Then, if I said yes, Ed would go to Mr. Halas and the old man would turn to Piccolo and say, "Pick, come here, Gale's tired. I think maybe you ought to go in for him." That was always kind of interesting, except it was a little tough for Piccolo to get into the games. By the time that ritual was finished the game would be over.

But after a while the coaches just let us do it by ourselves. And Pick got on to my ways and could tell when I wanted to take a blow. All I had to do was look over to the bench and he would see. He would know by the way I was standing in the huddle, by the way I hung my head. If I made a long run, starting at one side of the field and ending on the other, he'd know to come in for a play. And he was always around the side lines ready to come in.

There were times, of course, when this didn't work to Pick's advantage. Once, against Minnesota, I had just finished running what we call a "sucker play." On a sucker play the guard doesn't block the defensive tackle. He tries to pull the tackle the opposite way, making the tackle think he's leading a sweep or something. He takes the tackle with him and the runner shoots through the hole. And I shot through for 40 yards. Naturally, I was tired and Pick went in.

In the huddle our quarterback, Jack Concannon, called, "Same play," and Pick's jaw hit the ground. After a tackle has been had on a sucker play—which you never call more than once a game—you know the tackle wants to kill somebody. He just wants to sucker somebody himself. And Piccolo got hit good. He came out of the game and his nose was bleeding and his eyes were watery and he was muttering something about being the biggest sucker of all.

But the worst moment for Pick came in a game against Detroit in 1967. We had played the first game with the Lions at Wrigley Field and beat them 14–3. Afterward their linebacker, Wayne Walker, came out with this comment: "Every time the Bears play us they nickel-and-dime us to death. This time we're gonna get 'em."

So we went to Detroit about three weeks later and they tried very hard to get us. It was a pretty physical game—a tough game. It was one of the most physical, most vicious games I've been in since I've played pro ball. They were punching and gouging and twisting legs in there and getting away with a lot of stuff the referee couldn't see.

In the fourth quarter we had a 14-point lead and I decided to get out. I really wasn't that tired, but I said to myself, We're ahead, our defense is playing good ball, enough to hold them, I'll take a blow. With eight minutes to play, we punted and I came off and said to Pick, "Finish it up."

That puzzled him because it was not like me to leave a game with eight minutes still left. The puzzle was solved right away the first time he carried the ball. He hit into the line and someone started twisting his ankle and another guy started punching him in the guts and Alex Karras was hollering at our center, Mike Pyle, "When the season's over I'm coming to Chicago and I'm gonna kill you." And Pick came back and said, "This is one of the great favors you have done for me over the years, Gale."

166

And, in the summer of 1967, we began rooming together. In Birmingham, Alabama.

I was in the room when Pick came in. "What are you doing here?" he said.

I said, "We're in together."

He was a little surprised, but I had known about it. They had asked me if I had any objections to rooming with Brian. I said no, none at all. I had been rooming with a fellow who got cut, and I think Pick was rooming with a quarterback, Larry Rakestraw, and they decided maybe they ought to room guys together by position. But I think Bennie McRae, one of our cocaptains, also suggested that they start some integrated rooming, to get a little better understanding with the guys. And Pick and I were the first on the Bears.

But it really didn't make any difference. I think they tend to make too much out of it. Friends like to room with friends, and it has nothing to do with segregation or anything like that.

You can bet we didn't have dinner together in Birmingham that weekend. We joked a lot about it, but we went our separate ways. I don't know if we ate dinner with one another but a couple of times that first year. It was always that when we got into a place I'd call the guys that I normally went out with and he'd call the guys that he normally went out with and we'd split. It was just that he had his friends and I had mine. I think we were both a little unsure about the whole thing at first. And I guess I was a little distant that first year. I think once people get to know me I'm easy to get along with. Pick always knew that on the day of a game I liked to be left alone—just let me be—and this is what he did. But by the end of that first year we had both loosened up quite a bit.

I think he actually helped open me up because he was such a happy-go-lucky guy. He always had a joke or two in him. One day he read me this letter he had just received from a guy in Chicago who actually signed his name. It went: "I read where you stay together with Sayers. I am a white man! Most of the people I know don't want anything to do with them. I just don't understand you. Most Italians I have met say that they stink —and they really do!" And Pick couldn't resist his own P.S.: "Well," he said, "that's true, of course, you can't get away from that."

He was always getting in a dig about something. Like we'd be having breakfast in the coffee shop and a waitress would say to me, "Can I ask you your name?" And before I could answer, Pick would mumble, "They all look alike."

When Pick heard that Vince Lombardi had taken over in Washington, he said he thought he would like to play a little bit for Lombardi before his career was over.

"I can arrange that," I said.

"Would you?" he said. "I'm tired of playing in your shadow. I want to be a legend in my own time."

But he never was that much in my shadow. He meant a lot to the Chicago Bears. One game in 1967 he got the game ball for his performance against Minnesota. He had a way of playing a good game when I was having a good game. When I was going well, I'd be making a lot of long runs and so I'd be taking a blow more often and maybe my playing time would be a little less. And Pick would come in and play a helluva game. You'd have to say he was an opportunist. The day I tore up my knee against San Francisco Pick came in and ran for 87 yards on eighteen carries, and caught four passes for 54 yards.

And he did a beautiful job the rest of the year. Against New Orleans he rushed twenty-one times for 112 yards. He ended up rushing for 450 yards, a 3.8 average. He had a favorite line then: "I won't get you sixty [meaning 60 yards in one run], but I'll get you ten sixes." Every time I saw him that year and into 1969 he'd look at me and say, "I won't get you sixty, but I'll get you ten sixes." And he'd burst out laughing.

He was really a comfort to me during the 1969 exhibition season and into the regular season, especially those early games when the writers had written me off. He was one of the few guys who seemed to have confidence in me, who built up my morale. He would read what they were saying about me and he'd say, "Don't worry about them. You're running fine. The holes aren't there, you know, just keep your chin up." Which I was trying to do, but it wasn't always easy.

And he knew I was tight in those early days, wondering if I had lost something, and he did his damnedest to loosen me up. One time in camp a writer asked about my knee. "There's one big difference in Gale now," Pick said, standing right beside me. "He runs all right until the knee starts to wobble."

The trouble was that a lot of writers began to believe that. We have one local writer who is always sneaking around, trying to pick up conversation among the players. He wants to know everything and he always edges in trying to hear what doesn't concern him. So one day after practice we saw him coming. I put my back to him and Pick made believe he didn't know he was there, and he started in.

"It really feels that bad, huh, kid?" he said.

I said, "Yeah. I don't know if I can make it."

"Well, don't worry about it. Hell, I filled in for you last year. I'll do the job. The team will get along O.K., Gale. We can do it."

"Well, I hope so, but I'm just not so sure. Damn knee. I may have to hang it up after the season."

"Well, what the hell," Pick said. "It's your fifth year. You've got your pension in."

That writer stole away, not sure that he had heard right and wondering, probably, Was it a put-on, or should I write it?

It's ironic the way things happen. Because of my injury and my mental state afterward, I got to know Pick even better and became closer to him than almost anybody else on the team. And then when he became ill, it seemed that our friendship deepened and we got to understand each other even better. And that's when I found out what a beautiful person he really was.

In July, when we report to camp, we all have to take complete physicals. And of course Brian had one and he had a chest x-ray and nothing showed. Brian didn't smoke, didn't drink much, and he always took good care of himself. And when Ronnie Bull tore up his knee in the Detroit game, Piccolo was switched to fullback and played alongside me and was doing a helluva job.

But just about this time he began to develop a cough. It wasn't much at first. He wouldn't cough much at night, but he'd get up in the morning and start to cough, maybe four or five times, then stop for a while, then start again. Later he was coughing at night. He would excuse himself every few minutes —because, I guess, he thought he was disturbing me.

We went up to Minnesota on November 2, and the cough got a little worse. It was kind of cool and damp, and he figured maybe he was catching cold, so he got a prescription from one of the team doctors and started taking cough medicine. Then we played in Pittsburgh, and he still had the cough. And in the Atlanta game it really got bad.

It was warm down there, and he coughed so bad that he almost lost his breath a few times. Dick Gordon was sitting on the bench next to him. Brian was hacking something awful, and Gordon just couldn't believe it. He looked at Pick and said, "How the hell are you playing?" But he played the whole game and played well and he scored a touchdown.

And at this time he could still joke about it. He would get this coughing jag and then say to Ralph Kurek, another of our running backs and a good friend of Pick's, "I think I'm having a coronary."

Kurek, who's nuts, said, "Try this heart massage. I use it all the time when my heart stops."

Pick got back at Kurek by spraying his roll-on deodorant with a sticky substance, "Firm Grip." Every day he'd load it up with "Firm Grip" and Ralph never caught on to it. Pick swore that Kurek never raised his arms once he put that stuff on.

The Tuesday after the Atlanta game Pick decided he better see Doctor L. L. Braun, our medical doctor. Maybe he just needed a stronger cough syrup or something. So he went to the doctor's office at Illinois Masonic hospital and Doctor Braun wasn't in. Louis Kolb took Pick upstairs for a chest x-ray.

He threw the x-ray up on the light, and Piccolo, no medical man, nevertheless knew when an x-ray wasn't right. He saw a big spot on his left lung, a clear area where all the rest was dark. He said, "Hey, doctor, what's this?"

Dr. Kolb said, "I don't mean to be an alarmist, but it's something that shouldn't be there. But we'll have Dr. Braun come down and look at it and we'll see what we can figure out. Don't worry about it, it could be a swollen gland or something."

Piccolo told me he waited an hour or so, because Dr. Braun was busy, and while he waited, he said, he sat there looking at that x-ray and just wondering about a lot of things.

Finally, Dr. Braun came around, took a look, and told Pick he wouldn't be playing the game Sunday against the Baltimore Colts. He thought Brian had better stay in the hospital for some tests.

And he did. The chest specialist came in and looked down Pick's throat with a tube and he couldn't see anything. So they made an incision in his chest. And that's when they discovered it was a tumor. And it was malignant.

The doctor told Pick that he apparently had had a tumor there all his life, lying there benign, and for some reason it just decided to take off.

The first time I heard about the seriousness of Brian's illness was Friday night, when Coach Halas called me at home. He said, "Brian's very sick. He's got a malignant tumor in his chest that's got to come out. We're sending him to New York to the best hospital in the country for this type of tumor."

I was stunned. I was absolutely stunned, and shocked. I just didn't know what to say, or think. After practice Saturday, I went over to the hospital to see him. He was in a fantastic mood. "I'm ready to play, man," he said. "It's just a little cough, you know." He was disappointed that he couldn't play. His wife, Joy, was with him and she was in good spirits, too. I really didn't know what to say to him. We kidded around a bit and then I left.

That night, the night before the Baltimore game, Mr. Halas called me again. He said, "Gale, I think maybe you ought to say something to the team before we go out tomorrow, try to dedicate the game to Brian. You're Pick's roommate. I think it would be appropriate."

And I said I would. The more I thought about it, the more I liked the idea. Because I think a lot of the fellows didn't realize just how sick Brian was. There had been no announcements in the papers, and the Bears wanted to make no announcements until Brian got to New York and was operated on.

I had never in my life talked to a team. I don't consider myself a leader. All the leading I do is by example, by the way I go out and play the game. And I didn't know how it would go. I was a little nervous, but that didn't matter. I wanted to get something across to the guys, that was all.

Sunday morning I went to church, which I seldom do during the football season. I went mainly to pray for Brian.

Before we went out for our pregame warm-up, I told Jim Dooley I wanted to say something to the team about Brian. He said it was O.K. So after the warm-up and just as we were getting ready to go back on the field, Dooley told the team, "Gale has something to say to you."

I just told them that we have a tradition after a winning game to give a game ball to the outstanding player of that game. I said, "As you all know, Brian Piccolo is very, very sick. If you don't know it, you should know it. He's very, very sick and he might not ever play football again. And I think each of us should dedicate ourselves to try to give our maximum efforts to win this ball game and give the game ball to Pick. We can all sign it and take it up to him. . . ."

About this time I was getting pretty choked up, and they probably didn't even understand the last part of what I was saying, because I had started to cry.

As we went on the field, they started playing "The Star-Spangled Banner" and I couldn't help crying then. We were going to kick off, so I went to the bench and just leaned over with my head down, sobbing. Jim Ringo came over to me and said, "Gale, I've been in football for twenty years and never heard anything like that before." And Abe Gibron came over and said it was a great thing to do.

And then I went over to Ross Montgomery, who was my backup man now, and I told Ross that although he was a fine football player he might as well not suit up because I wasn't coming out of this game. I was going to play this game for Brian.

And we went out and we played ball and we should have won the damn game. We had them by a touchdown with six minutes to go and John Unitas came in and drove them 80 yards. Then, as we were getting into field-goal range, they intercepted a pass and they got the field goal and we lost the game. But most of the players had given their all, I knew that.

After the game, Linda and I went to the hospital to see Brian. He was leaving the next morning for New York, and a bunch of the players came by. Mike Pyle was there with his wife, Ronnie Bull and his wife, Jack Concannon and his wife, Ed McCaskey was there, Jim Ringo, and Ralph Kurek and his wife. McCaskey ordered a bunch of pizzas and a few beers and stuff and everybody sat around.

Linda and I stayed for two hours. At one point, Pick, Concannon, Kurek, and myself went upstairs to see this little girl who had dived into a shallow swimming pool and broken her neck. She was about thirteen and was paralyzed from the neck down. She had kind of become the darling of the Bears, because every time a player came to see Dr. Fox he would send him up to see this girl. Mainly because of the girl, Brian said, he wasn't as concerned about his own troubles. The next morning, the day he left for New York, he went into the girl's room to give her a signed photograph of himself. She was asleep and he left it. Some weeks later we heard that the girl had passed away.

We talked a lot that Sunday. We clowned a little bit, but it was sort of a serious mood, considering Pick's normal disposition. But he was in fine spirits. Listening to him, I found it hard to believe that here he had played football so long without getting knocked out by an injury and, all of a sudden, this terrible thing had struck him down. It was a tough thing to believe that this kind of thing could happen to him. But he was such a strong person. He just said, "It's a tumor and it's got to come out, and it's got to come out now." And he was loose about it because that was his way. He's always been loose about things. His attitude was, What's the use of getting solemn and serious? It doesn't change things. He said he felt he was fortunate in that respect because he knew a lot of people who just couldn't look at things that way. He said he was resigned to anything that happened to him. He felt, he said, that all our lives are plotted out in advance and nothing we do can change things. His only concern, he said, was for his wife and his three small daughters.

What he was really doing, I think, was carrying through the I Am Third philosophy of life. Really carrying it through. And yet it was a very positive attitude. And I think you have to be that way. I wasn't really impressed by Brian's courage because I knew Brian. I knew he was a very courageous person, and I expected that of him.

Pick flew into New York Monday and they operated on him on Friday. Dr. Edward Beattie, who is a famous specialist on such tumors, performed the operation. He told Brian beforehand that he might have to quit playing football for a couple of years. Pick knew that would be the end for him. Because if he laid out two years he would be trying to make a comeback at twenty-eight. So he told the doctor, "Well, listen, don't worry about it. We won't talk about it now. We'll wait and see."

Dr. Beattie also told Pick the tumor figured to be the size of a baseball. When they got it out—after a four-and-a-half-hour operation—it was closer to a grapefruit.

We had a Saturday game in San Francisco, and right after the game I flew back to Chicago, then into New York for an appearance. Sunday morning I went in to see Pick.

Same old Piccolo. He had watched the San Francisco game—it was on national television—and he gave me hell for not fielding a punt that went on to roll 70 yards. He said, "I kept yelling, 'Gale, pick it up, pick it up.'" Well, I caught hell from Abe Gibron for not picking it up, too.

Considering everything he had gone through, he looked well and he was in his usual good spirits. The room was full of flowers. "I don't have any oxygen for myself," he said to me. And he had gotten thousands of cards and letters. Then he showed off a personally autographed picture and album he had received from Frank Sinatra. He flipped over Sinatra.

And, naturally, he showed me his scar. It made my knee look like nothing. It was a wicked one, coming almost from his throat down to two inches above his navel, with another scar from the middle of his sternum to just under his armpit.

Brian's attitude after the operation was so phenomenal it made me feel all the worse about how I had acted just after my knee surgery. The day after I was operated on Pick and Bobby Joe Green came to see me. Bobby Joe was still on crutches from his knee surgery and he had a struggle to get to my room. And I just lay there and said nothing. Pick tried to make small talk, but it was like talking to a wall. Pick was so mad. He told me later, "Gale, I really felt like saying to you, 'you're a miserable S.O.B. and I won't come and see you again. Just lay in there and be miserable and feel sorry for yourself.'"

It was true. The first day or two I was terrible. Pick would say something that would normally get a chuckle, and it was like I was deaf. I lay there like stone.

And here was Brian Piccolo, after probably the most critical moment in his whole life, in fine spirits, cool and hopeful and so positive about things. He really helped lift *your* spirits.

He spent fifteen days in the hospital in New York. Pete Rozelle visited him on Thanksgiving Day and brought an auto-

174

graphed book about professional football, *The First Fifty Years.* And he watched part of the Viking-Ram game with Pick. I expected that from a man like Rozelle. He's a straight, down-to-earth guy. A helluva man.

When Pick got back home he naturally took it easy for a while. The doctor said he could go outdoors and do anything he wanted as soon as he felt up to it. And he did make one of our last practice sessions, before the Detroit game, our next-to-the-last of the season. And the guys were all glad to see him.

We talked on the phone a lot and Linda and I visited him a few times, and he seemed to be making terrific progress. He had gotten his weight back up to 188 and was getting ready to play a little golf and start working out a little in the gym.

When I got back from the Pro Bowl game in Los Angeles I called him. I had been named MVP on offense in that game, and Piccolo said, "I missed the first half. I was at a meeting at the country club. But somebody there had been watching it and was saying what a great game Sayers was having. So when I got home I turned on the TV. As soon as it goes on, the nigger fumbles. That's when I turned you off. I didn't watch another play. Typical nigger play."

I couldn't stop laughing on the phone. "You're terrible," I said, "you're so bad. You haven't changed at all. You're as big a racist as you've ever been."

Shortly after, he went out to play in the Astrojet golf tournament in Phoenix, in which they pair a pro-baseball player and a pro-football player from the same city. Pick was paired with Ernie Banks of the Chicago Cubs. "Wouldn't you know?" he said. "You can't get away from them."

When he came back from the golf tournament he called me to tell me about it. He also said that he had to go back to New York for more tests. He had discovered a lump on his chest.

That night we played basketball together. The Bears had a team, if that's what you want to call it, and Pick was player-coach. He played pretty well, too, and he was a very tough coach. He pulled me out of the game for taking those 80-foot shots. Well, I'm a guard. When you're a guard you can't get under the basket and you have to take the long shot. I was pretty bad, though, I admit it.

He was in good spirits, as usual, he was the same old Pick, playing down his little lump, which turned out to be a big swelling under his chest.

He went to New York, and they put him on medicine for a while. I came in and spent some time with him. His wife, Joy, was staying with him, and we took in movies, went to a couple of New York Knick basketball games, and ate pizza, which was Pick's favorite food.

They hoped that the medicine would reduce the tumor, but finally they decided he had to be operated on. He was operated on once, and a few weeks later he underwent his third operation.

Ed McCaskey and I flew into New York to see him before his second operation. He was coughing quite a bit and all the medication and stuff had weakened him physically. But mentally he was as strong as ever. I thought to myself, If anybody can lick it, it's got to be Pick. He can do it.

It happened that I have the same blood as Pick—B positive—so I gave a pint. A couple of days later, just before he was to undergo his second operation, he was telling friends about how Gale Sayers had given him blood.

"I don't know what it is," he said, "but lately I've gotten an awful craving for chitlins."

As much as they cut into this man, as much as he was inflicted with terrible pain and discomfort, as much as he suffered because of this wicked disease that struck him like a thunderbolt flashing out of a clear sky . . . as much as he was faced with all these tortures, his spirit would not be destroyed. That was the beautiful nature of Brian Piccolo.

There was the time, just before he went into the hospital again, that he sat down at home and wrote a letter to Freddy Steinmark of the University of Texas. Steinmark had played on Texas's 1969 national-championship football team. Just after the season they discovered that Steinmark had bone cancer. They amputated his leg. And Pick sat down and wrote him a letter. I asked him what he said to the boy.

"I told him that I, more than any other football player, understood a few things that must have gone through his mind. Because I had gone through the same thing. I told him never to lose courage and to remember that there was always hope."

At the end of May I came into New York to attend the

Professional Football Writers annual dinner and receive the George S. Halas award as the most courageous player in pro football. I had wanted Brian to attend with me if he was strong enough, but the day I arrived in New York was the day Brian and Joy left the hospital to go back home. He had finished a series of cobalt treatments and the doctors said he could spend a few weeks at home, then return to the hospital for more treatment.

One reason I wanted Brian with me at the banquet was that I intended to give him the trophy right there. But at least I was able to tell the audience something about Brian Piccolo.

"He has the heart of a giant," I said, "and that rare form of courage that allows him to kid himself and his opponent, cancer. He has the mental attitude that makes me proud to have a friend who spells out the word courage twenty-four hours a day of his life."

I concluded by saying, "You flatter me by giving me this award but I tell you here and now that I accept it for Brian Piccolo. Brian Piccolo is the man of courage who should receive the George S. Halas award. It is mine tonight, it is Brian Piccolo's tomorrow. . . . I love Brian Piccolo and I'd like all of you to love him, too. Tonight, when you hit your knees, please ask God to love him. . . ."

The next day I flew back to Chicago and called Pick on the phone. He had read about the speech in the paper and the first thing he said to me was, "Magic, you're too much. If you were here now I'd kiss you."

I said, "Yeah, well I'm glad I'm not there."

The next day Linda and I did go to see him. He was wearing shorts and sitting on the couch and he looked very small. But his spirits were as high as ever. Virgil Carter and his wife dropped by and we talked football and I cracked a couple of jokes, which was a big upset. "Gale, what is this?" Pick said. "I'm supposed to be the joker around here."

We left feeling better about him because he kept us in a light-hearted mood. He cheered *us* up. I'm glad of that last memory of Pick, since I was not to see him again.

He and Joy went to Atlanta to see their little girls, who had been staying with Joy's mother. He got very sick down there and they immediately flew back to New York.

Joy told us later that he had suffered a great deal the last week of his life. She said that up to then they both still had hope, but that last week, coming back to New York, they knew the end was near. And Brian faced up to it and started talking about it. "You know I love you, Joy," he said to his wife, "and I hope I have been a good father to the girls." And he told Joy things he would like for his girls. And when Joy would start to cry Pick would cheer her up the only way he knew how—by ridiculing his own condition. "Joy, can you believe this?" he'd say. "Can you believe this, Joy? Nobody would ever believe this."

I wanted to come in to New York to see him but at that time my parents were involved in an automobile accident. My mother got off light with some broken ribs but my father suffered a fractured skull and was in a coma, and I flew to Omaha to see them. And when I got back to Chicago I had a temperature of 104 and they put me in the hospital with a strep throat.

Tuesday morning, June 16, at six-thirty, Linda called me at the hospital to tell me that Brian had passed away a few hours earlier. A few minutes later I got another call from Ed McCaskey, who had been in New York with Joy and Brian until the end. I couldn't talk. I wasn't able to say a word to anyone the rest of that day.

I was discharged from the hospital that afternoon. When I came home I found that my trophy had arrived from New York. I sat down and wrote Brian's name on a piece of paper and pasted it over mine on the trophy. The next morning I went to the wake with the trophy and gave it to Joy and told her I wanted it buried with Pick. Joy said no, she wanted to keep it because it meant so much to her.

The funeral was held that Friday, a clean lovely morning in Chicago, and I went through it like a sleepwalker. I was one of the pallbearers along with Dick Butkus, Ralph Kurek, Ed O'Bradovich, Mike Pyle, and Randy Jackson. I think the only thing I remember about that funeral service was one line recited from the scripture: "The virtuous man, though he dies before his time, will find rest."

It was at the cemetery, as the priest was delivering his final words, that I broke down. He referred to the trophy and to our friendship and it was too much for me. I couldn't control myself. I just started to cry.

As soon as the service was ended, Joy came over to me and put her arms around me and we embraced and I told her how sorry I was. "Don't be sorry, Gale," she said. "I'm happy now because I know Brian is happy, and I don't have to watch him suffer any more. He's through suffering now."

She comforted me. I thought to myself, if she can really be that composed, Brian must have really given her something. And I thought, well, he gave us all something, all of us who were privileged to know him. And that helped compose me.

FOR DISCUSSION

1. In our culture it is rare that men express love for one another, yet there is nothing awkward about Gale Sayers saying "I love Brian Piccolo . . . ." What makes it acceptable in this situation, and awkward in others? Why do men have trouble expressing affection? How do sports in general offer a means of releasing affection?

2. How did Pick's training in sports prepare him to face death?

3. Discuss other athletes you know about who died during the peak years of their careers.

INTRODUCTION

The poems that follow all explore the effects of a sport on a man's later life. Each athlete tries to add it all up: what does it all mean? We meet Flick Webb, the ex-basketball star who now works in a filling station; an aging tennis player who can't seem to realize that he's past his prime; and a poet who used to be a linebacker. Each man's hour in the sun has passed. Or has it?

Ex-Basketball Player

John Updike

Pearl Avenue runs past the high school lot,
Bends with the trolley tracks, and stops, cut off
Before it has a chance to go two blocks,
At Colonel McComsky Plaza. Berth's Garage
Is on the corner facing west, and there,   5
Most days, you'll find Flick Webb, who helps Berth out.

Flick stands tall among the idiot pumps—
Five on a side, the old bubble-head style,
Their rubber elbows hanging loose and low.
One's nostrils are two S's, and his eyes   10
An E and O. And one is squat, without
A head at all—more of a football type.

Once Flick played for the high school team, the Wizards.
He was good: in fact, the best. In '46,
He bucketed three hundred ninety points,   15
A county record still. The ball loved Flick.
I saw him rack up thirty-eight of forty
In one home game. His hands were like wild birds.

He never learned a trade, he just sells gas,
Checks oil, and changes flats. Once in a while,   20

As a gag, he dribbles an inner tube,
But most of us remember anyway.
His hands are fine and nervous on the lug wrench.
It makes no difference to the lug wrench, though.

Off work, he hangs around Mae's Luncheonette,   25
Grease-gray and kind of coiled, he plays pinball,
Sips lemon cokes, and smokes those thin cigars;
Flick seldom speaks to Mae, just sits and nods
Beyond her face towards bright applauding tiers
Of Necco Wafers, Nibs, and Juju Beads.   30

The Old Pro's Lament

Paul Petrie

Each year, the court expands,
the net moves back, the ball
hums by—with more spin.

I use my second serve,
lob deeper, slice more,   5
stay away from the net, and fail
to win.

As any fool can tell,
it is time
to play the game purely   10
for the game's sake—to applaud
the puff of white chalk,
shake hands,
and grin.

Others retire   15
into the warm corners of memory,
invent new rules, new games,
and win.

Under the hot lances
of the shower, I play each point over,   20
and over,
and over
again.

Wisdom is the natural business
of old men—   25
to let the body go,
the rafters, moth-eaten and decayed,
cave in.

But nightly in dreams I see
an old man   30
playing in an empty court
under the dim floodlights
of the moon
with a racket gone in the strings—
no net, no ball, no game—   35
and still playing
to win.

To an Athlete Turned Poet

(for James Dickey)

Peter Meinke

Fifteen years ago   and twenty
he'd crouch   linebacker   gang-tackler
steel stomach flexing for
contact   contact   cracking
through man after man   weekend hero   5
washing the cheers down
with unbought beer

and now his stomach's soft   his books

press out his veins as he walks
and no one looks   10

but deep in his bone stadium
the roar of the crowd wells
as he shows them again
crossing line after line
on cracking fingers   heart red-   15
dogging with rage and joy over the broken backs
of words   words   words

FOR DISCUSSION

1. Describe briefly the life that each athlete is living now.
    What problems do they face? How do their solutions differ?
2. Sports somehow, sometimes, enable us to "win over," to
    conquer, those things that bother us the most—particularly
    the fact that all of us are mortal. Have the men in these
    poems won in this sense? Justify your answer.
3. How does the poet John Updike feel about Flick Webb?
    How do Flick's surroundings contribute to the picture the
    poet is trying to create?
4. We are told that we stress winning too much in our culture.
    Do you see traces of this attitude in the "old pro"? What is
    your final impression of him?
5. James Dickey now writes poetry—you will recall "In the
    Pocket" in the preceding chapter. Do you find it hard to
    believe that writing requires the intensity and the ferocity
    of football? Is this an inflated comparison? Explain.

Issues in Sports

CHAPTER FOUR

In an old Patty Duke–Jim Backus movie called "Billie," the hero is a young girl who wants to join the high school track team, which happens to be all male. After Billie makes the team by excelling in the time trials, she is sent to a separate dressing room to change clothes. Her father and mother enter, and Billie exclaims, "They treat me like a girl!"

"Darling, you are a girl," says her mother.

"I don't care," says Billie, "I want to be an equal."

Her father, incredulous, replies: "She's discovered a whole new sex—boys, girls, and equals."

Well, why not? Is it only coincidental that Billie is also the name of a prominent woman tennis player who, in addition to possessing a devastating forehand, shares the belief that boys and girls should receive equal treatment on the playing field? The outcome of the Patty Duke movie is not as clear-cut as Billie Jean King's career in tennis. Although the movie's Billie wins everything from the javelin to the 100-yard dash over male competitors, she ultimately decides to give up track for a guy named Mike. Still, the movie reflects the change in womens' attitudes toward sports.

As we look ahead, we must acknowledge that sports often reflect issues of concern to our society at large; and today we must deal with such questions as the rights of minority groups, and the rights of a *majority* group: women. Other questions include the use (and abuse) of athletes, and the right of the athlete to challenge established patterns of authority. Perhaps the most disturbing issues are: Do sports provide a common meeting ground where all members of our society are judged on ability alone? Are women treated fairly in sports? Must an athlete submit to authority for the sake of the team, or can he still remain an individual? In this final chapter of *Sports Literature* we endeavor to recognize the ways that sports and society, in handling these questions, complement and illuminate one another. If we can identify and exorcise the abuses in one area, perhaps we can do the same in the other.

In dealing with the issue of race in sports, Tom Meschery seeks to blur the difference: "The sweat pouring from our bodies/is neither black nor white." But there are disturbing stories elsewhere. Jack Olsen offers us "A Look at Life on the Black Side," and the view is not pleasant.

A similar issue—sometimes called Locker Room Lib, or "sexegration"—is discussed in selections such as the one on Ms. King in this chapter and Ms. Fasteau's piece in the next chapter. Schools today spend millions of dollars more on boys' sports than on girls' sports. A recent court case in Syracuse, N.Y., for instance, charged a school board with allocating $90,000 for male sports and $200 for female sports. Thus, the issue of money becomes paramount if teams are kept "sexegrated." Can schools *afford* to give each sex an opportunity to participate in competitive and interschool activities? Can they afford *not* to? At a recent conference with *Sports Illustrated* editors, sociologist David Riesman *(The Lonely Crowd)* was asked about the role of athletics in career development. He surprised his audience by saying that men and especially women who want to get ahead in the business world should participate in athletics: "The road to the board room leads through the locker room."

Another familiar dispute is also represented in this chapter. Today's coach has had to adjust to players who no longer accept his authority as absolute. He has had to learn to talk to his players, to understand them. Or has he? Max Rafferty discusses the way he wants it to be. Dave Meggyesy has his own ideas.

As you consider the selections in this chapter, we urge you to keep an open mind; try not to take a stand on an issue until you have heard all sides. Occasionally, we commit ourselves to positions without examining our motives, or without hearing the other man or woman.

186

INTRODUCTION

Tom Meschery played bruising basketball in the NBA for a number of teams: Philadelphia, San Francisco, Seattle. He was rough. There were regular scraps between Meschery and other players around the league. Yet, Tom has gentler feelings and things to say off the court about the men he knew in the basketball wars. This poem says something about his view of black and white in the men who play the game.

As It Should Be

Tom Meschery

A black hand supports
the white body of a fallen teammate.

The ball that scored the winning goal
was placed in motion by a gray hand.

The sweat pouring from our bodies   5
is neither black nor white.

FOR DISCUSSION

1. What are the ways in which Meschery emphasizes the closeness among athletes? What does he mean by "a gray hand"?
2. Do you agree with the poem's central idea? Do you think that Meschery is a realist or an idealist or what? Justify your answer.

INTRODUCTION

One of the hardest-hitting series of articles to appear in a sports publication in this century was "The Black Athlete: A Shameful Story," written for *Sports Illustrated* by Jack Olsen. The article that follows is a selection from that series, which cut through the cliché that sports is a panacea to end the ills between blacks and whites. In some instances sports seem to be just another arena for acting out racial conflicts that extend far beyond the outcome of, say, a football game. Olsen's case is a strong one, richly documented with interviews and anecdotes that make the reader abandon spectator status and get involved.

"I Didn't Know What a Birthday Cake Was": A Look at Life on the Black Side

Jack Olsen

That whites and Negroes live in two separate worlds is a bland axiom for whites and a grim fact of life for Negroes. The troubles of the Negro athlete in a white world stem largely from the failure of whites to examine the axiom; their unconscious assumption is often that the black athlete on entering the white world leaves his own. But the facts of life never yield so easily, and the divisions between the worlds remain. They are deeper than most whites can imagine, for they involve wholly different attitudes toward even such basic matters as food, money and responsibility.

To white athletes food is something that is ladled out three or more times a day, consumed and largely forgotten. To Negroes, food is a fascination, a preoccupation, an obsession. "Our colored athletes will spend their last dime on food," says Bobby Dobbs, white football coach of the University of Texas at El Paso. "They are a people that can go and eat in a chow hall, but if they've got any money later that night, they will be over at the Wiener schnitzel or the fried chicken place. I don't think the white race puts that premium on food. It's more important to a Negro. Some people say that's because Negro children go hungry a lot. But I just think it's inherent with their race. That's what they live for, is to eat, I think."

One is always meeting members of the sporting establishment who feel that certain characteristics of the average Negro are "inherent with their race." Tags and nickel slogans are popular in the world of sports, and the Negro athlete spends his life in a tight mesh woven of the white man's prejudices, clichés and sweeping simplifications. Only rarely does anyone in sports stop to puzzle the problems out, to approach Negro problems as social problems, and then more often than not he will be a Negro himself, like Melvin Rogers.

"They say we like to eat," says Coach Rogers, "and I say I agree; brother, we love to eat. And you take any white American who was brought up poor in the depression years and you'll find somebody else who loves to eat, and that's how simple the problem is. The depression never ended for the Negro; hunger is something he lives with, and he's gonna shovel that food down any chance he gets. Two years after he becomes financially stable, he's still shoveling that food down, trying to fill that hole in his stomach. Ten years later he's not much different. Inherent in the race? Not any more inherent than poverty."

The boys who go out for Coach Rogers's baseball and basketball teams at Eula D. Britton High School in Rayville, Louisiana, sometimes make him shake his head sadly as he stands in front of them trying to make the first cuts from his squads. "There are about two hundred boys in the high school, and from those two hundred you lose about fifty right away: polio victims, mental or physical defectives, a few with rheumatic hearts, some with asthma. Out of the remaining hundred and fifty, you find maybe fifteen or twenty who are good enough to play ball. The rest of them just can't make it. Diet is one of the main reasons."

One year Coach Rogers put a 6-foot-tall boy into a rigorous

I Didn't Know What a Birthday Cake Was 189

training program to strengthen him for basketball. The program called for long-distance running, starting with the mile and working up to the 5-mile run. The boy ran and ran, but he was never able to get past the 2-mile barrier, and it almost broke him in half physically to run that far. One morning Coach Rogers visited the boy's home in Rayville's Blacktown. "They were having beans for breakfast. The mother was cooking bread, and she explained that the bread she cooked in the morning was for the whole rest of the day. I asked her what else they had besides bread, and she said, 'Oh, mostly just bread. And sometimes a little greens.' Well, it was too late for me to do anything about that boy in high school. But look what happened. He's four years out of high school, twenty-two, twenty-three years old, and he's just now reaching his full growth. He's playing for a neighborhood basketball team, and he's plenty good. And he'd have been all that big and all that good in high school, if he had been eating something besides bread and beans."

One year the teachers at Eula D. Britton made an informal survey and found that the average student was coming to school without breakfast. "So we started a program serving juice in the morning, and next year we're going to try to serve more than that," Coach Rogers says. "But you run into certain problems. Some of these kids have almost never had milk; they can't afford it. Now they get milk automatically with the twenty-cent school lunch, and they won't drink it. They haven't had a chance to develop a taste for it. They wind up passing it along the line to the next kid. So I tell my athletes to get in line behind those kids that don't drink milk. Somebody's got to drink it; might as well be my athletes!"

Indeed, the technique of hustling extra food at lunchtime has become a fine art with Negro high school athletes, most of whom come from the same deprived homes as the other Negro students and yet require more than a normal amount of sustenance. Rogers is not the only coach who instructs his athletes in special techniques for getting extra milk. At Don Chaney's high school in Baton Rouge, the athletes were advised to get in good with certain girls who had not developed a taste for milk and others who refused to eat beans in public because they felt it was socially degrading. "Some days I would have six or seven cartons of milk," the lanky Chaney recalls. "I'd even carry a few back to class with me. And beans! I could get all the beans I could eat."

At Don Shanklin's all-black high school in Amarillo, the athletes learned how to make sweet eyes at the cafeteria assistants in order to win bigger helpings. Willie Cager of the UTEP basketball team used to take a quarter in lunch money to school in the Bronx and try to run it up to fifty cents in the crap game that always went on in the hall. "Usually I made it," he says. His teammate Willie Worsley cultivated the Jewish students at De Witt Clinton High School in the Bronx. "Jewish fellows don't eat too much at school," Worsley explains. "They get so much to eat at home they're just bored by the cafeteria food. So there was always plenty of meat and stuff left over, and I got plenty."

But not every Negro athlete is so lucky, or so clever. Some achieve years of athletic success on diets that would not sustain Tiny Tim. Bill Myles can show you dozens of them. Myles is a Negro who played center for Drake University's football team and returned to the black world as football coach at all-Negro Lincoln High School in Kansas City, Missouri. "Sometimes I go to coaching clinics and hear some white coach tell me all the problems he has with the white fathers—they complain that their sons are being discriminated against or that some other man's son is getting bigger write-ups in the paper. How can I talk to those coaches about common problems? My problem isn't how to deal with an irritated father, but to go out and buy a box of Cream of Wheat and half a dozen eggs, so that one of my players and his family can eat for another day. As for newspaper write-ups, most of my kids and their parents never even read a newspaper."

Myles laughed. "Last winter, the basketball coach at Southwest High School told me about one of his boys coming up to him and saying, 'Coach, you're lucky to have me at practice today. I almost went to Paris with my father for the weekend.' Imagine a father doing that for a son! When I want to reward my kids I tell them that if they win I'll take them to McDonald's for hamburgers. Or I may tell a boy, 'You score a touchdown and I'll buy you a barbecue dinner.' But *Paris*! What do you think of that?"

During 1967 Myles began to realize that he had a potential

I Didn't Know What a Birthday Cake Was   191

professional athlete on his hands, a boy who could run the 60-yard dash in 6.2 seconds and the 100 in 9.7, and who rushed for 960 yards and 13 touchdowns in his senior year; the boy had half a dozen colleges panting after him. One day Myles went to his address and found that he was living in a friend's car and scrounging for food on the streets. Myles got the boy a job at the school so he could afford an occasional warm meal. As soon as the boy began eating, he began doing better work in the class-room. "He'd been spending too much of his time figuring out how to eat," Myles says. The boy's name is Robert Buford.

The night before he was interviewed, Robert Buford got caught in the rain, and while he was running home he tripped and fell in the gutter. In the house he began to ache all over, so he changed clothes and went back out in the rain to go from door to door looking for aspirin. After a fitful night's sleep he cadged a glass of orange juice and went to his classes at Lincoln High. He had no money for lunch. In the afternoon, Coach Bill Myles tucked Buford into a cot and under two blankets. He lay shaking and quivering through the interview—a very black boy, slightly built (five feet ten, 163 pounds), with a Floyd Patterson haircut (close on the sides and full at the front), a large nose spread over the middle of his face, completely unmatching miniature ears and quick smile that revealed an uneven line of white teeth. He said it was a long story, how he wound up living in a car:

"When I was young I was shipped to my grandparents' and my aunt's a lot. I never did be around my father and mother very much. Everything was pretty nice when I was small till my mother and father separated, and then they started taking me here and there. At that time it was only me and my brother and my sister. My brother's in Omaha now and my sister's in Chicago and I'm here in Kansas City. From six years old on I have been shipped around. I stayed with my mother for about three years and then I came back to my father and stayed with him till I got thirteen years old, then he went to Denver, so I stayed with my other auntie. Then I went to Denver with my father. Then I came back. Then I went to Great Falls, Montana, to stay with my moth-er for a while. She wanted me to stay for good but I didn't want to. She was having another . . . another baby. I told her I wanted to come back to Kansas City, so she brought me back.

"Then I lived with my grandfather and grandmother. I stayed with them until my grandmother died. Then all of a sudden my grandfather started putting me out of the house and all like that. Then I went back to my auntie and then after that, I went to my cousins, after me and my auntie had a misunderstood. Then I came back. Then my auntie just split and I began to stay by myself. I spent the nights with my friends for a while, and then I started staying in cars. I didn't want to go to Omaha and live with my father because Omaha is not fun, like it is down here in Kansas City. It's real bad in Omaha because my brother is always getting into so much trouble. And if I go up there I would be in the same thing. Down here my friends will talk you out of it—and tell you to keep going on.

"I stayed in different cars every night till the beginning of last football season, when it started to get cold. I only had the clothes I was wearing. The only time I could take a shower was when my body started to odor and when I went into a friend's house they would smell me (that would be embarrassing), and they would tell their son to have me take a bath at their house. Sometimes I felt ashamed 'cause I hate to come to anybody's house like that. And then I would go right back out in them cars again. Now that I have twenty-three dollars a week coming in from a job at school, I live in a one-room apartment with a stove and a icebox, a bed, a chest and a table.

"For Christmas, my uncle got a Ban-Lon shirt for a gift and he passed it on to me. My grandfather gave me five dollars, and he said he was going to give me something else for Christmas, but I haven't got it yet. My father didn't give me nothing for Christmas. When I realized my father wasn't giving me nothing, it made me feel kind of bad. So I went on and tried to forget about it and do the best that I can, just as though he had gave me something.

"The people in my family were surprised that I kept on going to school after they put me out of the house. They thought I was going to do like my brother and quit school and hang out in the streets like they said I'd been wanting to do for a long time. Ever since I was small, when I first went out for sports, my people has always been throwing things and hitting me and beating me, saying that I'm lying that I stayed out late because of practice, that I was just hanging out in the street. When I tried to tell them, they never listened. So when I got good in sports, then they kind of brag on me, and that is what I hate. Now that I am doing something, they say, 'This is our boy, he did this and he did that.' They always say that. So the only people I ever ask to help me is the coaches.

"Every year we have a dad's banquet for the football players, and there never is many dads that show up. But last year my father came up from Omaha and I felt real proud because the year before I didn't have nobody to come up. The last time that I saw my mother was five years ago. Sometimes I have hatred for her and the man she's living with. He beats her all the time, and then I feel sorry for her. So far I know she's got seven kids.

"When I start having kids, I ain't gonna do them like I see most parents. I'm gonna help them out when they're small, and when they get a little older I'm gonna still help them. Like I need my father's help and he's never around. I'm gonna be around. My father had a habit of always beating on me till I started fighting back. I might whip my own kids, but I won't go half-crazy when I do it. I always gonna keep my kids close and feed them and always think about them.

"I been in trouble, yes, but not a whole lot. I have only been in jail once. When I was young I was arrested two or three times for riding stolen bicycles. And then I was caught in an old house getting copper and stuff to make money. The big time was when my brother went to Kansas and stole a car. I was driving it and got caught. They put me in jail for a day even when I told them I didn't know the car was stolen. Back before I wanted to be a professional football player, I always wanted to be a hustler. Every time you would look up, the hustler would always have money and was always driving these big cars. Then I met this man who worked in construction and had money and a big car too, so then I said I wanted to be in construction. Everything I saw I wanted to be. That was before I started playing football. Then I wanted to be a professional football player, and I still do.

"When I'm gonna play in a game or run in a track meet, I try to always get lunch. I have to bum money—ask people to give me a nickel or a dime—and most of the time I don't eat. I never eat breakfast, and sometimes I miss the lunch meal and the evening meal too. I used to starve a lot. But I would keep on trying.

Before games I'd always go around and try and get something to eat. I was always sick, but I never showed it. I would try not to run lazy so they wouldn't know nothing was wrong.

"This year the coach got me a job, helping out around the school, and then when I set a new meet record at an indoor track meet the school nurse baked me a birthday cake with my name on top of it. I didn't know what a birthday cake was, and it wasn't my birthday anyway, so she told me to pretend it was. We cut my cake at school and it lasted about five minutes, but it was good. School's not really such a bad place. I wake up at six o'clock and get to work at seven. I clean out the gym and then I talk to the fellows. My first class is metals and it starts at eight-fifteen. We're working on the vise now. We made our screwdrivers and our tool trays. After that I go to English class and I don't like it. I got three right out of one hundred on my English test. Most of the time I don't read. I don't write much either. After English I go to woodwork and after that I go to lunch. Then after lunch I have choir and then woodwork again and then gym. I don't go to gym that much. They do a lot of baby stuff, and most of the time I skip sixth and seventh periods and go play pool. The biggest thing I learned in high school was how to run with a football. I learned a little in class too; I used to get a thrill cutting open frogs."

Talking to Buford (he does not like to be called Robert or Bob, just Buford), one begins to get a chilled feeling. All through his recital of misery and despair, he sounds neither miserable nor desperate. And suddenly one realizes that Buford is merely describing life as it is. He knows no other. Moving from a grandmother's place to a cousin's place to parked cars to a friend's house to a one-room apartment is *normal*; never eating breakfast is *normal*; barely knowing how to read is *normal*. There is not a hint of self-pity about Buford, nor does he compare himself to other, luckier boys. He knows no luckier boys. In Buford's lexicon, a bad boy is one who goes to the penitentiary for a long term. A hungry boy is one who has not touched food in two or three days. These are everyday definitions in the Negro ghetto of Kansas City.

Buford will not graduate from Lincoln High School—he will receive a certificate of completion that says merely that he was a good citizen and endured his allotted time in the halls of learning. He is a special student and goes to special classes. According to Coach Myles, Buford's mentality is average: "He just can't read." But he has heard about college, and he is desperate to go, not only for social reasons but as a stepping stone to pro football. "The only people who put the college idea into his head were the college coaches," says a Lincoln teacher, with the air of a man who sniffs disaster. But Buford is exhilarated by the idea; he thinks he will go to junior college to catch up and then accept the best scholarship offer.

Ten years ago, Robert Buford would have breezed right out of the Kansas City ghetto and into any one of dozens of colleges that wooed him. Nowadays standards have been tightened, and it will not be so easy for him to attend college. But attend he will. Robert Buford represents too great a temptation to certain American schools that are selling themselves to the public on the basis of their athletic reputations. Some institution somewhere will yield to the temptation he offers, and Robert Buford, with his woodworking credits and his slow reading speed and his near inability to write, is more than likely to wind up on a tree-lined campus, posing as Joe College.

Buford represents an extreme, but by no means can he be considered atypical. Every year hundreds of Robert Bufords find themselves on the campus, drowning in a sea of problems: money, where to get it, how to handle it; schedules, how to meet them; temptations, how to avoid them; classes and homework and meetings and chalk talks, and practice, practice, practice. Do most of them learn how to solve the problems? No. The gulf is too wide. Most Negro athletes remain on the black side forever.

Coaches go through agonies trying to shepherd their black athletes across this gulf, and seldom succeed, and for their troubles they usually have only themselves to blame. Coaches are paid to win, not to solve social problems, and if a Negro with straight D's in electric shop can run the 100 in 9.4, there is always a coach willing to recruit him. And when the trouble starts, it is the fault of the Negro, "inherent in the race," never the school. Listen to a typical coach:

"I recruited him myself, drove two thousand miles to get him. Fixed it up so he could go to a high school in town to bring his grades up. So he comes here and all of a sudden he's married, and he hasn't got a penny to his name. So I lend him money. I move the boy and his wife into my own apartment. My wife and I are feeding them, cooking their meals; they're living with us. Finally we go out and get them an apartment, and I pay their deposit. The athletic director calls me in and he says, 'Cut that out! You're gonna get fired if you keep it up!' But I pay the kid's first month's rent and buy him a month's supply of groceries. The next thing I know, his wife's pregnant, and we get him fixed up with the doctor, no bills, no nothing. And after all this, we find out two things: the kid isn't gonna pass his courses, and the way things are going in his private life, he isn't going to help us on the playing field, either. Now is that ungrateful or not?"

One morning this particular athlete woke up to find himself in a strange town, married, nineteen, a father, living in a tiny apartment, and stripped of his athletic scholarship. At college he had been an independent operator for the first time in his life, and he had failed. How could it have been otherwise? His previous life in the ghetto had taught him only that money was something you won in a crap game or slipped from a woman's purse, and responsibility was something that happened on the other side of town. Who was to blame for his situation? The coach will swear he was blameless, and pull out the IOU's to prove his point.

In every college that recruits Negroes, financial problems are commonplace. To the average Negro, perched way across there on the other side of the gulf, money is another country. He knows as much about handling cash as the average white student knows about handling Norwegian rats; they are equally rare in their cultures. "Here's a kid that came to this university without a dime," says a track coach about a black world-class athlete. "Now he has a 1966 car. His apartment is out of this world. He spends thirty or forty dollars every chance he gets. He's got the very best of clothes. He's got two television sets. One for the bedroom and one for the living room. Big ones. Consoles! He bought a five-hundred-and-fifty-dollar RCA stereo, the best money can buy. I slip the kid money whenever I can. I made him money on the indoor circuit. I'm not supposed to, but I did. He wants everything, but he hates to pay the price. So he's up to his ears in debt." The athlete is handling money for the first time. He is like a looter standing in front of a broken pawnshop window. His needs are greater than his sense of responsibility. For the poor, it comes with the territory.

"Negroes are prone not to accept their responsibility and this is because of their heritage," says a Southwestern university athletic director. "It'll come with education. Say they've got a telephone, they make long-distance calls. They're indiscriminate about it, they don't realize you've got to pay, and they're prone to get over their heads, and then they think, 'Well, I don't really have to pay this today or tomorrow. . . .' I fault the business people. These kids'll go into a store and get credit. They buy things and they don't seem to realize they have to pay, and this aggravates us."

Negro athletes are constantly aggravating their coaches, and few coaches take the time to dig down very far and find out why. It is simpler to announce that a lack of responsibility is "inherent in the race," like a love of fried chicken or a predilection for candied yams and sowbelly. A Midwestern coach whips out a list of athletes who are behind on their laundry bills. There are seven names, all of them Negroes. "Do you get the message?" he says.

Another Midwestern coach discusses the subject: "I would say in all honesty that 99 percent of the disciplinary problems on this team are caused by Negroes. Things like being late to class or study hall, delinquencies in small debts, failing to do the required work, things like that. And the last guy to turn out for practice, just at the last second, is usually a Negro. It's almost as if they're testing you to see how far they can go. Most of them simply have not been educated in responsibility. They aren't so much in rebellion against authority as they are just plain irresponsible."

Another coach bristles with anger when he discusses the Negroes on his team; one wonders why he recruits Negroes at all, but then one remembers that this coach is a winner, a *nationally known* winner, and it is the Negroes who have been winning for him. He seems to approach them as a necessary evil. "They drive me crazy, off the record," he says. "I wake up at night screaming. Little things. The Chinese water torture. Not long ago one of our Nigra athletes looked like he was gonna flunk right out of school. He wasn't passing anything. And we sorely needed this boy on the team; I mean he was *crucial.* So we sat down and discussed the problem and came up with a solution. We would get him tutors, and the athletic department would foot the bill. I mean private tutors; every college kid's dream. Never showed up! Night after night the tutor'd be there and the boy wouldn't show. And then the Nigras go around telling how they never get an opportunity!"

"Well, about this problem of irresponsibility," says Don Chaney, "up until very lately the Negro knew he was gonna be chopping cotton or running around hauling the white man's trash, or something like that, and he knew he wasn't gonna go to college and he knew he wasn't gonna get a good job and he knew he wasn't gonna get out of the slum he was raised in. *Well, he doesn't have much to look forward to, does he?* So they call him lazy and irresponsible. But there's one little thing a human being has to have, and that little thing is hope: H-O-P-E. If you take all hope away from him, he's gonna say, 'Well, why should I jump up and hustle and almost kill myself when I'm not gonna get anyplace anyway?' Then you hear white people saying that the Negro isn't punctual. Well, if you're gonna spend your life chopping cotton, it doesn't make much difference if you're punctual or not, does it? That cotton's still gonna be there waiting for you, isn't it? That sun still be shining whether you're five minutes late or ten minutes early, am I right?"

Harry Edwards, the militant Negro professor from San Jose State College, says, "You talk about accepting responsibility. Well, I say to you, you take a newborn black child and you put him in a big black box with a closed black top and you open up that top when he's twenty-one, and you say, 'Now, boy, you go do my work!' Is that a fair thing to expect him to measure up to a white child who you never put in a closed box?"

FOR DISCUSSION

1. In Olsen's article many people say uncomplimentary things about black athletes. Yet the overall tone of the piece is

compassionate and sympathetic. How is this achieved? Cite specific techniques.

2. How effective is the use of personal experience here? Is the story of Buford, for instance, an isolated case? Or is it a typical experience used for effect?

3. The phrase "inherent in the race" appears several times in Olsen's article. Why does the author do this? What is the eventual effect of such repetition on your own attitudes about heredity and environment?

4. Write an essay describing the first time you encountered discrimination in any form. How did you react?

5. If the black athlete has suffered abuses, as Olsen indicates, who is to blame for the problem?

INTRODUCTION

If female recognition in sports has increased in recent years, the movement's superstar—on and off the court—is Billie Jean King. She has everything that Gloria Steinem represents, plus a powerful backhand. The article on Billie Jean that follows is of interest because it humanizes a giant in sports. It is a study of a woman who demolished the brash Bobby Riggs on the tennis court and made it look easy. Bud Collins chronicles the radicalization of Billie Jean, and along the way we get a glimpse of the politics embedded in a sport that has been lobbying against women for a long, long time.

Billie Jean King Evens the Score

Bud Collins

"When did you start beating your husband?"

This is a reverse of an old, tired question, but if you asked it of Billie Jean Moffitt King, she would have to respond: "From the beginning. Always have, and always will."

In fact, she could beat very nearly all the men in the world with her tautly strung racket, and with strokes that—along with extraordinary competitiveness, speed, and reflexes—have powered her to prominence during the five years that women's tennis has been a professional game. Twice in those years, she won Wimbledon (which is tantamount to the world title) and the U.S. Open at Forest Hills. For two years in a row, she earned over $100,000 in prize money, the only woman ever to top $100,000. Altogether her prize money has totaled more than $350,000, a record exceeded by perhaps a half-dozen men in those same five years.

But an enumeration of numbers and deeds, of bank deposits and championships cannot convey the excitement of Billie Jean in action any more than a financial accounting and an itinerary of bravura performances could capture the essence of Isadora Duncan on stage. Kindred spirits, these two artists, now that I think about it: Isadora and Billie Jean charging through life, knockouts of athleticism and grace, demanding of self both physically and emotionally, making all the moves, and having to make them their way.

They were much more than a great tennis player and a great dancer. Their impact was and is much broader, deeper. Billie Jean King has done even more for women in tennis, for instance, than another courageous Billie back in 1929—South African Billie Tapscott who liberated the female leg, scandalizing Wimbledon by daring to appear without stockings.

And that's not the half of it. As the La Pasionaria of the women's revolution in tennis, Billie Jean may not have had to fight the battle of bare legs, but she has had to knock the stuffed shirts off numerous men who control this lucrative sport-and-business. They're still trying to resist, but she's still knocking away at their paternalistic maneuvers, thereby earning an adjective that used to be applied to Isadora Duncan by the Establishment of her day: notorious.

Notorious? Really? Not that nice little fat girl from West 36th Street in Long Beach, California; the tomboy whose mother used to drag her from football games, leaving the boys secretly thankful for being spared any more tackles by Billie Jean.

Yes—not only notorious, but radical. Billie Jean winces at the word. She knows her mother, Betty Moffitt, is not pleased by references to her radical daughter. Betty wants her to start producing some grandchildren. (Well, so have most of her opponents, at one time or another, and a lot of her male colleagues. As Rod Laver said four years ago: "Billie Jean ought to quit and have babies. Tennis is all right for a woman for a while, but after twenty-five, it's not feminine. That's the time to be raising a family.")

So what made this little girl from Long Beach grow up to break all the rules? What radicalized her into a spokeswoman of sport?

"The radicalization of Billie Jean King?" Billie Jean smiles and stirs her coffee. We are sitting in a motel restaurant in Mas-

202

sachusetts, waiting for a tournament practice session to begin. "That's a pretty overworked phrase, isn't it?" she goes on. "I'm not radical—I'm just aware. I've come a long way, baby, that's all," she laughs, pleased with the advertising phrase. "That's one place where I disagree with some feminists. They think 'you've come a long way, baby' is a demeaning and offensive line; that it's not accurate about women's real position. But I think you've got to be a little pragmatic. Without Virginia Slims and the money and encouragement they've poured into the women's tennis game, we'd be nowhere. We'd be at the mercy of male officials as we always have been.

"I don't smoke, and I don't approve of smoking, so it was a real moral conflict for me when Slims came into the picture to back our tour. I wasn't sure I should lend myself and my name to it. I joined in kind of reluctantly on a wait-and-see basis, and I came to realize that Slims was doing us and the sport so much good that I'd have to live with my misgivings. You give a little to accomplish something big.

"And this is what bothers a lot of people about me," Billie Jean continues thoughtfully, "not that we've come a long way, but that I want us to make pragmatic, hard decisions because we've got a long way to go. I keep telling the girls in tennis —there I go, but I can't help saying 'girls'—I keep telling them that we can't be satisfied yet. Sure, I made $119,000 last year and about a dozen of the top girls were up there in high five-figures, but we're still getting hassled by male officials, and we still have to fight twice as hard as the men do to get fair treatment. We haven't made it yet.

"I guess this why-isn't-Billie-Jean-satisfied-after-all-she's-made feeling is shared by a lot of people. They're the ones who call me radical and notorious and a tough broad. That's the image I have; that's what the press has done for me. It's what they do for anybody outspoken.

"But I'm not down on the press. Where would I be without them? Press treatment of me—good and bad—has helped the game, and that's what I'm trying to do. But don't forget the press—the sporting press—is male, and they are not going to take kindly to a lot of things I say.

"There is a terrific double standard with sports reporters.

They ask me when I'm going to retire and raise a family. Do they ask a baseball player that? They ask me about my abortion. Do they ask a football player if he's had a vasectomy? They want to know about my marriage, because Larry and I are apart so much [husband Larry King is a lawyer with an office in Berkeley]. That's none of their business, although I'll answer any question, even if I resent it. But do they ask male athletes all about their domestic lives?"

Billie Jean pauses to sign an autograph for a waitress, and orders another cup of coffee. "I get along fine with the press," she concludes, in spite of everything.

Better than fine I would add; as a man in the sporting press, I know. Reporters come away from their first encounter muttering, "What a broad. What quotes. Can she play as well as she talks?" The answer is yes; sometimes even better.

I say as much, and ask Billie Jean what her experiences with reporters have been. "They write their stories," she explains, "and sometimes they're writing about somebody I don't recognize. It happens," she shrugs, "when you're in the public eye. You don't sue. You're glad they spelled your name right, and hope they use a picture and a big headline. Girls in tennis are still struggling for space, for attention. Once at a press conference, a guy asked, 'Doesn't it upset you, as a feminist, to look around today and see not one female reporter?' Nope. It's always been that way—I'd never really thought about it. Oh, occasionally there's a woman or two. But you know, the time I really choked was when I went to some kind of Women's Movement affair, a breakfast, I think, and there wasn't a single man in the audience. I didn't know what to say. I'd never spoken to an all-female audience before. I told them I wasn't used to it; I was speechless."

"But not for long," I say.

"No, not for long—but it *was* different. So I don't think I'm particularly radical or notorious or tough."

Nor do many people who meet her and take the time to converse. "Gee, she's quite a nice person—not at all as I'd imagined." How many times have I heard that reaction to Billie Jean? We of the press often unintentionally distort crusaders for effect, causing readers either to love them or hate them. Then

204

they show up in person, whereupon we learn that they're all right, or bloody tedious, or both. Yes, Billie Jean can be tedious when she gets too preachy, but that's the risk a crusader takes.

Whatever we may do to her, Billie Jean is regarded as a godsend to reporters. When you're desperate for a quote or a story, she'll give you five. Still, I do confess to practicing some of the discrimination she charges: the sin of last-paragraphing in the coverage of tennis tournaments, for instance. Check the current and forthcoming newspaper accounts of Wimbledon and Forest Hills, and you'll see what I mean. The stories will begin with details of the leading men's matches of the day, and then, somewhere at the bottom, a few lines will be allotted to the women. Occasionally they get the lead; usually on days when the men don't provide any news. But typically they're treated as also-played—or even left out entirely if space is tight.

It's always been that way. The press plays up the men, assuming that women players are of minor interest. Tennis officials have done the same thing, even though tennis was first introduced in this country in 1874 by a woman named Mary Outerbridge. But the game was run for the men—still is, basically—and the administrators soon considered themselves damned gallant for permitting the women to tag along at all.

When I say that tennis is a male operation, I urge you, for confirmation, to check the lengthy rosters of command positions in the USLTA (United States Lawn Tennis Association), the governing body of the sport in America, or the ILTF (International Lawn Tennis Federation), the world governing body of which the USLTA is a member. You won't find a single female in a significant position—or in any position at all in the ILTF. Yet these bands of officials—largely old, out of touch, and only slightly more progressive than the International Olympic Committee and Ronald Reagan—try to supervise female tennis. And their organizations benefit from the "sanction fees" or obligatory fees paid to the USLTA and ILTF by tournament sponsors. (These fees are supposed to simply assure that major tournaments aren't scheduled at the same time, but actually, they are also a source of profit and control.)

Recently, in a frightened response to the clamor for female autonomy, USLTA President Walter Elcock appointed three women to his executive committee, but they still will have to sit in deliberation among thirty men. Despite this radical gesture (radical for the USLTA, that is), Elcock has stated that he won't rest "until we get *that woman* out of the game"—meaning Gladys Heldman of Houston, publisher of *World Tennis* magazine. It was she who lured Virginia Slims into tennis and founded the female pro tour in 1970. She's bright, resourceful, well connected, persuasive, hard-nosed, and opposed to the male tennis establishment. You can understand Elcock's aversion, because Heldman has clout.

If tennis politics is beginning to sound Byzantine, then the truth of this big business is beginning to come through. Perhaps this is the time to do a brief summing up of tennis politics, female division. Brief because even for the insiders, the subject is confusing. Still, Billie Jean is at the heart of the conflict, so I shall try to explain.

Until 1970 when the Slims tour came into being, practically all tennis tournaments had male and female events, with the women playing second racket in regard to attention, remuneration, and playing conditions. United but unequal: that was the system. At the end of 1970, however, Billie Jean, Rosie Casals, Nancy Gunter, Ann Jones, Francoise Durr, and a few other disenchanted notables complained about the disparity in prize money. The ratio favored the men as much as ten to one.

Publisher Gladys Heldman sympathized, and talked Virginia Slims out of some sponsorship money for three women's tournaments. That's when the war with the USLTA began; a conflict hot to this day, though there have been several uneasy truces.

The trouble was simple: the Slims tournaments conflicted with the traditional USLTA events that the leading players were expected to grace with their poorly paid presence. Playing elsewhere for decent (higher) prize money than offered by the USLTA events was regarded as a boycott by ungrateful women whom the USLTA had been chivalrous enough to build up in the first place.

Furthermore, the appearance of a full-blown Slims circuit in 1971 was regarded as a direct economic threat. For the first time, the women would get a fair shake in money and publicity on their own. They and Gladys Heldman were thumbing their sunburned noses at the USLTA because, understandably, Heldman didn't want to pay the exorbitant sanction fees demanded by the USLTA. That was why the Slims tournament had to be separate—and therefore a threat.

So the Slims players became renegades. It's true that, from time to time, the breach was patched, sanction fees were adjusted and paid, and Heldman was even appointed czarina of female pro tennis by the USLTA. But all along, Heldman envisioned the women on their own, mistresses of their own destiny. Last autumn, she shafted the USLTA and ILTF (so they said) by forming the WITF (Women's International Tennis Federation), which amounted to a female union. After all, if anybody needed a union it was these women, but the USLTA was no more gracious than the first Henry Ford regarding the United Auto Workers.

Right there the lines hardened. Both the newborn WITFers on the Slims tour and the USLTA declared, "You're either for us or against us." The USLTA threw together a prize-money tour of its own, stealing several Slims promoters in the process, and invited all non- and anti-WITFers to join. The idea was to discourage women from signing with WITF-Slims by ruling them ineligible for USLTA–ILTF events if they did. Most WITFers didn't care, but there were some players who did: crucially the prize young plums, Chris Evert from Florida and Evonne Goolagong from Australia. Ineligibility from USLTA–ILTF meant confinement to the Slims circuit, and being banned from the historic events at Wimbledon, Paris, Rome, and Forest Hills; the "name" championships.

Had Evert and Goolagong gone with WITF, there would have been no war. Billie Jean & Company would have won. The USLTA–ILTF would have been forced to respect the women's union, just as they do the men's ATP (Association of Tennis Pros).

But when I ask her now about the two holdouts, Billie Jean says, "I can't blame Chris and Evonne. When you're young, you don't understand the struggle—and for them there hasn't been much of a struggle. We've paved the way. The money is all there for them and at that age [Evert is eighteen; Goolagong, twenty-one] you don't want to buck the system. I wouldn't have. It wouldn't have crossed my mind then, either."

Goolagong is influenced by her guardian, Vic Edwards; Evert by her father, Jimmy Evert. Both men are—well, *men* in their outlooks. They are very protective of these young women, and don't care to throw them onto the picket line. "Jimmy Evert isn't money-motivated," says Billie Jean, "and he believes that I'm purely money-motivated. He worries that his nice little girl will become like me. I understand that, and Chris and I get along. One day she'll see that we all have to stick together."

Edwards and Papa Evert are also fearful of Gladys Heldman. They suspect that she is too manipulative and erratic, though brilliant; not the person they would like to see steering the game their charges will one day dominate.

Billie Jean respects this caution, but she and other WITFers remember well that, when they were taking so much crap from male officials, suddenly there was Gladys Heldman, riding to the rescue, smoking a Virginia Slims. At this writing, both sides have just worked out a compromise that will allow the WITF–Slims gang to appear on the Establishment playgrounds, and the USLTA to collect some sanction fees. Under the agreement, Billie Jean will be able to defend her Wimbledon and U.S. Open titles. "I'm glad there's peace," Billie Jean says, "but we've still got to stick together and form a strong players' association that all the girls will join; it must be so good that no girl can afford to stay out. I would have missed Wimbledon terribly if we had been banned. That's where it's all at for me. We just can't give in on the principle of a women's union.

"You mature before you realize that. That's why I can't blame Chris Evert for taking the easy way with the USLTA at eighteen. How old was I in 1964?" Billie Jean thought a while. "Twenty, and playing at Forest Hills. That's when we were amateurs. Of course, we were getting paid 'expense money' but only a few of us got even that token amount; only four women at Forest Hills in 1964. I remember Stephanie DeFina, one of the better players, coming to me all upset because she wasn't getting any expenses. I said, 'Okay, let's get the best players together and insist on expenses for all of us. No expenses, no play, and I'll stick with you even though I personally am getting good expenses. Either we all get something or none of us plays.' I was talking strike, I guess, although I didn't use the word.

"Stephanie was aghast. She said, 'Gosh, suppose we do it, and they won't let any of us play.' Our 'strike' never got beyond that. That's where we were only a few years ago. It was amateur tennis, and the officials wanted to keep it that way. I made pretty good money, but I wanted to be a pro, and I said so."

Ever honest, Billie Jean did rap the system and the officials in those days, thus reaping their enmity early. She urged that professionalism be approved in tennis, as in other sports. Now it has been. But, amateur officials still won't accept the inevitable corollary: that they can't and shouldn't oversee pros. (Billie Jean, who will be thirty in November, turned pro in 1968, a radical move in itself at that time, since open tennis, permitting pros to mingle with amateurs in the biggest championships, was just beginning to be recognized by the ILTF.)

"At first, when I was becoming aware, I blamed the system," says Billie Jean, "but when I began to analyze it, I realized the 'system' is men.

"Do you know when that fact first came to me? I was eleven. The 'radicalization' doesn't go back that far, but some realization does. There I was, a little kid at the Los Angeles Tennis Club where Perry T. Jones was the boss of tennis in Southern California. A lot of champions came out of his program, and he was strict. I played in the Southern Cal sectional, my first, and we were supposed to have our pictures taken. But Mr. Jones pointed to me and said, 'Not you. You're not properly dressed.' I didn't know what he meant. I didn't come from a tennis family, but I learned you had to wear an all-white outfit, and my mother had made me a pair of shorts that I wore with a T-shirt. I was clean and neat and eager, but Mr. Jones didn't approve. He told me that I had to wear a tennis dress to have my picture taken. I had to wear the correct costume.

"That turned me inside out. He didn't hurt my feelings or make me bitter, but I realized it didn't matter how you played, or how hard you tried—you had to dress the way this man wanted. What kind of attitude was that?"

Presently, she got a tennis dress. "But Mr. Jones never gave me a dime to help me travel. All the money went to the promising boys. Fortunately, some people in Long Beach chipped in. Otherwise, I'd never have got to the big tournaments you need to make a name. And you know, we found out at Wimbledon last year that something as stupid as Mr. Jones's policies hasn't changed. Rosie Casals was censured by the tournament committee for wearing a dress with purple designs on it instead of plain white. In 1972 at a professional tournament!

"Men may have their ideas on how we should act, but they're not going to dictate to *me*." Suddenly, Billie Jean sounds like Muhammad Ali proclaiming, "I ain't gonna be what you want me to be."

"Men have this image of you," she continues, "and they don't want you to change, to grow. They like you best when you're young and cute and you don't ask questions. That's where Chris Evert is now. If you're sexy, that's even better. Ability just isn't the key with the press."

True enough. The best press always has gone to "glamour girls of the court": Gussie Moran and her lace panties, Karol Fageros and her gold lamé panties—to name a couple of ordinary players whose physiques drew more coverage than the skills of champions. "I think maybe that I and the other pros on the Slims circuit have helped that," Billie Jean goes on. "We're recognized for our ability and the prize money we've won, which is the way we want it: recognition as athletes, pros, not for our looks. Do the reporters care if a football player is ugly as long as he can block, tackle, and do his job? An athlete has to perform. Measure us that way; not on sex.

"Measure us on money, too. That's the American way, the reason I worked so hard in 1971 to be the first woman to make over $100,000 in sports. Not for the money alone, but for me and the game, as a symbol of what a girl tennis player could do. People took notice. They could see the Slims tour was in business. Sure, it was an ego trip, too. But I wanted to establish women's pro tennis, and making one hundred grand is the way to America's consciousness. Even more so than having great looks and a great figure.

"Men read about me and they say, 'Hey, those broads must be able to play to make that kind of money. Let's go watch them.' They're suddenly less likely to say, 'Let's go out and look at legs.'

Although, that's okay, too, if it's not the main point—and we have some good legs on the tour."

Actually, Billie Jean is considerably more attractive than she was ten years ago when I first met her. Trimmer, warmer, deeper, and more sure of herself, she is therefore sexier, if you'll pardon my porcine instincts. Is this a tribute to tennis, feminine politics, money, or love?

Billie Jean says "thank you" for the compliment, but doesn't know the answer. "I do know this—in spite of all the grievances I have about men in the tennis Establishment, I'd be nowhere without Larry.

"Larry is the only one who urged me to be myself, to do what I had to do, to make the most of my talent and follow my goals. He's been behind me all the way. He's lucky, and he doesn't seem to have any of the male hang-ups; he laughs along with people who call him Mr. Billie Jean King."

Larry King, a year younger than Billie Jean, met her when they were students at California State at Los Angeles in 1962. They married three years later, and he now manages her affairs, including their education-oriented TennisAmerica—a camp, clinic, and tournament promotion business. Whenever she weakens, he gives her encouragement and help.

"Larry's more Women's Lib than I am. He's secure, and his attitude has given me strength," she explains. "When we were married, he told me anything I did was okay with him. I offered to give up everything for him and settle down. I thought that's the way it was supposed to be, but he told me, 'Don't waste your talent.'

"The other day, I found an essay I wrote when I was fifteen. The theme was 'Where will you be twelve years from now?' I wrote that I'd be married with four kids.

"Now, I don't know if I'll have any children. I'll admit that I'm not sure of myself about that. These are the childbearing years, and you wonder if you'll want them when it's too late. My mother keeps asking when I'm going to have a 'normal' life. But this is my life. This is normal for me. Nobody asks my brother, Randy [Moffitt], who pitches for the San Francisco Giants, when he's going to settle down to a 'normal' life.

"Larry and I got married too young. I was twenty-one, but

we'd been going together for more than two years, and you know, people expected you to *do* something about it. We should have lived together but we were hung up on Puritanism.

"Now Larry kids me, 'Let's get divorced and live together.' But we love each other even though we're apart so much. People want permanence, romance, but things change. We don't have to be together all the time to be sure of each other. We spend a fortune on phone calls, but we're free. That's important. I have a healthier concept of love now.

"And I guess I'm more than just a tennis player—all the Slims girls are. We're showing the gains women can make in a male-dominated area. That's the good thing about sports, and where women are like blacks. Blacks and women have to plug harder just to get equal treatment, and sports is a place where everybody can see those gains."

Billie Jean gets up to leave at last. It's time to go to practice, and she is rarely late. She has this huge, heavy black suitcase filled with her gear that she lugs around the world, and I try to lift it for her. "Ugh, Billie Jean," I say, giving up.

"That's okay," she says as she hoists it and begins walking to the car. "Men are funny. I don't mean you and the suitcase." (She didn't expect chivalry from a newspaperman, after all.) "No, I was thinking about the money. When we were amateurs, and made our private under-the-table deals with tournament pro- moters, I haggled pretty good and got almost as much as the top guys. They didn't mind because nobody knew. But now that it's all out in the open as prize money, the men players hate like hell that we make so much, and that we're still agitating for equal pay in tournaments we play together, like Forest Hills or Wimble- don, where nobody can prove who draws more at the gate—men or women. Arthur Ashe says men should make more because they support families. How do you like that?

"But I love to be around the men, love to watch them play. I didn't like the idea of going our own way. Larry told me we'd never get anything until we did. He knew the men would never let a promoter split the prize money down the middle, or give us nearly as much as the men. He could see that back in 1968 when open tennis arrived. 'You girls will have to prove yourselves alone,' Larry predicted. 'If you're an attraction, the public will buy it. If you aren't, you might as well forget a pro career. The men want all the money in the tournaments they play.' Larry was so right."

Walking toward the car, Billie Jean resumes the chronology of her radicalization, taking it up in 1970.

Like any female visitor to Rome, Billie Jean has been pinched, but she didn't scream until May of that year when she arrived at Il Foro Italico for the Italian Open. First prize for the women's singles was $600 compared to $7,500 for the men. "That's when I began thinking *boycott*. So did Rosie Casals, Esme Emanuel, Ceci Martinez, and some others.

"There was no alternative. By the time we got to Forest Hills four months later, we were boiling. Everywhere the ratio was insulting; worst of all in the U.S. at the Pacific Southwest Open in Los Angeles where it was ten to one. We decided we wouldn't play the Southwest. Gladys Heldman provided the alternative through Virginia Slims, with a tournament in Houston where the money was about five times as good. That was the start."

Total prize money for women's tennis throughout the world wasn't much heavier than $50,000 in 1970, only a fraction of the money won by men. The Slims circuit in America alone was worth over $300,000 in 1971 (with other sponsors joining Virginia Slims for separate events, such firms as K-Mart, British Motors, and Four Roses. The catch-line in Charlotte, North Carolina, for the Four Roses Classic was "cigarettes and whiskey and wild, wild women"). In 1972 the Slims dough was $525,775, and this year it's over a million. The 1972 men's prizes totaled about $4 million. Other tourneys, shamed and pressured by the Slims operation, and also aiming to keep rising youngsters from joining Slims, have raised their women's purses remarkably.

"There's still a lot of inequality and discrimination, which is why we can't relax," says restless Billie Jean. "We should get equal money for the few giant tournaments where men and women are together. Last year, at the U.S. Open, Ilie Nastase got $25,000 for winning, compared to my $10,000—and I'll bet I drew more people and more publicity than he did.

"Then there are the little, subtle discriminations that hurt. Like at Forest Hills for the Open, there's no masseuse or trainer for the girls. The men have one. They told me, when I needed treatment that, okay, I could use the men's masseur. So I went up to the men's dressing room with a committeeman leading me because my eyes had to be closed to walk through in case somebody was naked! Oh, wow.

"Another thing: when Rosie Casals and I played the Southwest in 1971, we were in the finals against each other and we had a hassle with the umpire. The officiating was terrible, so we both walked off. We were fined $2,500 by the USLTA and suspended. All right, except for one thing: no man has ever been fined and suspended for walking out, and Pancho Gonzalez did it as recently as February at a tournament in Florida. Double standard?"

At the car, Billie Jean joins Rosie Casals to head for the courts; a practice session for the Massachusetts Virginia Slims Championship at Quincy. She continues: "We've brought tennis to towns that never had pro tournaments before—Oklahoma City; Columbus, Georgia; Boca Raton, Florida; Birmingham, Michigan—and succeeded. Our minimum prize money for a tournament is $25,000, no thanks to any of the officials trying to keep us down. The publicity is terrific, and it's all ours."

No more last-paragraphing. When a Slims tournament comes to town the women get all the paragraphs.

"If we don't get satisfied, things will get even better. That's why I keep traveling like a madwoman, talking, making appearances, promoting. It's all good for me, but it also pulls the girls and the game along with me.

"I think," says Billie Jean, looking to the future, "we're grabbing the kids. Those twelve-, thirteen-, and fourteen-year-olds. When they get ready to turn pro, they won't worry if it's a 'normal' life. No men are going to assign them their roles; they won't go through that phony amateur bit like I did, and I don't think they'll line up with the wrong people like Chris Evert has done—though I don't think she'll turn her back on us for too long, either. These kids are *really* going to be liberated."

And with that, she went off to work.

Billie Jean's vision is enough to make all those ILTF-type males either repent or lobby the Surgeon General to put a "dangerous to health" label on the Virginia Slims tournaments as well as on cigarettes.

But even those old-fashioned men have covered some distance in merely three years, since Billie Jean sneered at the Italian who handed her $600 worth of lira for a big win at Rome. The Family Circle Cup at Sea Pines, South Carolina, paid a $30,000 first prize in May, and gave the WITFers their first significant TV exposure. By the last income tax deadline, Margaret Court had crossed the $70,000 mark, intent on becoming even more popular and prosperous than Billie Jean. In fact, Court, the clear leader of the current Slims tour because injuries have slowed King, was ahead of male players like Rod Laver, Stan Smith, Ilie Nastase, Ken Rosewall, and Arthur Ashe in prize money—for the moment at least.

"You got to be kidding," said Erik van Dillen when I told him Margaret Court's total. He is a young pro who had earned $10,400 to Court's $70,000 in the same period of time, an amount that wouldn't have put him in the female top ten. "Margaret Court has made more money than anybody? Even us guys?"

There was disbelief in his voice. It was a whole new game.

FOR DISCUSSION

1. Currently, in Washington, the high court of the state is deciding whether three teen-age girls should be allowed to play interscholastic football. In view of what you have just read, would you vote yes or no? Discuss.
2. Althea Gibson was a tennis player; so is Billie Jean King. What common characteristics do you see between these two women?
3. How would you respond to the topic, "Where will I be twelve years from now?" How do you think the goals of women have changed since Billie Jean wrote on the same topic?
4. Billie Jean is considered a maverick of sorts in the world of tennis. Is she noncomformist in other ways?

Olga Connolly, captain of the U.S. women's track and field team at the 1972 Olympics, is a champion discus thrower and advocate of women's athletics. Taking a sane look at the furor which surrounded "The Battle of the Sexes," the match which pitted Billie Jean King against the aging court hustler Bobby Riggs, she argues that women cannot compete with top caliber men. But this truth should not hinder women's participation in organized athletics because *some* women can defeat *some* men in *some* sports. Everything, after all, is relative.

Destroying a Myth

Olga Connolly

When Billie Jean King so skillfully defeated Bobby Riggs in tennis, she helped destroy some of the myths about the unsuitability of women in keenly competitive sports.

She demonstrated anew that athletic excellence by women can deserve the recognition traditionally reserved for men.

She showed again that physically, as well as psychologically, women can handle the stress of training and of competition just as men do.

She showed that athletics has not masculinized her. The smooth definition of her muscles only underlined the beauty of a well-conditioned, vibrant human body.

Her concentration was flawless. Tactically and technically, she dominated.

Mrs. King did not prove, however, that women can match men's records or compete successfully against truly well-trained men. After all, Bobby's game falls far short of the men's world-class tennis caliber.

We have to keep in mind that the athletic battle of the sexes was dreamed up as an entertainment, a moneymaking gimmick, in no way concerned with aiding the development of women's sports. While it stole headlines, it has not moved other women's athletic events to the forefront of sports news.

Bobby's victory over Margaret Court evoked inordinate cheers from male chauvinists; Billie Jean's revenge put women's liberationists into equal ecstasy. That is all right for the social fun of it.

But in serious athletic competition, where the human organism is taxed to the utmost, men and women athletes just cannot be mixed. A claim that a woman is physically inferior is a voice of prejudice, but a claim that she is identical with a man is a voice of ignorance. If we are to achieve a physically fit nation, with both men and women deriving the greatest benefits from sports, emotional attitudes must give way to the sensible understanding that a woman differs anatomically, physiologically and biochemically from a man.

The structural differences between the sexes significantly influence the results of their athletic training. Among children, differences are negligible. In adolescence, however, the situation changes dramatically. While training under an identical work load, a young man develops far greater muscular power, and at a far faster rate, than a young woman of the same body weight. While the male hormone plays a key role in the boy's strength development, its precise action and other factors involved are not fully understood. The man's muscle ends up with smaller stores of fatty tissue than a woman's. It also seems that the proportions among certain chemical constituents within his muscle differ from a woman's, and result in different responses to identical training stimuli.

Man's blood contains more red cells and hemoglobin and therefore has greater oxygen-carrying capacity. That, plus the larger size of his heart, gives a man the potential for greater endurance than a woman.

None of the above should be used as an argument for ANY man's physical superiority to ANY woman. I could take on a 300-pound football player and defeat him soundly in discus throwing, because I would be in a fine physical condition and would possess skills in my event that are far superior to his. Similarly, being a fairly good basketball player in fine physical condition, I could defeat a fairly good man basketball player in poor physical condition.

On the other hand, were I to compete against a man of my age and size whose conditioning and skills in a sport were similar to mine, I would lose. Though I am capable of a superb condition within my feminine realm, I would have less strength, speed and endurance.

It is important to know, however, that with dexterity, speed of learning skills, or reaction time to a visual stimulus, there are no sex differences. Pistol shooting, for example, is a "unisex" sport.

Comparisons aside, a woman can acquire very high levels of fitness. There is no logic to any assumption that, by virtue of femininity, a woman has an excuse for lacking the power, speed and endurance needed for outstanding performance in most sports.

Male-female relationship in most sports can be compared to that between a heavyweight and a lightweight boxer. Both are judged for excellence solely within their categories. They need not be matched to prove themselves.

In my opinion, we do not need more battling between the sexes. We need their cooperation in building meaningful, year-round programs for girls interested in athletics. We need civic organizations that will sponsor girls' as well as boys' teams. We need a sports system where outstanding women, instead of being special cases, will be the final products of a broadly based pyramid of girls who will be developed through sequential, demanding, and imaginative physical education programs in schools and communities.

As women are being encouraged to utilize their full potential in jobs and professions, they need to acquire and generate all the energy and the sense of well-being that exercise lends to the men.

Shows such as "The Battle of the Sexes" promote spectatorship. But what we need in this society is participation. Now that Billie Jean has put Bobby Riggs in his place, we ought to give both the male and the female youngsters of our nation an equal opportunity for an unlimited physical expression through sports.

FOR DISCUSSION

1. In serious athletic competition, "men and women athletes just cannot be mixed," says Olga Connolly. Yet at San Diego State University a woman athlete won a place on the men's volleyball team; at Yale a female student shattered 122 years of tradition by joining the all-male diving team; and across the country, girls are taking up sports in increasing numbers because of the success of superstars like Billie Jean. What sort of guidelines do you think should be established for mixed competition in this time of change?

2. Pistol shooting is referred to as a "unisex" sport. What are the requirements of a unisex sport? How many additional unisex sports can you think of?

3. Ms. Connolly says that we need "civic organizations that will sponsor girls' as well as boys' teams." If such organizations cannot be found, do you think that Little League teams, for instance, should open their dugouts to qualified girl players? (New Jersey courts recently ruled that this must occur.)

4. If a girl pursues athletics, does she forgo some of her femininity? How do you define "femininity"?

5. Olga Connolly's article was first published in the *Los Angeles Times* sports section. Imagine that you are a male chauvinist reader, writing a protest letter to the *Times's* editor about Ms. Connolly's philosophy.

INTRODUCTION

Olga Connolly calls for meaningful, year-round programs for girls interested in athletics. Women's own attitudes toward sports are changing. Many feel that by being shortchanged with inadequate sports programs in high school and college, they are handicapped later in life. Certainly athletics is one of the areas in which discrimination against women is most visible. One can measure the amount of gym time that girls get in school. One can count the number of coaches they have. One can total up the monies allocated to women's sports. Brenda Feiger Fasteau paints the picture more explicitly.

Giving Women a Sporting Chance

Brenda Feigen Fasteau

For the first few weeks of the season, two eight-year-old girls longingly watched the practice sessions of a Montgomery, Alabama, boys' football team. Finally, the coach broke down and let them play—but just for one season. I admire the stubbornness and audacity of these two little girls. I am also angry and sad that the same obstacles face them that faced me twenty years ago —when I was their age.

I wonder if they wish, as I once did, that they were boys. When you're that young, it's hard to see the value of being female because boys are permitted to do almost everything girls do, but not vice versa. It is especially hard when you love climbing trees and playing games, but are expected to play with dolls instead.

At about thirteen years of age, it becomes even more painful, as boys, almost overnight, seem to grow stronger and bigger than girls. Although I was fairly good at sports and was on the girls' varsity field hockey, basketball, softball, and tennis teams, I was never as good as the best boys. It was small consolation that I was better at some sports—horseback riding and water-skiing. (Perhaps because these sports weren't as popular with boys.)

In athletics as we know them, the average man will probably beat the better-than-average woman. Scientists chalk it up to testosterone and the retention of nitrogen in men's muscles, which make them bigger and bulgier than women's. Even if this is true, the unhappy fact is that sports have been designed for men's rather than women's bodies—which means the emphasis is on strength. We have yet to see major promotion of sports utilizing women's unique flexibility (because of our less bulgy muscles) and better balance (as a result of our lower center of gravity). Gymnastics is the only widely practiced sport where women can outperform their male counterparts—especially on the balance beam.

I still haven't fully accepted what it means to be smaller and weaker than most men. From a practical point of view, it shouldn't matter; but it always has inhibited my activities in ways that make strength and sex matter a great deal. For example, in college I learned to play squash. When I got to law school, I discovered that women were banned from the university's squash courts. By disguising myself as a man, I managed to invade the courts with a classmate who is now my husband. We had fun, but I never beat him.

Still, as I remind myself, that may have been as much a matter of opportunity as biology: he's been able to play squash wherever he's wanted to and on courts where I wasn't allowed because of my sex.

Exclusion of women in sports is a concrete and difficult problem. But most young women never reach the point of challenging their exclusion from their college's athletic facilities or varsity teams. By that time, they have been well conditioned to think of gym as a drag—often doing dancing and exercises, instead of playing football, soccer, basketball, and baseball. From early childhood on, girls are discouraged from taking pride in active and strenuous use of their bodies; boys, meanwhile, are encouraged to get "into condition," to enjoy their athletic ability.

Then there are the subtle discouragements: the unenlightened suspicion that a woman's interest in athletics violates the docile female stereotype and indicates lesbianism (remember the rumors about gym teachers?); the insinuation that if she shows too much interest in sports she may not be able to catch a man; and the general scoffing at women's athletic achievements. One Chicago high school teacher points to clear-cut evidence of sex discrimination in sports. "In the latest edition of the school paper, there were five articles on football and no mention at all of the girls' tennis team which had won its last three matches."

I don't mean to suggest that sports should become for women what they have been for many men: a display of aggression, a proof of toughness, and a kind of primitive communication that replaces emotional intimacy. Sweating, swearing, and grunting together as they play, men manage to create a fellowship which they find hard to sustain elsewhere. And sports provide men with yet another vehicle to test domination and preeminence. ("Let the best man win.")

Women, however, often do communicate with each other in noncompetitive, nonathletic situations; they are generally better able to express emotion, and seem to care less about beating each other into submission. Our self-images (unless we are professional athletes) aren't much affected by winning a tennis match. While this may reveal something positive, it also unfortunately indicates that women are conditioned not to take themselves seriously in sports.

Of course, the majority of men do not take the sportswoman seriously, either. I notice that whenever I'm interested in playing tennis with a male partner, no matter how well matched we might be, he invariably prefers to play against another man no better than I. Partly, this reflects his fear of losing to a mere woman. But, in a deeper sense, playing with another man seems to reinforce his own competitive sense of masculinity. If he beats another man, he's somehow more of a man himself. If he beats me, it's irrelevant, predictable. Losing is a blow to his ego whether it's to me or to a man, but it's a diversion to play with me; the real contest is man-to-man combat.

However, there are encouraging signs that participation in sports is becoming important to women of all ages. Women are beginning to demand their rights as athletes. In New Jersey, for instance, the State Division on Civil Rights found probable

222

cause in a case brought by a local National Organization for Women chapter because girls were barred from the all-boy Little League team. Most often, sex discrimination charges are filed when girls want to engage in a particular sport which a school offers only to boys. Lawsuits or the threat of legal action have led many schools to accept girls on boys' teams, especially in non-contact sports.

One of the highest courts to rule on the issue of integrating high school teams on the basis of sex is the U.S. Court of Appeals for the Sixth Circuit. In the case of *Morris v. Michigan High School Athletic Association* last January, that court affirmed a lower court order that girls may not be prevented from participating fully in interscholastic noncontact athletics. As a result of the desire of Cynthia Morris and Emily Barrett to participate in interscholastic tennis matches, many high school girls have benefited. In addition, after this complaint was filed, the Michigan Legislature enacted a law guaranteeing that all female pupils be permitted to participate in noncontact interscholastic athletic activities and to compete for a position on the boys' team even if a girls' team exists.

New York and New Mexico now also have new regulations which call for the integration of the sexes in all noncontact sports wherever there is a high school team for boys but not for girls. And lawyers of the American Civil Liberties Union have caused at least five other states—Connecticut, New Jersey, Indiana, Minnesota, and Nebraska—to integrate noncontact sports in their high schools. As a result of litigation, female track stars in Connecticut and Minnesota have made their way onto the men's teams. A young Minnesota woman is now on the boys' skiing team of her high school; another has joined the boys' tennis team of hers.

The Indiana Supreme Court, responding favorably to a class action by a female high school student wishing to play on the boys' golf team, held that the Indiana High School Athletic Association rule against "mixed" participation in noncontact sports was a denial of equal protection under the 14th Amendment to the United States Constitution. (Any institution receiving federal or state money may be in violation of the equal protection clause of the 14th Amendment if it discriminates against women students and coaches in athletic programs; sex discrimination in schools which receive federal funds also violates the Education Amendments of 1972 which recently became federal law.)

In New Jersey a high school sophomore successfully challenged a rule of the state Interscholastic Athletic Association that prohibited high school women from competing on varsity tennis teams. A pilot program has begun in New Jersey to allow girls to compete with boys for positions on varsity teams and to encourage schools to upgrade physical education programs for girls. Specifically, the ruling makes clear that outstanding female athletes receive opportunities for training and competition at their ability levels. Lawsuits have also been won in Louisiana and Oklahoma.

In many of these cases there are no girls' teams, so it's easy to decide that interested girls must be allowed to play with the boys. It is more difficult to resolve the question where a girls' team and a boys' team exist for the same sport. If the highly talented girl athlete is encouraged to join the boys' team at the high school level, why not at the college level? Or in the Olympics and other amateur athletic competition? And if at the Olympics, why not in professional sports?

Unfortunately, no American woman would have made the Olympics if the team had been integrated and if the same criteria for selection were applied to both sexes. The very best men—the ones who enter the Olympic tryouts—are still better than the very best women. And certainly at the professional level, women in direct competition with top men would be in trouble in almost every sport. It is debatable whether Billie Jean King, the Number One woman tennis player in the world, would even make the top ten if male and female professional tennis players competed against each other.

At the professional level, the point is occasionally made that because women aren't as good as men, the purse in women's tournaments is legitimately smaller. This argument overlooks the fact that women pros, such as Ms. King in tennis, draw crowds just as large, if not larger, than the men they can't beat and that such women regularly capture the headlines in sports columns.

224

In any high school or college, integrating teams on an "ability only" basis could result in a new form of exclusion for women players. It would effectively eliminate all opportunities for them to play in organized coached competition.

Obviously, therefore, school athletic training programs have to be developed to balance the scales, and equal financial attention must be paid to both sexes. To begin with the human resource, coaches of women's teams must be paid as much as coaches of men's teams. A woman high school basketball coach recently produced figures showing an allocation by the Syracuse Board of Education of $98,000 for male coaches and $200 for female coaches. Discrepancies between women's and men's salaries may violate not only the 14th Amendment to the Constitution but virtually every piece of legislation in the area of sex discrimination in employment and education. Scholarships, too, must be equalized. The first and, it seems, the only university to establish an athletic scholarship for women is the University of Chicago.

As for the students themselves, Minnesota and Utah lawsuits are asking that equal resources—money and personnel—be devoted to physical education for girls and boys. From the first grade through college, girls and boys should have gym classes together with equal access to athletic facilities and instruction. Students, regardless of sex, should be encouraged to perform to the best of their individual ability.

Until puberty, there are insufficient height or strength differences between girls and boys to justify predominately female or male sports below the junior high school level. Girls and boys from an early age should be taught judo or other skills which convey a sense of their own individual strength and agility. If at some point girls and boys prefer different sports, they can individually separate themselves according to these preferences.

Until there is a relaxation of the external cultural pressure for males to prove their masculinity, boys may well choose sports like football, wrestling, and boxing. In any case, a girl wanting to play football should be permitted to try out for the boys' team if an entire girls' team cannot be formed. Girls with the skills to make the boys' team should have the opportunity to play. I am now arguing in court for the right of a woman student at City

College in New York to participate in a men's basketball course because there is none offered for women.

That only noncontact sports are considered suitable for sex integration is nonsensical. As one proponent for the integration of contact sports puts it: "If we are worried about girls' breasts and internal organs, then give them chest and belly protectors. We haven't spared our male football players any expense in that department. We can't declare that because we think many or even most girls cannot or will not play in certain sports that *none* may therefore be allowed to." To match this myth about women's participation in contact sports, there is also a long-standing controversy over the definition of "contact sports." (Baseball and basketball are considered contact sports.)

Because girls have not enjoyed the same physical and psychological opportunities as boys to develop athletically, I believe that resources must be made available for at least two interscholastic teams per sport: one for girls and one for boys. While sex-segregated teams may sound like the long-discredited, separate-but-equal doctrine, it is through a process of careful elimination that this policy emerges as the most viable. The four other alternatives listed below are simply *not* equitable:

1. A system involving ability-determined first- and second-string teams will undoubtedly result in two mostly male teams and no greatly increased participation for females.
2. A first-string team that is sex-integrated to absorb top talent of both sexes plus a second-string all-girl team would increase girls' participation but it runs afoul of boys' rights by excluding them from the second team.
3. If the first-string team is based solely on ability and the second-string team members are evenly divided, boys and girls, the system ends up favoring boys again by assuring them representation on what amounts to one and one-half out of two teams
4. The quota solution requiring half boys and half girls presents both practical and psychological problems: intrateam ostracizing of the girls who dilute the overall performance, and interteam exploitation of the "weaker" sex members of the opposing team.

So we're left with the separate-but-equal solution. While it may penalize the outstanding female athlete who must play on girls' teams regardless of whether she qualifies for the boys' team, it has the singular advantage of giving boys and girls an equal opportunity to compete interscholastically. This is, in my view, an adequate response to the argument that in sports, as in other areas, women should be compensated for past discriminations. The contention that women should be allowed to try out for men's teams, even if there are comparable women's teams, is potentially unfair to the men who can't make the men's teams but might make the women's teams. Even more importantly, it cheats the women's team which would lose its best athletes to the male squads, thus setting women's sports back even farther.

Where girls' sports are taken seriously at the high school and college level, the results are striking. Throughout Iowa, for instance, girls' basketball draws the bigger crowds. The coaching is excellent, and the facilities and equipment are first-rate. Because women's basketball is a matter of state pride, high school and college women in Iowa eagerly try out without feeling the traditional stigma and scorn so frequently associated with women's sports.

Marcia Federbush of Michigan suggests an Olympic-style system to solve the inevitable imbalances of participation, resource allocation and spectator interest: the girls' varsity and the boys' varsity would *together* constitute the school's varsity team. On the same day or evening both teams would play their counterparts from another school (alternating the game order since the second game is inevitably the star attraction). At the end of the two games the point scores would be totaled. If the boys' basketball squad won 75–70 and the girls' basketball team lost with a score of 60–80, the final school score would amount to a 15-point loss.

The girls' and boys' teams would travel together and use the same facilities. They would enjoy equally skilled (and equally paid) coaching staffs, equal budgets, game schedules, uniforms, equipment, combined publicity attention, and a shared spotlight.

Clearly, when interdependence leads to team success, the primary advantage would be the shared commitment in *two* strong separate-but-equal teams.

FOR DISCUSSION

1. Brenda Feiger Fasteau says that sports have been designed for men's rather than women's bodies, with an emphasis on strength. How would you redesign any popular sport to accommodate female players?
2. The rules for girls' basketball differ from those for men's basketball. Can this approach be used in other sports as well? Explain.
3. Is Ms. Fasteau's contention that one reason men prefer to play against other men because they fear "losing to a mere woman" accurate? Discuss.
4. The author is a lawyer. How would a lawyer defending the status quo in sports argue against the points raised by Ms. Fasteau?
5. The author says that "from the first grade through college, girls and boys should have gym classes together with equal access to athletic facilities and instruction." Write a theme on why this program should or should not be implemented at your own school.
6. Is the Federbush proposal for an Olympic-style system of team play a fair solution to the problem of intersex competition? Or does it create problems of its own? If so, what are these problems?

INTRODUCTION

Max Rafferty, once State Superintendent of Schools in the state of California, is for a return to the basics. In the speech that follows, he advocates a return to the "basics," especially in terms of the rules that exist—or used to exist—between coaches and their players.

Try to keep in mind the questions that have been raised by the preceding articles: how could these problem areas be affected by attitudes like Rafferty's?

Interscholastic Sports: The Gathering Storm

Max Rafferty

There are two great national institutions which simply cannot tolerate either internal dissension or external interference: our armed forces, and our interscholastic sports program. Both are of necessity benevolent dictatorships because by their very nature they cannot be otherwise. A combat squad which has to sit down and poll its members before it reacts to an emergency has had it, and so has a football team which lets its opponents tell it whom to start in next Saturday's game.

Ridiculous, you say? Yet both these ridiculous things are happening, or threatening to happen. If you're up on the news at all, you're familiar with the problem the army and marines have been having in recent months with men who go on hunger strikes and who refuse to obey orders on the battlefield. You should be even more familiar with what's happening on the athletic field.

To pinpoint what I'm talking about, let's look at a couple of examples of how sports are being pressured and used to do things they were never intended to do at all.

First, let's look at the "Great Pumpkin," as his Oregon State players call coach Dee Andros. Andros is of Greek descent, like Spiro Agnew, and he's just as good at football coaching as Agnew is at pointing out the faults of the news media, which is pretty darned good. Unfortunately, Andros has a problem.

For twenty-one years, he's had an invariable rule that his gridiron gladiators look the part. His squads have always enjoyed sky-high morale, much of it due to the fact that the players are encouraged to regard the team as more important than the individual player, and the combined effort more valuable than the heroics of the loner. Long ago, the coach banned the freak-out as an acceptable avocation for Oregon State footballers.

In other words: if you want to play for me, fellows, no girlish necklaces and cutesy medallions, no Iroquois scalp locks, no hair-mattress beards, and no Fu Manchu mustaches. You can sport these execrable excrescences and still go to Oregon State, but you can't massage your egos thus publicly and still play football for Dee Andros. Period.

At least right up until last spring it was "period." The Battling Beavers of OSU won a lot more games than they lost, and what's far more important they managed to win them while looking like decent human beings instead of like fugitives from a Barnum and Bailey sideshow.

They were shaven, they were shorn, they wore men's clothing rather than feminine fripperies, and they actually looked as though they bathed once in a while. In short, the varsity players stood out like lighthouses alongside the campus activists, many of whom look and smell as though they had recently emerged from ten years' solitary confinement on Devil's Island.

And this last is undoubtedly what triggered Andros's current crisis.

It seems that some hulking lout on his squad decided to defy the team's personal appearance rules and to sprout a luxuriant thicket of facial foliage which viewed under his helmet and behind his face guard made him virtually indistinguishable from a gorilla. The coach said: "Shave it off or shove off." The player refused and appealed to Oregon State's president on the grounds that his civil rights were being violated.

Instead of backing up his coach and telling the hairy one to get lost, the OSU prexy appointed a Commission on Human Rights to investigate the coach, thus firmly establishing the president's credentials as an even bigger ass than the exhibitionist player. The commission dutifully censured Andros for showing "insufficient sensitivity to the sacred right of adolescent show-offs to break coaching rules."

Kindly note at this juncture that nobody at Oregon State is compelled to play football. Note also that the coach's rules have been part of his winning formula for more than two decades, and are well known to almost everyone in the state of Oregon. The alternative is laughably simple, and it's true on every campus and for every sport: if you don't like the rules, don't go out for the sport.

Now just where does the decision by the Human Rights Commission's driveling academicians leave Dee Andros? What's the future of a coach whose players now know he may be road-blocked and face-slapped by some ad hoc committee every time he tells them to do something they don't want to do?

I can't think of a better way to destroy a fine football team, can you? Or a fine coach, for that matter. But maybe that's the whole idea.

Up to now, I've never known that exquisite sensitivity to a player's pampered ego was one of the prerequisites for a good coach. I've always thought a coach's job was to make men out of wet-behind-the-ears boys.

Can you imagine the expression on gruff old Knute Rockne's face if some cap-and-gowned buffoon had called him "insufficiently sensitive"?

Second, along the same lines but with even more unsavory overtones, there's the recent case of Stanford University's foray into the unlovely field of religious persecution, with athletics playing the role of unwilling patsy. It seems that Stanford recently and scathingly severed athletic relations with Brigham Young University because of one of the fundamental tenets of the Mormon faith: that the descendants of Canaan are ineligible by Old Testament mandate to hold the highest offices in the Church. Inasmuch as those descendants are held by long tradition to be black, Negroes are thus disqualified from taking their place as priests and bishops of the Mormon faith.

Result: not many Negroes are Mormons. Additional result: no black football players at BYU. So Stanford joins several other colleges in a kind of anti-Mormon coalition which is boycotting the Utah school until it mends its allegedly wicked ways, and they are presently writing unctuous letters to each other congratulating themselves on their own virtue.

So far, so good. But let's carry the story one step further. The coalition isn't trying merely to get Brigham Young to put Negroes on its football team. If that's all there were to it, you wouldn't be hearing a single squawk out of me, because I firmly believe that all education, and athletics in particular, should be completely integrated and conspicuously multiracial. Unlike some southern schools which the coalition somehow didn't get around to denouncing, though, BYU is perfectly willing to do just that, has in fact featured black athletes on some of its past teams, and is currently looking for some more. No, what the coalition is really demanding is something far, far, different. It's that the church of the Latter Day Saints repudiate part of its established dogma, given to it a century and a half ago, according to its scriptures by divine revelation.

Now this is quite another matter. What on earth would you do if you were athletic director in a case of this kind? Brigham Young University, you see, is a Church school. Its policies must perforce reflect the teachings of that Church, and cannot contravene them. In effect, the Church *is* the school, and vice versa. So the coalition isn't just demanding that a sister school simply change an athletic policy; it's conducting an organized boycott of a deeply held theological belief, and this sort of religious persecution in the final third of the twentieth century is absolutely intolerable.

It's as though the coalition were to boycott an Episcopalian college because we Episcopalians don't permit females to be bishops, or to put pressure on a Jewish university because Judaism won't allow ham sandwich munchers to become rabbis. I don't happen to agree at all that the color of a man's skin should keep him from becoming a priest, a bishop, or a pope, for that matter, in any church. But I don't happen to be a Mormon, and what the Mormons devoutly believe is simply none of my Episcopalian business. Neither is it the business of athletics in general, or the coalition in particular.

232

So long as BYU keeps up its academic standards, behaves itself properly on the playing field, and opens its classrooms and its athletic teams alike to all who qualify for entrance regardless of color or race, it's as outrageous for the coalition to use athletics to interfere with a church's right to practice its own faith as it was for the jolly jesters of the Third Reich to interfere with the German Jews' right to practice theirs. The BYU students, incidentally, have an impeccable record in regard to the criteria I've just listed, and what's more, stayed soberly in class last year while the Stanfordites were bloodily occupying administration buildings and raising hell generally.

Ah, well. Football is supposed to teach players sportsmanship, fellowship, and fair play. I'm sure BYU can find other schools beside those of the coalition to supply this desired mixture, and which won't also expose its players to the added and unwelcome ingredient of religious intolerance.

My purpose in bringing these incidents before you tonight is simply to remind you of their increasing frequency. At San Jose, Wyoming, Washington, and a dozen other distracted colleges, players have challenged their coaches, walked out on their own teams, and boycotted their own schools, all in the name of some social, economic, or political grievance which the sport in question had never had anything to do with and with which it was never set up to cope.

As athletic directors, you're up against more than just a challenge to your authority or that of your coaches, a temporary roadblock in the path of bigger and better athletic competition. What's facing you in the very near future is the possible elimination of school sports altogether, if only because sports as we know them cannot survive their transformation into a mere tool of various activist groups with their own nonathletic axes to grind.

It's ironical, in fact, that those who hate athletics the most are the ones currently trying to use athletics for their own ends. These, of course, are the "Let's-give-aid-and-comfort-to-the-Communists" agitators, the hairy, loud-mouthed freaks of both sexes who infest our campuses today like so many unbathed boll weevils. The activists and the pseudointellectuals have created a myth—a kind of antiathlete cartoon caricature which I'd like to analyze briefly.

The stereotype is that of the muscle-bound and moronic athlete. Of late he has receipted for so many "avant garde" jokes that he has become a permanent cliché, like the college widow and the absent-minded professor. Yet when one puts the myth of the jug-headed, oafish muscle man under the cold light of logical analysis, it doesn't hold up worth a nickel.

The beard-and-sandal set claims the athlete is stupid. Yet in every high school where I've ever worked, the grade-point average of the varsity players was higher than that of the student body as a whole.

The lank-haired leaders of our campus revolutionists sneer at the varsity letterman for his allegedly juvenile enthusiasms and his willingness to die for dear old Rutgers. But they themselves are quite openly and ardently guilty of enthusiasms for such strange causes as raising bail money for Mario Savio and paying Joan Baez's taxes, and they seem ready to die at a moment's notice for a smile from Kosygin or even for the slightest relaxation of the built-in scowl on the face of Mao-Tse-Tung. By comparison, dying for Rutgers has its points.

Their intellectual vials of wrath are constantly overflowing onto the hapless head of the athlete because of his hopeless philistinism and his alleged inability to communicate with his peers save in monosyllabic grunts. Yet the halls of Congress and the board rooms of giant industrial complexes are alike populated by a striking number of ex-athletes who seem to have no difficulty whatever in communicating. And the philistine mentality of such former contenders on the playing fields as Douglas MacArthur, John F. Kennedy, and Justice Byron "Whizzer" White may be left safely for history to judge.

As another football season ends and another basketball season begins, I have to confess a lifelong fondness for the amateur athlete. Over the past thirty years, eight of which were spent as a high school coach and athletic director, I've seen a remarkable number of athletes fighting and even dying for their country, and remarkably few of them ending up in jail or taking the Fifth Amendment before a Congressional investigating committee. They seem to be conspicuously absent, too, from Communist-inspired demonstrations and Filthy Speech Movements.

They are, in short, above-average, decent, reasonably pa-

234

triotic Americans. Maybe that s why they're under increasing attack from the kooks, the crum-bums, and Commies.

I'm not too worried about the outcome. The love of clean, competitive sports is too deeply imbedded in the American matrix, too much a part of the warp and woof of our free people, ever to surrender to the burning-eyed, bearded draft-card-burners who hate and envy the athlete because he is something they can never be—a *man*.

Our greatest soldier-statesman of the twentieth century once had this to say about athletics and the men who follow its rigorous and rewarding discipline: "Upon the fields of friendly strife are sown the seeds which, on other days, on other fields, will bear the seeds of victory."

As athletic directors, you have a decision to make. The college syndrome I have noted and documented in this brief talk is spreading into American high schools even as we meet together tonight. Your choice is simple: you can back up your coaches' authority to do with their teams what coaches have done for the last hundred years, or you can play a cowardly game of patty-cake with the activists and watch your sports program go down the drain with your own jobs going right along with it.

I didn't come here tonight to make you feel good, but rather to do two things: warn you, and promise to help. Little enough of idealism and faith and cheerful willingness to fight on steadfastly for the right remains to us Americans in these, the sick sixties. Interscholastic sports, rising surprisingly and increasingly above their age-old status as mere games, serve today as the staunch custodians of these treasured concepts out of our great past.

If you elect to cop out on all this and to let your teams be used for their own sinister purposes by those who are the enemies of all athletics, you will deserve exactly what you will get, and you will receive no sympathy from me. But if you decide to stand your ground and fight for the future of American sports against those who would destroy everything you've worked for all your lives, then indeed you will have formidable allies: my own department; the vast majority of our state legislators; above all, the millions of Californians who love athletics and who believe with all their hearts that it symbolizes the clean, bright, fighting spirit which is America herself.

Interscholastic Sports: The Gathering Storm   235

A tough job, this one which I am urging upon you? You bet. But you are tough men, or should be. These are rugged times, and we need rugged men to stand up to them. My own job, over the years, has not been exactly a bed of roses. All you and I can do is to lower our heads and do our level best, keeping the goals of our great profession constantly before our mind's eye, disregarding as best we can the barrage of the opposition, striving to keep our feet despite the shell holes and the booby traps, satisfied if the end of each day finds us a little closer to our hearts' desire.

When I grow tired, as I occasionally do—when I get discouraged, as once in a while happens—when the slings and arrows of our common enemies get to me, as they do now and then—there is one never-failing source of inspiration upon which I learned long ago to rely, and which always sends me back into the fray with renewed strength and a stout heart.

It's a very simple thing. I merely close my eyes and call up from the depths of memory my old teams—the myriad faces which have passed before me for so many years—the bright, fresh, questing faces of the kids with whom I lived and worked for so long. Those strong, eager boys, so willing to learn, so wrapped up in the joy of playing the game for the game's sake, the only way it ever should be played. I look back upon the long parade of faces, and in my mind I see the countless more whom in reality I will never get to see—the youngsters of California —your own teams—thronging in their untold thousands from the redwood country of the north to the great desert which lies along our southern border.

And suddenly it's all worthwhile. What men ever had more children than you and I to work for, to hope for, to live for? More than two million boys—the joy, the hope, the whole future of our state. It's a family worth fighting for.

I recommend it to you.

FOR DISCUSSION

1. Rafferty is addressing an audience of coaches here. How does his language reveal his awareness of his audience? On what bases does he appeal to that audience?

2. Is the tone of the speech appropriate? How would the speech be received by a gathering of coaches today? Explain.
3. How appropriate or accurate is Rafferty's comparison of interscholastic sports to the military?
4. Assess the logic of the speech. Are there places where the logic breaks down? Explain.
5. If you were a coach and a group of your players refused to obey the rules for beards and long hair, how would you talk to them as a group? Write a short speech with this audience in mind.

INTRODUCTION

Dave Meggyesy played as a linebacker for the Cardinals from 1963 to 1969. Then he left the game abruptly and wrote a book called *Out of Their League.* In it he called football "a circus for the increasingly chaotic American empire." He said, "The game has been wrapped in red, white, and blue. It is no accident that some of the most maudlin and dangerous pregame 'patriotism' we see in this country appears in football stadiums." Meggyesy hit the sports establishment harder than Mean Joe Greene mauling a quarterback on a rough day. In the excerpt that follows, Meggyesy confines his punch to college athletics.

Football and Education

Dave Meggyesy

Shortly after I graduated from high school I went down to visit two cousins in Baton Rouge, Louisiana. One of them had played defensive end for the Chinese Bandits, on the Louisiana State University national champion team of 1958. His younger brother, Gary, who was entering LSU in the fall, was a high school All-American. My cousins' house was near the LSU campus and we spent a lot of time during my visit hanging around with some of the big-name LSU jocks like Billy Cannon and Warren Rabb. Gary and I worked out every day with many of the LSU football players, doing a lot of calisthenics and running. One morning we were working out by Tiger Stadium when Head Coach Paul Dietzel and a few of his assistants wandered by. They asked some of the players who I was and that afternoon they called Gary's home and offered me a scholarship. Though I was still planning on going to Syracuse on the football scholarship they had offered me, I was very interested in LSU. They were the National Champions and Baton Rouge was the most football crazy town I had ever seen. The people were falling all over their feet to be with or to know football players. I told Dietzel I'd accept his offer, and he told me my parents' signature on a letter of intent would be needed before I could be officially awarded a scholarship. He tried hard to get me to handle the whole thing by mail, and Gary's parents also wanted me to stay in Baton Rouge, but my parents insisted I come home and talk the whole matter over with them.

By the time I got home I was really in a turmoil. I called Coach Bell at Syracuse to tell him I had decided to go to LSU. He asked me how I could do such a thing to him after he had personally recruited me. Within five minutes after I stopped talking with Bell, Ben Schwartzwalder, the head football coach at Syracuse, called. As usual, he did not waste words. "Boy, you fly up here immediately. We'll pay for the plane," he told me. "Just get up here by tomorrow." No sooner had Schwartzwalder hung up than I received a call from Col. Byrne, head of the Air Force ROTC program at Syracuse. The Colonel said he had just talked with Ben Schwartzwalder and was calling because he had learned I was interested in becoming a jet pilot. He personally assured me I would be able to go through the Air Force ROTC program and could enter flight school when I graduated from college.

I arrived in Syracuse the next day and was met at the airport by Jim Shrieve, the freshman coach. He took me to my room at the Hotel Syracuse and then left, saying he would return with Coach Bell at six o'clock for dinner. I waited around by myself for about two hours feeling anxious as hell. About six Bell called to tell me they were waiting for me in the hotel dining room. I walked down and saw what seemed to me to be the entire Syracuse coaching staff sitting there with one empty chair reserved for me. Schwartzwalder, the head coach, whom I had met only briefly on my recruiting trip to Syracuse, was at the head of the table. Seated around him were Bell, Shrieve, and Joe Szombathy, the end coach who was there to play on my ethnic sensibilities because he too was of Hungarian descent. The chair reserved for me was directly across from Ben and I couldn't escape his gaze. Ben talks in this raspy, gravelly voice. His head is usually lowered and he peers at you over the top of his glasses. Bill Bell sat there, asking every few minutes how I could do this to him. He looked hurt. The waitress came over to take our order, but Ben shooed her away. She must have known I was starved, for she came back about every ten minutes. Ben never took his eyes off me, never stopped talking. "Boy, we had great plans for you," Ben would say, and Szombathy or Shrieve would second him. They really came on heavy against LSU. Shrieve told me, "Dave, if you told us you wanted to go to Notre Dame, or some other fine school, we wouldn't say anything, But we would be doing you an injustice if we didn't object to your going to LSU." Even though the public schools I had gone to in Ohio were always all white, they made a big point of telling me "There will be no colored students at LSU." After a while they began to focus on how Syracuse was a small school with a limited number of scholarships and how it would be impossible for them to give my scholarship to someone else at this late date. I finally agreed to go to Syracuse. They were all smiles and assured me how happy I would be. Then Ben finally allowed the waitress to come over and take our orders.

The next morning Coach Bell picked me up at the hotel to take me to the airport for my flight back to Ohio. Col. Byrne, the Air Force ROTC commander whom I had talked to briefly on the phone, was with him in the car. When we arrived at the Syracuse airport, Bell drove over to the National Guard hangar, and Col. Byrne got out to speak with some of the guardsmen stationed there. He asked me if I would like to sit in a jet, so I climbed up, and he spent a few minutes explaining the controls. Once I was back in Solon, Coach Bell would call me every week to see how I was doing and to tell me how personally pleased he was that I was going to Syracuse. He assured me he would do anything he could to make my four years at Syracuse as enjoyable as possible. I would always reassure him that I was coming to Syracuse, and thank him for the personal interest he had in me.

For incoming freshman football players, practice began at Syracuse on September 5th even though classes did not start for another two weeks. I took a train from Cleveland to Syracuse and arrived tired from a night made sleepless by excitement and anticipation over the beginning of college. After collecting my luggage I immediately telephoned Coach Bell who had insisted that I call him the minute I got into town so he could pick me up

240

at the station and get me settled in the football living quarters. His phone rang for a very long time and I was just about ready to hang up when he answered. Our conversation went something like this: "Hello Coach Bell? This is Dave. I just arrived and I'm down at the train station." There was a long silence and I started to get a little nervous. "Do you realize what the hell time it is?" he growled. "Yes, Coach, it's about 6:20 in the morning." By this time he was really pissed and told me to meet him at the Syracuse Gym around 9 o'clock. Since I didn't know my way around town, I asked him how I should go about getting there. "I don't care," he responded, "Just don't ever wake me up this early in the morning again."

We had two practice sessions a day for a week and didn't get our first break until freshman orientation day. It seemed like we had been at Syracuse for ages, and right from the start we didn't feel much fellowship with the other freshmen. When I saw them running around the quadrangle in their orange beanies it hit me how different I was. On the one hand, I felt somewhat superior, but on the other hand they made me realize I was part of a select group of individuals brought there to play football, not to have a "normal" college experience.

The following day we had to register for courses. Syracuse had a special remedial program, ostensibly designed to help freshmen entering with academic deficiencies. But the coaching staff encouraged me and the other freshmen football players to enroll in this program because it lasted through the whole year and consisted of mainly "mickey mouse" courses requiring little work.

Joe Szombathy, the varsity end coach, was also in charge of the athletic tutoring program. He would take the freshmen football players' class cards and simply fill out the courses he wanted them to take. Szombathy not only enrolled most of them in the remedial program, but decided on their courses with one of the main criterion being whether or not they interfered with afternoon football practice. I had searched through the course catalogue for classes I wanted to take, then filled out my own course card and presented it to Szombathy. He was furious. "What the hell do you think you're doing, Meggyesy?" he shouted at me. "We want you to take these other courses so you'll be sure to be eligible. You can always take the other courses next year." But I was conscious of not wanting to be identified as a stupid jock, and I refused to allow him to sway me. I simply wanted to take the courses other freshmen were required to take.

We finished an undefeated freshman season. Meanwhile, the varsity was 7 and 0 and the number-one ranked college team in the nation. It was exciting to be a part of the football program at that time for it seemed all the energies of the university were being channelled toward making sure we won the National Championship. Most of the varsity players had stopped going to classes and were devoting full time to football. Besides the regular afternoon practices, much of the day was spent in special team meetings. The athletic department had complete backing from the administration in this quest for a national championship. Les Dye, the Director of Admissions, had started at Syracuse as a football coach and made sure good players were admitted. Eric Faigle, the Dean of the School of Arts and Sciences, was an avid supporter of the football program and no professor was about to incur his wrath and rule a player ineligible simply because he wasn't attending classes or taking exams. Even though most of the players hadn't seen a classroom for some time, no one was declared ineligible and the team went on the win the National Championship and defeat Texas in the Cotton Bowl.

Syracuse recruited top football players regardless of their academic ability, and the athletic department's biggest jobs were to get the football players admitted and then to keep them eligible. I remember one citizenship course which all Syracuse freshmen, including football players in the remedial program, were required to take. I knew most of the other players hadn't been to class or done any studying and I couldn't figure out how they were going to pass the exam. Then, just before midterms, we had a squad meeting with one of the tutors hired by the athletic department. The tutor didn't exactly give us the test questions but he did give us a lot of important information. He told us cryptically that if we copied down what he said we would do all right on the exam. He wasn't joking: when I took the exam I discovered he had given us the answers to the test questions. When the general tutoring session broke up the tutor asked about

242

ten ball players to stay. These were the guys who were really out of it and made no pretense about being students. They had neither the ability nor interest to do college work. I don't know exactly what kind of help they got after we left but I do know it was this kind of tutoring that kept them eligible for four years.

There were even less ethical techniques than these. For example, my brother, Dennis, who also came up to Syracuse on a football scholarship, flunked his freshman year. He was told he would have to get six units of "A" during summer school to get back in school and be eligible for football. After registering for summer school, Dennis immediately drove back to Ohio, where he spent the summer working for a Cleveland construction company. He returned to Syracuse in September with six units of "A" for courses he never attended.

By the time I graduated, I knew it was next to impossible to be a legitimate student and a football player too. There is a clear conflict, and it is always resolved on the side of the athletic program. Nearly every major university in the country has an employee within the athletic department who supposedly provides athletes with tutorial assistance. At the University of Texas, he is known as the Brain Coach while at Berkeley he has the more prestigious title of Academic Coordinator. Whatever he is called, his task is always the same: to keep athletes eligible by whatever means necessary, even if it involves getting them an early look at exams, or hiring graduate students to write their term papers or take finals for them.

Most athletes are accustomed to being on the take and think the system works for them or that they are somehow beating it. But the reality is quite different, and, as in most other things, the athlete is far more sinned against than sinning. He is a commodity and he is treated with unbelievable cynicism. The minute his eligibility expires, the athletic department's concern for his welfare suddenly evaporates. The free tutoring stops and an athlete finds himself faced with a flock of difficult classes which somebody has put off to keep him eligible. He finds himself encased in the stereotype of the dumb jock and psychologically devastated. Of the twenty-six players who got scholarships in my freshman year, only John Mackey (now an all-pro end with Baltimore), Gene Stancin and I graduated with our class.

We lost to Army in a game played in New York City, 9–6. I got a big thrill out of playing in the home of the New York Yankees, but I'll always remember that game for something else. Mark Weber had suffered a succession of knee injuries during the season, and there was some question about whether he would be able to play against Army. Mark was seriously thinking about quitting football. About a month earlier, he had asked Ben to cut him in on some of the money other players were getting. Ben flatly refused. Mark and I talked about it a lot, and he decided to stick it out because it was his last year.

He didn't even finish that year. In the second half of the Army game, Ben sent Mark in to receive a punt—something he was almost never called on to do. Mark caught it and started up field. One of Army's big tackles got a clean shot on his bad knee and just tore it up. Mark was carried off the field on a stretcher. It just didn't make sense to have a big, heavy guy with a bad knee returning a punt which everyone knows is one of the most hazardous plays in the game. Mark never played football again.'

Schwartzwalder and I appeared together on a couple of radio and television shows shortly before my sophomore season ended. Since I had won honorable mention All-American honors, he was touting me as the next Roger Davis—Syracuse's great All-American lineman who also came from Solon High. I took the praise, but, especially after what happened to Mark Weber, I wasn't playing football for any great love of the game but primarily to win approval. I still felt ambivalent about hitting. At times I didn't want to touch anyone or to be touched. On other occasions I felt great pleasure and release from the sheer physical violence of the game. Sometimes after getting a clean shot at the ball carrier, I would feel this tremendous energy flow and not experience the pain of contact at all. I sometimes could psych myself so high I would feel indestructible. Like most of the other players, I had been introduced to a system of rewards—psychological and material—and I played mainly for them. The intrinsic joy of physicality got shunted into the background. Even now, after playing for fourteen years, I can't really say if there is any basic worth to the game. I just can't separate the game from the payoffs—approval, money, adulation.

The process of questioning, which eventually made me decide to get out of football, really began after my successful sophomore season. I had performed well and gotten recognition, but there was no real satisfaction. Shortly after the season ended, I began making friends with graduate students and people in the liberal arts. When Schwartzwalder found out about this he called me into his office. "Dave, you have a great football career ahead of you," he began. "But if you hang around with those beatniks you're going to destroy yourself." I told him they were my friends. "That may be true, Dave, but it doesn't look good for our football team for you to be hanging out with those beatniks." I assured him I would do nothing to hurt the team and left his office.

My beatnik friends, as Ben called them, hung out at a bar near campus called the Orange. Their view of the world and of life was completely different from the football ethic. At first I couldn't believe them. They were completely sacrilegious when it came to athletics. They would get drunk and go to the games to laugh at fans and mock the coach.

Some of them were drama students and they would do great imitations of Ben, whom they called "the pygmy paratrooper" because of his diminutive size and widely publicized war exploits. They would point out the cynicism and hypocrisy of the university's commitment to football. At the same time Chancellor Tolley was claiming to be guided by the highest religious and educational principles, he was hiring football players to gather prestige and money for the university. What my new friends were saying didn't make too much sense to me yet, but I enjoyed rapping with them. My association with these "beatniks" eventually became such a contradiction that I had to stop seeing them whenever I was playing. In the fall and during spring practice I would rarely stop in at the Orange, for I knew hanging around there would screw me up for football.

One of the justifications for college football is that it is not only a character-builder, but a body-builder as well. This is nonsense. Young men are having their bodies destroyed, not developed. As a matter of fact, few players can escape from college football without some form of permanent disability. During my four years I accumulated a broken wrist, separations of both shoulders, an ankle that was torn up so badly it broke the arch of my foot, three major brain concussions, and an arm that almost had to be amputated because of improper treatment. And I was one of the lucky ones.

When a player is injured, he is sent to the team physician, who is usually more concerned with getting the athlete back into action than anything else. This reversal of priorities leads to unbelievable abuses. One of the most common is to "shoot" a player before a game to numb a painful injured area that would normally keep him out of action. He can play, but in so doing he can also get new injuries in that part of his body where he has no feeling.

When I spoke to a group of athletes at the University of California in the spring of 1970, Jim Calkins, cocaptain of the Cal football team, told me that the coaching staff and the team physician had put him on anabolic steroids. Both assured him such drugs would make him bigger and stronger, and this is true. But they didn't bother to tell him that there are potentially dangerous side effects. "I gained a lot of weight like they told me I would, but after a month or so, these steroids really began to mess me up" Jim told me. "I went to the team physician and he admitted that there are possible bad side effects. I had complete faith in the coaches and medical staff before this, and I felt betrayed." And well he might, because steroids are known to have caused atrophied testes, blunting of sex drives, damage to liver and glands, and some physicians believe they are the causal agent for cancer of the prostate. And they are widely used.

The violent and brutal player that television viewers marvel over on Saturdays and Sundays is often a synthetic product. When I got to the National Football League, I saw players taking not only steroids, but also amphetamines and barbiturates at an astonishing rate. Most NFL trainers do more dealing in these drugs than the average junky. I was glad when Houston Ridge, the San Diego Chargers' veteran defensive tackle, filed a huge suit last spring against his club, charging them with conspiracy and malpractice in the use of drugs. He charged that steroids, amphetamines, barbiturates and the like were used "not for purposes of treatment and cure, but for the purpose of stimulating mind and body so he (the player) would perform more violently as a professional. . . ."

I don't mean that players are given drugs against their will. Like Calkins, most players have complete trust in their coaches and team doctors and in the pattern of authority they represent. Associated with this is the atmosphere of suspicion which surrounds any injured player unless his injury is a visible one, like a broken bone. Coaches constantly question the validity of a player's complaints, and give him the silent treatment when he has a "suspicious" injury. The coaches don't say, "We think you're faking, don't you want to play football?" They simply stop talking to a player and the message comes across very clearly. Most players want and need coaches' approval, especially when they are injured and can't perform, and it really tears them up when the coach won't even speak to them. This is especially true in college where the players are young and usually identify closely with the coach. After a few days of this treatment, many players become frantic. They will plead with the team physician to shoot them up so they can play. The player will totally disregard the risk of permanent injury.

Though we were supposed to be a superior team and were heavily favored, we just barely managed to beat Boston College. We celebrated after the game, not so much because we had won, but because the weight and pressure of a particularly rough season was behind us and we were looking forward to a return to normal life. No such luck: a few days later the Syracuse athletic department and the college administration announced that the team had accepted an invitation to play in the Liberty Bowl. Even then, straight as I was, my first reaction was that the coaches and administrators should play the game since they had accepted the invitation. This game, which was played in Philadelphia in the middle of December, was at best second-rate, and all it meant to most of the players was another couple of weeks of practice. But it was quite a profitable venture for the athletic department. The game was nationally televised, and even though both the teams—Syracuse and Miami—were mediocre, they were invited because each had one of the country's most exciting players—our Ernie Davis and Miami's quarterback George Mira, one of the top passers in the history of college football. The Syracuse athletic department would get a significant amount of the television money and they weren't about to pass this up simply because the players were tired.

Many of us felt that since we had to play we should at least get something out of it. After speaking to Ben, Dick Easterly, one of the cocaptains, informed us there were no plans to give the players anything. This made us even more angry, because we knew that players in the major bowls always received a wristwatch, a set of luggage, or something like that. We were in a murderously petty mood, and had a special team meeting without the coaches to discuss what we should do. Some of the seniors favored boycotting the game unless the athletic department at least gave us a watch, and decided to send the cocaptains to Lou Andreas, the athletic director, to tell him this.

The athletic department had never seen the ball players get together on their own before and this, coupled with the talk of boycott, made them quickly agree to give us watches—and before the game as we had demanded. That was a good lesson: one of the greatest absurdities in the football mythology is that the players' interest are identical with those of coaches and administrators.

After the season I began to think a lot about what the football program at Syracuse meant. The whole Liberty Bowl experience had made me realize the blatantly commercial nature of college football and see that the players had picked up these petty, small-minded values. But it was also clear that I was basically just a hired hand brought in from Ohio, and that if I began to question the values behind the game very loudly, I'd quickly find myself back in Solon. We were semiprofessionals, and the only reason the N.C.A.A. regulated scholarship money was to keep our wages down. We were a cheap labor pool that made great profits for the university while we were constantly told to be grateful for the opportunity we were getting. Still, standing out there like the pot of gold at the end of the rainbow, was the incentive of pro ball which helped keep the players from griping too loud or really organizing.

You hear a lot about how football scholarships allow poor kids to attend college. This may be true, but it isn't anything to be proud of. It's pretty obvious that this country could, if it wished, give everyone a chance to go to college. Actually, people should feel guilty rather than chauvinistic and elated when they see a scholarship awarded to a student who can throw a football 60 yards while one of his classmates with good grades who sincerely wants to attend college cannot do so for financial reasons.

It's not surprising that vast numbers of poor kids, black and white, throughout the country spend an inordinate amount of time and energy on athletics. Thousands upon thousands of them turn out for high school football every year, filled with dreams of gridiron glory and hopes of a college scholarship and immortality as a pro. Instead of talking honestly, most high school coaches play cynically upon these dreams and hopes. Figures released in 1969 by the N.C.A.A. present a sobering reality: only one out of every thirty high school football players ever gets a chance to play college ball. Most likely, fewer than one in one hundred get a full athletic scholarship.

My last semester at Syracuse was my most rewarding —mainly because football was behind me. I got a glimpse of what school could really be like, especially in a seminar on Education and Society, taught by Hank Woessner, one of the few teachers I met who had faith in the students' ability to involve themselves in serious work. Hank was the first teacher to discuss in the classroom some of the problems I had been struggling with privately during my years at Syracuse. He constantly provoked us to question the whole concept of education. He talked about what education should be ideally and the reality at Syracuse. I began having long discussions with Hank about my role as a football player at Syracuse and the relationship of football to the rest of the university. With his encouragement, I wrote a term paper on the role of college football in higher education. The paper showed that big time college football was completely antithetical to the professed aims and goals of higher education, saying in a scholarly way what I had been feeling on a personal level since my junior year. For the first time it occurred to me that questioning the system was not something to feel guilty about, but a sane response.

FOR DISCUSSION

1.   Does a college football player have the right to a "normal"

college experience? Is such a thing possible? Or does the football player, like the show business celebrity, automatically forgo normal experiences by consenting to perform in the first place?

2. Meggyesy says that the "process of questioning ... eventually made me decide to get out of football." Make a list of the things that he questioned, and discuss each item for its merits and demerits.

3. The late Vince Lombardi, coach of the Green Bay Packers (winners of six divisional championships, five NFL championships, and the first two Super Bowl games), once said "the individual has to have respect for authority regardless of what that authority is. I think the individual has gone too far. I think 95 percent of the people, as much as they shout, would rather be led than lead." How do you think Meggyesy would reply to this view of sports and life?

4. Lombardi's slogans have been repeated so often they are now clichés: "Winning isn't everything, it's the only thing"; "If you can't accept losing, you can't win"; "If you can walk, you can run." How do you think Meggyesy would respond if he were a player on one of Lombardi's teams?

INTRODUCTION

The following three articles, which appeared in the *New York Times* during March of 1974, present various views and facets of athletic recruiting. Some reiterate Dave Meggyesy's criticism, condemning recruiting as "a slave market." Others, such as Penn State football coach Joe Paterno, defend the practice—without its "excesses and abuses." In fact, one Harvard freshman, Sandy Climan, even advocates that recruiting extend to the high school scholar. As you sift through these differing opinions, weigh each against the values which you feel sports should embody. In making your judgments, take into consideration the clarity and objectivity of the news reporting in each selection. Watch carefully for false generalizations which may sway your opinion.

Athletic Recruiting: A Campus Crisis

Joseph Durso

America's college campuses, rocked by unrest in the nineteen sixties, are being shaken again by a new crisis: a frenzied "slave market" in recruiting and paying athletes.

Many educators warn that the crisis is approaching a public scandal, and they attribute it to a national mania in the nineteen seventies to "win at any cost."

But the cost is spreading far beyond the 50,000 athletes and coaches who are staging 32,000 basketball and 3,000 football games this year, or the hundreds of millions of dollars the games will generate. The cost, they say, is being paid in the growing corruption of high school students, in a distortion of the role of sports in education and in the moral climate surrounding all the schools.

Even successful coaches like Frank Broyles of Arkansas

have predicted that "if something isn't done, the lid is going to blow off." And, forty-five years after a historic study of identical pressures, the Carnegie Corporation, the Ford Foundation, and other national bodies are initiating new inquiries into the gold-rush world of college sports.

In a far-ranging survey of the campuses, a dozen writers for the *New York Times* have interviewed educators, athletic directors, coaches, students, alumni, and public officials.

Their report, which begins today, found that thousands of high school seniors are now sweating out their admission to college—while an elite group of quarterbacks and 6-foot-8-inch centers ponder which high-powered offers to accept before the deadline known as "national signing day." The witching hour for football heroes in the class of 1974 fell at 8 A.M. last Wednesday, and for all other athletes it will arrive at 8 A.M. on April 17.

Nobody denied that the grab-bag frenzy would open college doors to some students, especially black and women athletes, who otherwise might have stayed home. But to many critics, the system more often ends in exploitation of the young persons it supposedly is glorifying, even though schools like Ohio State spend $4 million a year on sports and U.C.L.A. budgets $500,000 for athletic scholarships.

"It's the worst I've seen in my twenty-three years of coaching," said Joe Paterno, whose football team earned $500,000 for Penn State in the Orange Bowl two months ago.

"It's not the kids, it's the system," said Digger Phelps, the basketball coach at Notre Dame, whose football team earned $420,000 in the Sugar Bowl and whose basketball team opened the national championship tournament yesterday.

"Football is just too big," said Tim O'Shea, a senior majoring in engineering at the University of Nebraska. "You know something has gone amiss when the stadium (which seats 76,000) is the third largest city in the state on a home game day."

"It's getting vicious again," said the Rev. Ed Visscher, basketball coach at Long Island Lutheran High School, one of the perennially best teams in the country. "The competition reminds me of the old slave markets, talking about 'things' instead of 'people.' Budgets are getting tighter, pressure is coming down from above, the schools are reaching the point of 'win or else.' "

In the stampede to "win or else," the *Times* team found, the symptoms of runaway professionalism at all levels of education include these:

Nine of every ten college athletic departments are running in the red. The chief reason: costs have doubled in the last decade, in some places in the last five years. The chief result: a steepening of the competition for high school athletes who might thrust a college into the national spotlight, the television picture, the postseason bowl games—or just into the black.

Eight colleges have dropped football in the last year, forty-one in the last ten years, because the pressure grew too great. Don Canham, athletic director at the University of Michigan, warned that if the trend continued, only the biggest would survive and "a super conference will develop out of the wreckage."

In their rush for the teenaged talent, universities are increasingly ignoring or sidestepping the nine pages of single-spaced rules that form the heart of the recruiting code of the National Collegiate Athletic Association. The chief rule says that a college may provide tuition, room, board, books and fifteen dollars a month for "laundry."

But some violations include payments to high school stars, tampering with their grades, forging their transcripts, finding substitutes to take their exams, promising jobs to their parents, buying them cars, and supplying them with football tickets that may be scalped for as much as $8,000 during their undergraduate careers. At U.C.L.A. several years ago, some eager alumni secretly posted a bounty of five dollars for every rebound off the basketball backboard.

The 664 schools in the N.C.A.A. are policed by only four investigators led by Warren S. Brown, who until recent years did all the policing himself. About twenty universities are publicly censured each year, and an undisclosed number are warned privately. Oklahoma has been placed on probation three times in the last seventeen years in football; Southwestern Louisiana, twice in six years during a sudden rise to prominence in basketball. Cornell, already on probation in hockey, has just admitted violations in basketball.

What it all adds up to, many educators agree, is a frantic hustling of the 300,000 football and 200,000 basketball seniors in the nation's 22,000 high schools—or, at least, of the few hundred of them who excel in the money sports. Some get "letters of interest" from colleges while they are still in the ninth grade; Rick Mount, now in the American Basketball Association, started getting letters in the eighth grade. Eric Penick of Notre Dame, when he was a star halfback at Gilmour Academy in Cleveland, was besieged by sixty-two college coaches the week after his last game.

Butch Lee, a high school senior in New York City, currently is weighing basketball offers from more than 200 colleges.

The rush is even reaching into sports that do not fill stadiums, like swimming, lacrosse and wrestling; and into sideshows that do not even qualify as sports, like rodeo and baton twirling. And women athletes have lately started a furor to get their share of the loot. At the University of Miami, fifteen scholarships are being offered in golf, tennis and swimming—and four hundred girls have applied from as far away as Hawaii.

But persons caught up in the system concede that it goes far beyond a cat-and-mouse game between a paid recruiter and an unsuspecting boy, or even a suspecting and possibly greedy boy. Coach and athlete operate at one end of the chase; at the other, supplying the external pressure, are college presidents trying to build stadiums or libraries; alumni trying to build the prestige of alma mater, and state officials trying to build a record with the public.

Whether their combined efforts result in more opportunities for education—or just more opportunities for money—is an open question.

Investigations Pursued

One critique of the situation is being pressed by the National Association of Basketball Coaches, which will report its findings in the next two weeks. The coaches have been polling twenty-five athletic directors, twenty-five former college players who were All-America selections in high school, twenty-five high school players who now have All-America ranking and the parents of twenty-five such stars.

They voted the inquiry during a wave of protests from the coaches themselves. Pete Newell, a longtime college basketball coach and now general manager of the Los Angeles Lakers, said: "The prevailing thought is that 'if he can do it, why can't I?'" Bob Cousy, who quit recently after a long career in basketball, said: "It wasn't worth it, the winning and losing and everything else."

When Jack Rohan resigned as Columbia's basketball coach last month, he said: "I leave with a great deal of sadness. Also, with a warning that you get the N.C.A.A. to come down hard on recruiting cheaters. Otherwise, we'll have a major scandal again."

Another inquiry has been started by the American Council on Education, with financial help from the Ford Foundation and the Carnegie Corporation and with some prompting from the Association of American Universities. In Ottawa, meanwhile, a major study of sports is being undertaken by the Association of Universities and Colleges of Canada.

The studies will be the first of such scope since 1929, when the Carnegie Foundation for the Advancement of Teaching issued a historic report on the fact that "college sports have been developed from games played by boys for pleasure into systematic professionalized athletic contests."

But any survey will have to cover a lot of ground to keep up with the continuing merry-go-round of college sports in the seventies.

When Louisiana State's football team went to the Orange Bowl in Miami, the fuel shortage forced the school to cancel the charter flight for the band. Commercial space was booked—at a cost of $25,000.

When Frank Navarro quit as Columbia's football coach in November, he was succeeded by Bill Campbell, who said (in a voice made hoarse from the constant recruiting speeches he had been giving for Boston College): "My main goal is to intensify recruiting efforts by alumni in all parts of the country. The alumni have to take an active part in luring kids to come to Columbia."

When the University of Oklahoma finished its football season under probation, an imaginative plan was suggested by the athletic director, Wade Walker: sell season tickets between the 40-yard lines to the highest bidders, with an opening price of $1,000. "When you compete with the Joneses," he said, "you'd better have a program like the Joneses."

And 28 Special Guests

When Notre Dame ended U.C.L.A.'s basketball streak at eighty-eight games in January, the great event was watched by a sellout crowd at South Bend, a national television audience, and twenty-eight special guests: high school football stars who were spending the weekend at Notre Dame, all expenses paid.

When Leonard Thompson, a twenty-seven-year-old golfer, won his first tournament as a professional last month (the Jackie Gleason Inverrary at Fort Lauderdale), he pocketed $52,000 and recalled his student days at Wake Forest. What did he study in college? "Golf," Thompson replied. "If you don't believe me, ask my professors."

But for total involvement nothing may reflect the trend more than the City of Petersburg, Va., where a 6-foot-11-inch high school senior is leading the country in promises. His name is Moses Malone, and he has been averaging 38 points and 26 rebounds a game while his basketball team has been winning by 50 points before standing-room-only. The offers include tuition, room, board, books, fifteen dollars a month for "laundry"—and a car, an apartment, and cash.

The post office even sent out a Christmas message inscribed, in the spirit of the times: "Greetings from Petersburg, home of Moses Malone."

To Moses, though, it was all a little heady, even though one basketball superscout described his potential as a member of the class of 1974 in these words: "He can lead any college program in the nation into the promised land."

Meanwhile, for the Brainy Nonathlete, a 'Financial Struggle'

Steve Cady

While college sports recruiters pour it on this month, scholars ponder the disparity between athletic adulation and academic neglect.

Scholarly frustration was put into words a few years ago by a man in Idaho who made a startling proposal at the monthly meeting of the Parent-Teacher Association.

He suggested that the local high school form a talent team made up of its most gifted students. The team, selected on the basis of rigorous performance tests, would be taught by staff members after school, wear special varsity uniforms, and compete against similar teams from other schools

The proposal was promptly attacked as undemocratic, impossible, too expensive, snobbish, and unfair to other children.

Yea, Team!

"But I'm not talking about a new program," the academician protested. "We've been carrying on this very program at our high school for years. We call it a football team."

The idea of a "brain" team has never found favor in an educational value system that lavishes its inducements on athletes. There's always room for an athlete, they say, but recruiters don't chase scholars the way they chase athletes. If they did, people like Sanford (Sandy) Climan's father wouldn't be borrowing money now to put him through Harvard.

Sandy, an All-America math wizard last year at Bronx High School of Science, would have been on everybody's blue-chip shopping list. And his father would be relaxing now instead of going into hock.

"Nobody made him a firm offer," said Jack Climan, a middle-income business agent for a community school board in the Bronx. "He got some letters, but nobody came to the house and said, 'We'll take you out to dinner, we'll pay your lab fees.' Nothing like that."

Climan still can't understand the lack of support. At Bronx Science, a hotbed of learning, nobody hit more academic home runs last season than his seventeen-year-old son. Sandy was valedictorian of a senior class of 850 (commencement address: "Mediocrity in America"), a National Merit winner, a Westinghouse talent search finalist, and one of one hundred students selected to attend the National Youth Science Camp. His Scholastic Aptitude Test scores of 750 put him in the top 1 percent of the more than a million students who took the same College Board exams.

"A very unusual boy with real promise for the future," said Melvin Adelson, assistant principal in charge of guidance. "Unhappily, American colleges generally don't pursue that kind of talent with the zeal they show for athletes."

While schoolboy athletes were getting their pictures in the paper for scoring touchdowns or sinking baskets, Sandy Climan was going one-on-one against tough guys like advanced-placement calculus (he pulled down a final grade of 100), writing papers about things like "Nth-ic Residues," and conducting an independent research project that discovered a new bovine brain compound capable of leading to a better understanding of degenerative brain disease. He also found time to be editor in chief of his school's yearbook and math bulletin.

Yet no plane swooped out of the sky to whisk Sandy to a faraway campus. No townspeople waited at an airport with signs lettered "We Want You!" Alumni celebrities never phoned him, and no smooth-talking recruiters ever promised him free tuition, board, cash bonuses, girls, apartments, credit cards, resalable football tickets, or even a summer job.

So his father and mother, Fanny, a hospital clerk, have curtailed their style of living to help meet an annual expense of about $6,000. Climan said his wife's entire salary "and then some" was going for that purpose.

Had offers of financial aid from other reputable colleges come, young Climan might not have waited for the no-aid acceptance letter that finally arrived from Harvard last April 15.

258

"A couple of times, I was ready to say 'Buy me' to interviewers from top colleges," he recalled recently on the phone from his freshman dormitory at Harvard. "I didn't want to be a financial burden on my parents. But nobody offered any money."

Unfortunately, the only team 5-foot-6 Sandy played for at Bronx Science was the debating team, and his final grade in gym ("I never enjoyed climbing ropes") was an undistinguished 80.

"I'm proud to help him realize his full potential," the older Climan said, "but something is wrong when top athletes are offered the goodies, and academic people aren't. It's criminal these things are happening."

His son, the youngest of three, takes a more philosophical view of sports recruiting: "Sure, your bright students resent it, but let's face it—athletes can draw money to a university. People like me couldn't do it unless we discovered a cure for cancer, something like that."

Even Federal grants and interest-subsidized loans are now geared almost exclusively to financial need, with academic achievement having no bearing.

Young Climan's rewards added up to $1,900 in various national scholarship awards and prizes, all of them one-shot deals that will expire this June.

"It's no picnic," he said. "It's a struggle financially, but at least I was able to pick up a few dollars being in math and science. My friends in literature and social studies and humanities, they're the ones that got completely demolished in the way of scholarship money."

Though Sandy regards the athletic scene at Harvard as sensible ("You can relate to the jocks here"), he still feels "a great deal of resentment" toward sports recruiting.

"It has a lot to do with anti-intellectualism in America," he said. "People would rather look at a football game than watch 'Meet the Press.' I guess that isn't going to change."

OPINION: A College Coach Tells Why Recruiting Abuses Happen

Joe Paterno

College football is a great game and I'm very happy to be a part of it. The recruiting excesses and abuses discussed on these pages the last week disturb me, as they do all people committed to sound intercollegiate athletics. But rather than elaborating on what has been written, I believe we can perform a more useful service if we first explore the recruiting syndrome from a coach's viewpoint—to try to give you a better insight into why we have the abuses and excesses and then suggest remedies to cure the disease.

Recruiting performs worthwhile functions. It introduces a university as an opportunity to a student-athlete with an ambition. It gives the player a chance to choose and to investigate different programs. It helps him to find the right institution for him, and it certainly introduces him to the world of mature decision making.

He weighs the importance of environment and facilities. He makes value decisions on sincerity and personalities. He has to analyze personal priorities, sorting out relevant considerations from irrelevant ones.

Winning Above All

The proselytizing also forces a young man to look at himself, especially where he truly wants his ambitions and abilities to carry him. He is being told by college representatives what is best for him (not really being asked what he wants). Self-analysis under this pressure is difficult.

How then does recruiting become a sinister practice that many times confuses, frustrates, emotionally disturbs, psy-

260

chologically damages, and even corrupts the people to whom it should be a useful experience.

Almost by definition, coaches are extremely competitive, and once they get involved in a recruiting battle they are determined to win. Without even realizing it, the proselytizing frequently becomes an end in itself and not a means of putting together a successful squad.

Don't be quick to criticize coaches, because this sophistry somewhat parallels the malady our leaders suffered in Vietnam. When you have fiercely competitive, personable coaches with great energy and ambition getting emotionally involved in the life of the prospect they are pursuing, you can see how easy it is for the recruiters to get carried away. Add to this the importance the athletic milieu places on the recruiting ability of a prospective coach.

Because we are not different from other segments of our society, often the word is "Get 'em; I don't care how, but get 'em." (Some of the personalities in Watergate resemble an aggressive head coach and his staff determined to make their team undefeated and national champions at any price.)

Just Can't Say No

It's all so tremendous for the high school athlete—a dream fulfilled for him and his family and everything for which he has worked hard. The college coaches descend on him, his school and his home.

At first the attention is wonderful. And then it starts to snowball. If one of our opponents drops around the school once a week, our staff is competitive. We aren't going to get outworked; we are going to get in there twice a week. A third school is just as determined and a fourth, etc., and the vicious cycle has begun.

Soon, the strain of the big decision starts to wear on the family, and they may begin to take sides. Advisers pop out of the woodwork. Each college makes it tougher and tougher to say no. Everybody is so nice (say what you want about college coaches, but we are good salesmen).

As the boy's indecisiveness mounts, the more resources we expend. After all, we have spent all this time, money and energy on him, and he hasn't told us no; maybe one more pitch will do it for us (the same mentality we saw with our involvement in Vietnam).

Finally, a school appears to be losing out. Accordingly, a coach whose job is on the line or who has been hired by a college president and told to win—not teach well, but win—may do what he believes the college president, the athletic director, the alumni, and friends of the institution want him to do.

He arranges for the prospect to be offered extra money, clothes, or other illegal inducements. He isn't really concerned about getting caught because the N.C.A.A. (National Collegiate Athletic Association) has ineffective investigation and enforcement apparatus.

Size of a Giant

The coach may directly make the illegal overture or he may have a friend or alumnus contact the player, appearing to do so without the knowledge of the coach. In some cases an overzealous supporter will take it upon himself to secure a prospect for his school.

Although there are such covert propositions, the present-day high school athlete has generally resisted the temptation and is turned off by this hypocrisy. Furthermore, I believe the coaches who do get involved in these activities are usually doing what their president and athletic coterie want done.

Through all this we build up the athlete. We exaggerate his ability; we flatter him; we idolize him; we kneel at his feet and tell him how great he is and how much we need him. We almost lead him to believe that if he doesn't come to our institution the entire university is going to collapse. We barely discuss what efforts he must make in his academic life.

These mendacious promises start a new vicious cycle. The youngster now develops distorted values about himself. We create imaginary utopias and don't prepare him for the realities of college life.

We compound our errors when we allow athletes to make unlimited expense-paid visits to campuses all over the country. Often, they are not really interested in all these schools, but they like the idea of traveling and being entertained.

The recruiting rat race is finally over. The youngster has been lionized, wined, and dined. He has been told how great he is and how much he is needed.

And, after the big buildup, he finds out he's just another player, just another student. He is not the star anymore. He has to make the team and study like everybody else. It's a tremendous letdown, and not every youngster can adjust to it. But many athletes do have the resilience and stability to bounce back.

How can we cure this syndrome?

First, the leaders of the N.C.A.A., college presidents, and athletic directors must realize their college coaches are under tremendous pressure to win and that there are no miracle coaches and no miraculous recruiters. These leaders cannot abrogate their responsibility to the coaches—too many administrators have ostrich tendencies. Coaches should not be fired arbitrarily and should not have their tenure based on won-lost record only.

Second, the N.C.A.A. must protect the coach and athlete by having strong and efficient investigation, enforcement, and punitive capabilities. N.C.A.A. investigators should make unannounced appearances on campuses. There is no sense having rules you can't enforce, and we can't begin to solve the problems of recruiting without a new approach to N.C.A.A. police activities. Penalties against the guilty must go right to the heart of the university, including the president. After all, the N.C.A.A. was organized by college presidents, but few ever attend N.C.A.A. meetings.

Third, more good high school players must be available to more schools. The N.C.A.A. took a giant step in this direction when it recently passed a national limit of thirty grants-in-aid a year for football. This will help, but twenty-five a year would be better.

Fourth, reduce the vicious-cycle patterns of recruiting. Do not allow the athlete to make paid visits to more than five campuses. Shorten the recruiting season. Make all university representatives refrain from contact with a prospect for one week prior to the date for signing the national letter of intent.

It is impossible to present these thoughts without appearing to cast oneself in the role of "holier than thou." That is not our purpose. Instead, we want to give insight and views on a major problem in intercollegiate athletics.

FOR DISCUSSION

1. The first article you read ("Athletic Recruiting: A Campus Crisis" by Joseph Durso) describes the nature and size of the problems associated with recruiting. What evidence surprised you the most? Do you think that the sample opinions represent all those involved in recruiting? Look at the article—particularly at those places where people are quoted directly—and support your answer.

2. By carefully selecting the language they use to present evidence, writers reveal their attitudes toward their subjects: how would you assess Durso's attitude toward his subject? What words and expressions have favorable or unfavorable connotations?

3. The article "Athletic Recruiting: a Campus Crisis" suggests some financial causes for the growing problems in sports. How would you, if you were a college coach or administrator, solve these problems?

4. Sandy Climan, in "Meanwhile, for the Brainy Nonathlete, a 'Financial Struggle',' claims that sports recruiting springs from the "anti-intellectualism in America." How true is this charge? Do you agree with Sandy Climan that we are not likely to change our national priorities? Why?

5. What do you think of the proposal in this article to start a local talent team? Why would you support or attack such an effort in your school?

6. Joe Paterno, in "Opinion," considers recruiting to be a basically worthwhile practice which needs reform. Evaluate his defense of recruiting, noting particularly his word choices and general style, and then correct or add to his list of suggestions for improving the recruiting system.

7. Paterno compares some coaches' "Get 'em; I don't care how, but get 'em" attitude to that of some of the per-

264

sonalities involved in the Watergate affair. What do you think of the comparison? Speculate further in this area, drawing a parallel between our national sports mentality (if such a thing exists) and the attitudes exhibited by the men close to President Nixon.

8. Write a letter to the N.C.A.A. giving your thoughts on the causes and the cures for the problem of sports recruiting.

INTRODUCTION

Have you ever wanted a favor from someone you didn't know especially well? If so, you probably ended up scratching out on the typewriter a letter that seemed acceptable; so you mailed it. Only after you read the carbon copy the next day did you realize how awkward you really sounded. So it goes. The letter that follows is a spoof of such a letter asking special favors for an athlete, something that Dave Meggyesy tells us is common practice. Beneath the spoofery, though, a serious message comes across.

He Tries Hard

William E. Stafford

Dear Coach Musselman:

Remembering our discussions of your football men who are having troubles in English, I have decided to ask you, in turn, for help.

We feel Paul Spindles has a chance for a Rhodes Scholarship. Although he has the academic record for this award, the aspirant is required to have a good record in athletics. Paul has trouble with athletics, but he tries hard.

We propose you give him special consideration and put him in the backfield of the football team. Thus, we can show a better record to the scholarship committee.

We realize Paul will be a problem on the field, but as you have often said, cooperation between our department and yours is desirable.

During intervals of study, we shall coach him as much as we can. His work in English Club and on the debate team will force him to miss many practices, but we intend to see that he carries an old football to bounce during intervals of his work.

266

We expect Paul to show good will in his work for you, and though he won't be able to begin practice till late in the season, he will finish the season with good attendance.

Cordially yours,

Chairman, English Department

FOR DISCUSSION

1. *Irony* means saying one thing, but meaning another. Do you see any instances of irony here? Where?
2. Assume that you are Coach Musselman. Write a reply to this letter, and be humorous in turn. (Give the English department chairman an appropriate name, for instance.)
3. Is honest effort, or "trying hard," reason enough for special consideration in a class? If ability is lacking, how much should effort count toward a grade?
4. Do you agree or disagree with the often-argued statement that athletes are inferior students? Discuss.
5. Compare and contrast any two sports, noting especially the intelligence of the players. Are some sports "dumber" than others? What role does instinct play in sports?